CAPITALISM,
SOCIALISM,
AND THE PROMISE OF
DEMOCRACY

CAPITALISM, SOCIALISM,

AND THE PROMISE OF

DEMOCRACY

William D. Barber

Printed in the United States of America.

First Printing 2019.

ISBN: 978-1-7341490-4-3 (hardcover)
       978-1-7341490-3-6 (softcover)
       978-1-7341490-1-2 (ebook)

Published by:
Laforest Products, Inc.
Dearborn Heights, Michigan

Front Cover Portraits: Adam Smith & Karl Marx

"I can't do this Sam."

"I know. It's all wrong. By rights we shouldn't even be here. But we are. It's like in the great stories, Mr. Frodo. The ones that really mattered. Full of darkness and danger they were. And sometimes you didn't want to know the end. Because how could the end be happy? How could the world go back to the way it was after so much bad had happened? But in the end, it's only a passing thing, this shadow. Even darkness must pass. A new day will come. And when the sun shines, it will shine out the clearer. Those were the stories that stayed with you. That meant something. Even if you were too small to understand why. But I think Mr. Frodo, that I do understand. I know now. Folks in those stories had lots of chances of turning back, only they didn't. Because they were holding on to something."

"What are we holding on to, Sam?"

"That there's some good in this world Mr. Frodo. And it's worth fighting for."

—LORD OF THE RINGS; THE TWO TOWERS
J.R. TOLKIEN

CONTENTS

ACKNOWLEDGEMENTS

I am very grateful to the following individuals who read drafts of this manuscript and offered advice and guidance on improving it. These include Timothy Bureau, Paul Jakary, Patricia Barber, Joseph Colwell, Paul Fisher, Sarah Barber, Anton Gnadt, and Mark Hilpert. Their insights and suggestions greatly improved this book.

I am also indebted to my teachers and colleagues over the years who engaged me and forced me to sharpen my ideas concerning economics. These include Louis Junker, James Hamilton, Stephen Spurr, Gangaran Kripilani, Robert Arnold, and Steven Winrich.

Lastly, I am indebted to all the students who enrolled in economics courses taught by me over the last 40 years. Their questions and insights forced me to become a better teacher and to learn how to better explain complex concepts in a more understandable manner. I often learned as much from them as they did from me.

Even with the help and support of all those above, I am sure that flaws remain. These are my responsibility alone.

PREFACE

Explaining complex subjects to individuals first becoming acquainted with a topic is challenging. There is a danger the complexity of the topic will immediately overwhelm, causing people to turn away. The way forward is generally to initially oversimplify the topic, making it more accessible. As individuals become familiar with basic concepts and ideas, the complexity and nuances of the explanations can be dealt with more thoroughly.

As an instructor of introductory Economics to college students over the past 40 years, I have had to deal with this challenge. Economics can be a tough subject for many. Numerous students who enroll in these classes do so with little enthusiasm and a great deal of trepidation. It is necessary to make the subject both interesting and accessible so they will become engaged and develop at least a tolerance, and perhaps a love, for the topic.

In writing this book, I was faced with the same challenge: how to write a book about important economic matters that will interest the general public without overwhelming people with the complexity of the caveats and nuances of the topic, which is easy to do with Economics. The key, again, is oversimplification; but that is also a danger.

The danger is exact truth can be lost; there can, indeed, be exceptions to the rule, caveats and nuances, that don't make something exactly, always true. The problem is allowing for every possible exception can take you down a rabbit hole that readers can get lost in. They end up believing no definitive statements can be made about anything.

Thus, my approach is to initially oversimplify. However, it is important to let your readers know you are doing so; there may be exceptions, caveats, and nuances that are not being explored. This can pique their interest to do further exploration on their own. However, I initially avoid getting into the complex details of the exceptions because there is a fundamental truth at the foundation of the explanation.

Critics will point to the oversimplifications in an attempt to discredit the fundamental truth of these explanations. But the explanations remain fundamentally true, and readers have been told there have been oversimplifications; there may be some exceptions, caveats, and nuances to what has been written.

INTRODUCTION

In recent years concerns and questions about Economics and economic systems have become a greater concern in the public discourse. It seems increasing numbers of people are becoming dissatisfied with the performance of the United States economic system and the global economy. There are real questions as to whether future generations will be able to achieve living standards above or at least equal to that of their parents. What has gone wrong and what can be done?

The distributions of income and wealth are two of the most contentious issues. Over the last several decades, both income and wealth have become increasingly concentrated in fewer and fewer hands.[1] From 1979 to 2015, income increases have been:

- Top 1%: 242%
- Next 19%: 78%
- Middle 60%: 46%
- Bottom 20% 45%.

From 1989 to 2016 changes in the share of wealth have been:

- Top 1%: + 9%
- Next 9% + 1%
- Bottom 90%: –10%.

As a result, millions are left struggling and are barely able to make ends meet while a small minority lives in almost unimaginable luxury. Many are denied basic needs such as access to affordable health care, the cost of higher education is out of the reach of many middle-class families, and the dream of owning a home seems unattainable. The cost of health care and education has saddled many Americans with crippling debt, undermining any hope of ever attaining any semblance of economic security. This lack of economic security has resulted in ever-greater divisions between citizens, a breakdown of civil discourse in politics, and demands for change.

There have been calls for fundamental changes in the structure of our economic system. Questions concerning the benefits of expanding global trade are raised. The use of tariffs as a protective device and the threat of trade wars dominate the news. Fundamental questions of the merits of a Capitalist system versus a Socialist system are being raised in a manner unseen since the Great Depression of the 1930s.

A problem preventing our ability to have a meaningful public debate on these issues is that for much of the public there is a lack of a general understanding or agreement on many basic economic ideas and principles. Without such understanding or agreement, it is not possible to have discussions that can move us forward and resolve the important economic issues we are confronted with.

As an instructor of introductory Economics on the collegiate level for the past 40 years, I have become increasingly concerned about this lack of knowledge among even the more educated segments of our society. The lack of understanding, lack of agreement, and misconceptions about basic economic terms, principles, and ideas are a major impediment to moving forward in resolving the economic and political problems confronting us.

This book is an attempt to begin to lay the groundwork for a more informed discussion of the economic problems and issues challenging us at the beginning of the twenty-first century. I start by defining, clarifying, and explaining important basic economic terminology and principles so there is an understanding of and, hopefully, agreement on the meaning of these important concepts. Next, a very brief history of early economic systems is discussed, which is followed with a discussion of early capitalist systems. I believe this is important because understanding our current economic situation requires having an understanding of how we arrived in the present situation. Also, to be able to discuss where we should be going in terms of changes to our economic system, it is important and necessary to have an understanding of where we have been.

I then turn to the topic of Adam Smith and the development of the ideas of Free Market Capitalism. A basic tenet of Smith is the crucial role trade plays in rising living standards, so I follow with a chapter on the expansion of trade in the late twentieth century since Smith's ideas are central to what happened. I next discuss the ideas and establishment of Socialist systems. This is followed by the history of the rise and fall of the Oligarchic Capitalist system in the late 1800s and early 1900s and its replacement with a system of Democratic Capitalism by Franklin Roosevelt's New Deal. A discussion of the expansion of the Democratic Capitalist system during the administration of Lyndon Johnson is then explored, followed by the problems of the early 1970s that led to Democratic Capitalism being replaced with a second era of Oligarchic Capitalism during the administration of Ronald Reagan. This is the economic system that has fundamentally existed in the United States since 1980. I then explore the current problems with the system of Oligarchic Capitalism and its replacement with either a new era of Democratic Capitalism or a system of Democratic Socialism to create a more democratic and equitable economic system.

It is important to note that because the book is about Economics, a primary issue dealt with is living standards. A basic assumption in Economics is that a primary goal of human beings is to achieve higher living standards. In the parlance of Economics this means human beings want to consume more. Consuming more necessitates higher levels of production. Thus, throughout the book, the assumption is that higher levels of production and consumption are desirable.

Therefore, when discussing these topics, important issues such as environmental concerns are dealt with only in passing. It is not that I don't recognize the importance of issues like environmental concerns; only that the purpose of this book is to focus on Economics. The tradeoff between higher levels of production and the resulting environmental damage certainly needs to be considered.

I also do not deal with the issue of whether higher levels of consumption (living standards) necessarily result in human beings being happier. While higher living standards, for the most part, would seem to be desirable, there are those who contend more is not necessarily better. Some studies have shown more does not necessarily translate into happier. I do not disagree; but, again, the purpose of this book is to focus on Economic concerns.

Ceteris paribus (other things being equal) is a hallmark of Economics. Assuming other things are equal, more production and more consumption are good. Of course, other things are rarely equal. More production leads to more environmental damage. More consumption does not necessarily translate into greater happiness. It is important that the reader understand this.

1

Economic Principles

Economic Fundamentals

Economics is a science, which means economists use the scientific method in their work. The scientific method involves the development of hypotheses and theories, the testing of these hypotheses and theories by gathering evidence, and the acceptance or rejection of the hypotheses and theories based on the results of the tests. In this way, knowledge in a field of study, like Economics, moves forward.

Science can be divided into two categories. The natural sciences involve the study of nature because they deal with the "nature" of things. Examples include chemistry, biology, physics, astronomy, and botany. Many of the natural sciences are characterized by the use of laboratory experiments as a way to test their theories and hypotheses.

The social sciences, also called the behavioral sciences, involve the study of human behavior. The cornerstones of the social sciences are psychology and sociology. Psychology deals with the study of individual behavior while sociology involves understanding group behavior. All other social sciences are derived from these two.

In political science we are concerned with how human beings behave in different types of political environments and the role different types of political institutions play in different political settings.

History attempts to understand past human behavior. When studying anthropology, the behavior of primitive peoples and the evolution of human beings are examined. Geography deals with how human beings interact with the physical world around them.

Economics is also a social science and so involves the study of human behavior—but what areas of human behavior? *Economics is the study of human behavior in relation to the acts of production, consumption, and exchange.*

- Production is the act of making commodities or capital.
- Consumption is the act of using commodities to satisfy needs and desires.[i]
- Exchange is the act of trading commodities.

A commodity is an output resulting from production used to satisfy the needs and desires of human beings. Commodities are often referred to as products. They can be divided into two categories: goods and services. Goods are physical, tangible things. Food, clothing, houses, and automobiles are all examples of goods. Services are non-physical and intangible. The services of a doctor, a barber, or a police officer are examples.

Capital is an output resulting from production which is used as an input for further production. Capital can also be defined as human-made aids to production. Types of capital are tools, machines, and equipment. Capital, and other inputs, will be discussed below.

So, Economics is concerned with understanding how human beings go about producing, consuming, and exchanging commodities, i.e., products. To more fully appreciate these ideas, one must have an understanding of the Economic Process.

The Economic Process

The Economic Process is the series of activities human beings must undertake to sustain themselves. In the Economic Process, human beings use resources for production to make commodities for consumption.

---

[i] Needs and desires are often referred to as wants.

| Use Resources | → | For Production | → | Make Commodities | → | For Consumption |

Resources are the inputs into production. They are the things used by human beings to make the desired commodities. Traditionally economists have broken resources down into three categories:[ii]

- The natural wealth of the physical environment (natural resources)
- Human effort, both physical and mental
- Capital, human-made aids to production; an output that results from production used for further production

Adam Smith, a renowned economist from the late 1700s, was the first to classify resources into these three categories. He referred to the natural wealth of the physical environment as *land*. Today we use the term natural resources. Examples are plant life, animal life, minerals, land, oil, water, and air. Smith used the term land because he was referring to things that came from the land. He used the term *labor* to describe the second resource, human effort. He called the third resource, human-made aids to production, *capital*. To this day economists still use the terminology of land, labor, and capital as the three types of resources available to human beings for production.

In the Economic Process, then, human beings use the resources available to them to produce desired products in order to consume them to meet their needs and desires. Economists are interested in understanding how this process works.

It is important to have a clear understanding of the importance of the Economic Process to appreciate that economics is fundamentally concerned with how human beings survive.

All human beings have to consume commodities in order to live. At the very least, human beings have to eat. They also need to consume shelter, housing, medical care, and many other products. In order

---

[ii] In the early 1900s economist Joseph Schumpeter argued there was a fourth resource, *entrepreneurship*. Entrepreneurship is a special type of human effort. It involves economic leadership, the organization of resources for production, and risk taking.

3

to consume, someone has to produce. *Every act of consumption requires an act of production.* If a person is going to eat, either they or someone else has to produce the food. If a person is going to have clothing to wear, either they or someone else has to make the clothing.

So, at its core, Economics is concerned with understanding something very basic: how human beings go about surviving in the world, i.e., how human beings go about producing and consuming the things they need to live.

People typically don't think about Economics in this way. Typically, Economics is thought of as being about money or business or investing or markets. Economics is not thought of in terms like production, consumption, and survival. While the study of Economics does involve the study of things like money and markets, it is important to appreciate that Economics is really about something more important and fundamental; it is about how human beings go about surviving in the world.

Exchange, Absolute Advantage, and Comparative Advantage

Exchange is not included as part of the Economic Process because it is not necessary for human survival. If a person was stranded on a deserted island, they would have to consume to survive. Since every act of consumption requires an act of production, they would also have to produce. However, because they were the only person on the island, they would not be able to exchange. So, everything they consumed they would have to produce themself. Thus, survival is not dependent upon exchange. While production and consumption are necessary for survival, exchange is not.

However, even though exchange isn't necessary for human survival, human beings have fundamentally always traded among themselves. The earliest groups of humans exchanged. But if exchange isn't necessary, why have human beings always traded?

The fundamental economic reason human beings exchange products is that, as a result of exchange, production, and therefore consumption, increases.[iii] This

---

iii   Human beings also exchange because they may not be able to obtain certain products due to reasons such as a lack of resources or environmental factors like weather. However, the fundamental economic reason for exchange is the increase in production and consumption that results.

increase occurs due to the gains from specialization. The gains from specialization are the increases in production resulting from specialization in the production of specific products. Let's go through an example to illustrate.

Assume two people are on an island: Person A and Person B. Assume there are two productive activities they can engage in: hunting and gathering. Table 1A illustrates the situation for these people.

Table 1A

	Time Spent	Hunting	Time Spent	Gathering
Person A	1/2	4 lbs	1/2	24 bu
Person B	1/2	8 lbs	1/2	6 bu
TOTAL		**12 lbs**		**30 bu**

Each person initially spends half of their time doing each activity. Person A is able to produce 4 pounds of meat and 24 bushels of fruits and vegetables per month, while Person B can produce 8 pounds of meat and 6 bushels of fruits and vegetables. Person A has an absolute advantage in gathering. Person B has an absolute advantage in hunting. Production would increase if they each focus their efforts on the area they have an absolute advantage in. Since Person A is the better gatherer, they should spend all of their time gathering. Person B, who is better at hunting, should concentrate all of their time on hunting. Table 1B shows the results when they divide their production in this way.

Table 1B

	Time Spent	Hunting	Time Spent	Gathering
Person A	None	0 lbs	All	48 bu
Person B	All	16 lbs	None	0 bu
TOTAL		**16 lbs**		**48 bu**

As a result of specialization, overall production has gone up. They now have 16 pounds of meat rather than just 12. The production of fruits and vegetables has also risen from 30 bushels to 48. The problem, however, is Person A has only fruits and vegetables while Person B has only meat. The solution is for them to trade with each other. Through specialization and trade, production rises, which leads to an increase in consumption.

The above is an example of absolute advantage. An absolute advantage exists when a person can produce more of a product with a given amount of resources than another person can. Person A has an absolute advantage in gathering while Person B has an absolute advantage in hunting. Each individual should focus their efforts on the activity where they have an absolute advantage.

What happens if one person has an absolute advantage in all areas? Would there still be a gain from specialization and trade? Table 1C illustrates this situation.

Table 1C

	Time Spent	Hunting	Time Spent	Gathering
Person A	1/2	8 lbs	1/2	24 bu
Person B	1/2	4 lbs	1/2	6 bu
TOTAL		**12 lbs**		**30 bu**

As in the previous example, each person spends half their time on each activity. However, in this case, Person A has an absolute advantage at both hunting and gathering. Is there any gain from specialization and trade in such a case?

For there to be a gain, the time spent on each activity needs to be rearranged so that production increases. Once again there can be a gain. Table 1D illustrates it.

Table 1D

	Time Spent	Hunting	Time Spent	Gathering
Person A	1/4	4 lbs	3/4	36 bu
Person B	All	8 lbs	None	0 bu
TOTAL		**12 lbs**		**36 bu**

Even though Person A has an absolute advantage in both hunting and gathering, there is still a gain from specialization. Person B now spends all their time on hunting. Person A, on the other hand, spends one fourth of their time on hunting and three fourths of their time on gathering. The result is that overall production of meat has remained the same at 12 pounds while overall production of fruits and vegetables has increased to 36 bushels. Through specialization and trade, overall production has risen, which leads to an increase in consumption.[iv]

This second example is a case of comparative, or relative, advantage. *A comparative (relative) advantage exists when a person's opportunity cost of producing a product is less than someone else's. Opportunity cost is the foregone benefit of the best available alternative.* It's what a person gives up to do something. The opportunity cost of meat is the fruits and vegetables which could have been produced. The opportunity cost of fruits and vegetables is the meat which could have been produced.

For Person A, it is not just a question of *if* they are better at both activities but rather a question of *how much* better. Person A has a 4 to 1 advantage in gathering, 24 bushels to 6 bushels, but only a 2 to 1 advantage in hunting, 8 pounds to 4 pounds. *Person A needs to concentrate their efforts on the activity where their advantage is the greatest, which is gathering.* This is reflected in the opportunity cost of the two products. Person A's opportunity cost of producing an additional bushel of fruits and vegetables is only one third of a pound of meat. Person B gives up two thirds of a pound of meat for each additional bushel of fruits and vegetables. Since Person A has a lower opportunity cost in producing fruits and vegetables, they should concentrate on gathering. *They have a greater comparative, or relative, advantage at gathering.*

Person B is at a disadvantage in producing both products. *Person B needs to concentrate their efforts on the activity where their disadvantage is the least.* Since they are at a 4 to 1 disadvantage in gathering, and only a 2 to 1 disadvantage in hunting, Person B needs to focus on hunting. Again, this is reflected in the opportunity costs of production. Person

---

iv   The amount of time spent on each activity can be adjusted so that the production of meat rises while fruits and vegetables remain the same, or so that the production from both hunting and gathering increase.

B's opportunity cost of producing an additional pound of meat is one and a half bushels of fruits and vegetables. Producing an additional pound of meat costs Person A three bushels of fruits and vegetables. Therefore, Person B should focus on producing meat. *They have less of a comparative, or relative, disadvantage at hunting.*

The examples of absolute advantage and comparative advantage show that, even though exchange is not necessary for survival, it leads to increases in production and consumption.[v] Therefore, exchange is a fundamental economic activity in which human beings have always engaged.

Although the above examples are extremely basic and over simplified, the core principle of the gains from specialization and trade illustrated apply to the complexities of the real world. The principles of absolute advantage and comparative advantage, which we have applied to individual people, also apply to countries. Just as with individuals, countries should focus their productive activities on areas where they have absolute or comparative advantages. When they do, production in the world rises, leading to rising levels of consumption across the globe. This has been a driving force behind the efforts in recent years to expand world trade. These important issues will be discussed at length later.

Production, Consumption, and Living Standards

It is critical to understand what is meant by higher levels of consumption. *We can equate higher levels of consumption with higher living standards.* If someone has a higher living standard than someone else, that individual consumes more.

The living standard in the United States is higher than it is in Mexico. This fundamentally means people in the United States consume more than people in Mexico. On average, people in the United States live in bigger houses, have more clothes, eat more food, get more health care, travel more, and have more cars than people in Mexico.

---

[v]   The ideas of absolute and comparative advantage were first developed by the renowned economist David Ricardo. See *The Principles of Political Economy.*

Increasing living standards is something countries and people throughout the world aspire to. This fundamentally means people want to consume more products. Since every act of consumption requires an act of production, the only way to increase consumption, i.e., living standards, is to increase production. How countries can increase production and, therefore, living standards is an important topic we will be covering in greater detail. However, it is important to note, at this juncture, one of the most important ways to increase production and, therefore, living standards is exchange, i.e., trade.

The Economic Problem

If Economics only involved human beings producing, consuming, and exchanging, life would be challenging but survival would be relatively easy. *The entire process is complicated, however, due to the scarcity of resources. Scarcity means resources are limited, which means commodities are limited as well. Economists refer to this as the Economic Problem.* As a result of scarcity, producing more of one product can mean having less of another. Scarcity of resources is the reason opportunity costs exist. If resources weren't scarce, society could produce more of everything.

As a result of scarcity and opportunity cost, human beings must make economic choices. The three basic choices that must be made are:

1. What to produce?
2. How to produce it?
3. Who gets it?

Somehow people and society must decide what products should be produced with their scarce resources. Should farmland be used to raise corn or wheat or oats? Should we build single-family homes or apartment buildings? What kind of cars should be made?

Once we know what commodities we want to make, we next have to decide how to make it. Should crops be harvested by hand, or should we first build complex harvesting equipment and then use it do the job? Should we dig ditches using shovels and picks, or should we first build heavy-duty ditch-digging equipment? There is more than one way to produce any product.

Once products are produced, a society must determine who gets to consume the products. Who gets to drive new cars? Who drives old cars? Who takes the bus? Who gets to lives in mansions? Who lives in new housing? Who lives in poorly constructed apartment buildings? Who gets to go to the Superbowl? Somehow these questions must be answered by a society.

The use of scarce resources to satisfy the needs and desires of human beings is the basic economic challenge. Decisions on how scarce resources should be allocated need to be made. Societies must have some method, some process, by which these economic decisions are made. There needs to be some type of system in place to make economic choices.

Economic Systems

An economic system determines how economic choices are made in a society. Different types of economic systems have existed over time. Each system is governed by principles that determine how economic decisions are made. *The dominate economic system in the world today is Capitalism, which is comprised of four basic principles:*

1. Private Property
2. Individual Freedom
3. Competition
4. Limited Government

The existence of private property is the cornerstone of Capitalism. People are allowed to own the resources used for production. Individual farmers and businesses own farmland. Private corporations like General Motors and Ford own automobile factories.

Second, individuals have a great deal of freedom in deciding how they use the resources they own. Farmers decide what crops to grow on their land. General Motors decides what kind of cars to produce in its factories.

Third, businesses are legally required to compete against one another. Companies are very limited in their ability to join together

10

to make decisions. There are laws preventing General Motors and Ford from getting together to discuss things like the prices they charge for the cars they sell, the wages they pay their workers, and the types of products they make. These same laws limit companies in their ability to merge together and become one company.

Finally, the role of government is limited. Government exists to pass laws to ensure private property rights are protected, individual freedom is ensured, and competition exists in markets. Government enforces these laws and, also, looks after the overall protection and survival of the system.

Other economic systems are based on different sets of principles. Private property and individual freedom may be severely limited. Competition may be restricted and, instead, private or government monopolies may be allowed to exist. The role of government can be much more expansive in overseeing the use of resources and decisions about production and consumption. We will discuss these other types of economic systems later in the book.

Production and Consumption in Capitalism

Understanding the critical relationship between production and consumption is one of the most important concepts in Economics. As stated previously, *every act of consumption requires an act of production.* Ultimately, the purpose of all production is for consumption. As Adam Smith stated.

Consumption is the sole end and purpose of all production...

—SMITH, 1776/1937, P. 625

Most production directly leads to the creation of commodities for consumption. However, some production is used for the creation of capital (tools, machines, and equipment) which is then used for further production. It is rational for some production to be used for the creation of capital because capital increases productivity resulting in greater amounts of commodities being produced for consumption.

Thus, production of capital indirectly results in an increase in the amounts of commodities produced and, therefore, higher levels of consumption, i.e., higher living standards. The production of hammers, saws, and ladders increases the productivity of people in building houses, which results in more houses being built. The production of plows increases the productivity of people in growing crops, resulting in more crops being grown.

Since all production is ultimately intended for consumption, over time the total amount of production in a society must be equal to the total amount of consumption. This eventual equality of the total amount of production and the total amount of consumption is an important principle which must be understood. The level of total consumption, i.e., living standards, in a society is determined by the total amount of production.

It is true that, over a *given* period of time, the total amount of production could be greater than the total amount of consumption. However, since the ultimate purpose of all production is consumption, the only reason for producing more than what is being consumed during a *given* period of time is so that at some *future* date consumption could be greater than production. In other words, production being greater than consumption now simply delays the time until that consumption will occur.

The production of capital is an example of delayed consumption. Rather than produce commodities for immediate (or future consumption), resources are used now to produce capital, which will be used in future production of commodities which will eventually be consumed in the future. As discussed earlier, this is rational since capital increases productivity resulting in even greater amounts of commodities for consumption (higher living standards) in the future.

So, over time the total amount of production will equal the total amount of consumption in a society. What, then, should be the relationship between production and consumption on an *individual* basis. What should be the relationship between an individual's level of production and that individual's level of consumption?

In a Capitalist economic system, an important basic principle is that, on an individual basis, the amount of consumption should be closely related to, and ideally equal to, the level of production. Since over time the total amount of production in a society must be equal to the total amount of consumption, for the most part, the same must be true on an individual basis. The more that an individual produces the more the individual should consume. *In other words, there needs to be a strong relationship between an individual's living standard and their level of productivity.*

The issue is if there are some individuals in society who are able to consume more than they produce, there then must be other individuals in the society who produce more than they consume. *Individuals who consume more than they produce must be subsidized by individuals who produce more than they consume.*

A basic desire or goal of virtually all human beings is to consume more, i.e., to increase their standard of living. For living standards to increase, production must rise. In a Capitalist system, the path to higher living standards for an individual is to increase that individual's production. Whether Capitalism is accomplishing this, how well it is accomplishing it, and problems with this approach will be discussed in later chapters.

2

A Very Brief History of Pre-Capitalist Economic Systems

Primitive Economic Systems

Primitive Economic systems are broken into two categories: Early Primitive systems and Later Primitive systems. Early Primitive systems were the first economic systems that existed. The primary economic activities engaged in were hunting and gathering. During this period, production was largely a collective activity. With the exception of clothing and weapons, human beings claimed little as their own.

Two events transformed the way human beings lived in the world, resulting in the development of Later Primitive systems and civilization. These events were the Agricultural Revolution and the domestication of animals. Human beings gradually learned how to grow the plants they wanted for food. They also gradually became able to control the animals they hunted as a food supply. They were eventually able to domesticate some of these animals and so could control them.

As a result of the Agricultural Revolution and the domestication of animals, human beings were able to build more permanent shelters and establish permanent settlements. If people can grow their own crops and control animals, they can stay in one place. If they can stay in one place, they can build better and more permanent shelters for themselves.

The Agricultural Revolution, the domestication of animals, and the establishment of permanent settlements all contributed to the growth of human population. The first two meant that human beings were eating better. The third meant that they were in out of the weather. If people eat better and are in out of the weather, they will live longer. Also, infant mortality will go down. As a result, population grew.

The establishment of permanent settlements and the growth of population contributed to the development of a private property system. Increasingly human beings laid claim to certain things as their own. They claimed certain houses, plots of land, and certain animals as belonging to them. This claim of ownership is a natural consequence of the building of more permanent shelters, the farming of certain plots of land, and the herding of particular animals.

Additionally, the growth of population led to people feeling more of a need to claim things as theirs. During the Early Primitive period of time, groups tended to be small, so individuals tended to know and have personal relationships with others in the group. In such a situation, individuals will feel less of a need to claim things as their own. However, as population grows, the relationships among some individuals within the group become more distant. There were individuals within the group who barely knew each other. In such a situation, individuals felt an increasing need to claim certain property as their own.

An important result of the creation of a private property system was the development of a class structure. When the amount of private property was limited, everyone pretty much was on equal footing in terms of what they had. As a private property system becomes more entrenched, some people accumulate more than others: more land, more animals, more clothes, bigger houses. In other words, some individuals in the group have a higher standard of living, i.e., they consume more than others.

The existence of a private property system and a class structure necessitates the development of a more complex political/economic structure in society. Roles within the society become more defined and specialized. The rights of people and the relationships between them become more clarified and enforced. And so, civilization develops.

Slave Systems

As civilization spread, groups came into contact with other groups. Often these contacts were peaceful and resulted in trade, which was beneficial to both groups. However, inevitably disagreement and conflict eventually occurred between some groups: conflict over land, territory, water, animals, or other resources. Conflict led to warfare. When warfare occurred, one group defeated another group. The victorious group confiscated the property of the defeated group. The victors took the land, the animals, and the other possessions of the defeated.

Inevitably the victorious group captured prisoners. The issue became what should be done with prisoners. Initially, adult male prisoners were probably killed. Females and juvenile males, on the other hand, could more easily be absorbed into the group, and so they were.

Eventually, rather than killing adult males or absorbing females and juvenile males into the group, these captives were made into slaves. As the benefits of slavery were increasingly recognized, some groups began to intentionally go to war to defeat other groups, confiscate their property, and capture slaves. This was the beginning of Slave systems.

In Slave systems there were two primary groups of people: masters and slaves. *Slaves were forced to produce more than they consumed. Masters were then able to consume more than they produced.* This was the purpose of having slaves, resulting in an increase in the living standard of the masters. *Economic exploitation occurs when people are forced to produce more than they consume so that others can consume more than they produce.* Slave systems were a type of exploitive system.

17

There were a number of important Slave systems that existed in the Western World[i]; the Egyptian Slave system, the Greek Slave system, and the last of the major slave systems in the West, the Roman Slave system.[ii] The Roman Slave system existed for about a thousand years; from approximately 500 BCE to 500 ACE.

The primary economic activity during the Roman slave period, as with all Slave systems, was agriculture. The key to economic power was the control of land.[iii] Powerful individuals, masters, controlled a great deal of land, which meant they could own lots of slaves, grow lots of crops, and support a large army.

Markets and trade existed during the Roman Slave period. It was primarily Mediterranean-based trade. Merchants controlled the trade. However, it is important to understand merchants were of secondary importance in the Roman Slave system; it was the masters who controlled the land and owned the slaves who were at the top of the economic ladder.

Eventually the Roman Slave system would collapse due to increasing economic, political, and social problems. Germanic tribes from Europe would surpass the Romans in political and military power. The Germanic tribes would first defeat the Roman armies in what is today Germany and Eastern Europe. This would be followed by Roman defeats in present-day France. The Germanic tribes would drive down the Italian peninsula, defeating the Romans in northern Italy. Finally, in 475 ACE, the city of Rome itself would be conquered. This would end Slave systems as the dominant form of economic system in the Western World.

---

[i]   This discussion will focus on the Western World since that is where the Capitalist system first developed.

[ii]   It is important to note that a distinction must be made between slavery as an economic system and slavery as an institution within other economic systems. With the fall of the Roman Slave system, slavery as the dominant economic system in the West came to an end. However, slavery as an institution within other economic systems continued to exist. It could also be said that slavery was a secondary system which existed within the dominant economic system, such as the Slave system in the southern United States that existed within the dominant Capitalist system at that time.

[iii]   Land in this sense means arable, agricultural land; not land in the Adam Smith sense of natural resources.

Feudalism

Feudalism, or the Feudal system, replaced the Roman Slave system as the dominant economic system in Europe. It existed from approximately 500 to 1300 ACE. *The most important characteristic of the Feudal system was that there existed a lack of trade.* There were two primary reasons why trade dried up in Europe after the collapse of the Roman Slave system.

First, the fall of the Roman Slave system left a political void with no central authority to govern. As a result, the situation in Europe became chaotic and dangerous. Second, the Romans had built roads throughout Europe; but once the empire fell, the roads were no longer maintained and, so, deteriorated. In an environment of no central authority to enforce laws and govern and with the system of roads in a state of disrepair, travel became dangerous and difficult. As a result, merchants were, for the most part, unable to come to Europe and trade. So, trade dried up.

There were two main groups of people during the Feudal period: lords and serfs. Lords were former leaders of the Germanic tribes. Serfs were former slaves and owners of small farms. The relationship between the lords and serfs developed out of the chaotic and dangerous environment which existed in Europe after the collapse of the Roman Slave system. Former slaves who had settled on land to farm and other owners of small farms were at the mercy of armed groups of soldiers who were members of the Germanic tribes and so needed protection from them. Former leaders of the Germanic tribes, who had armed soldiers under their control, could offer the needed protection.

In return for the protection offered by lords, serfs initially had one of two obligations. In some cases, serfs owed their lord a certain amount of crop at harvest time. In other cases, serfs owed the lord a given amount of labor to farm the lord's land. The serfs kept whatever crop they raised on their land, but they were obligated to farm the lord's land for a given number of days per week.

As time passed, the relationship between the lords and serfs developed into something more comprehensive. Eventually, the lords were responsible for looking after the general welfare of their serfs. Beyond protection, this meant the lords were obligated to ensure the serfs had roofs over their heads, had enough to eat, and to settle disputes among serfs. In return, the serfs served their lord in a broad, general way. Not only did they owe a share of their crop or were required to farm the lord's land, they were obligated to serve their lord in whatever way was necessary. Construction work such as buildings or on castles, digging moats, building bridges, fixing roads, or going to war to assist their lord were all part of their duties.

It is important to note serfs were not slaves. Unlike slaves who were owned by the masters, serfs were not owned by the lords. Serfs were not property; they could not be bought and sold like slaves. In fact, during the Feudal period of time, serfs had a fundamental right; *the right to remain on and farm the land*. Lords could not drive serfs from the land; serfs had the right to be there. However, this right to be on the land was also an obligation; *serfs were obligated to remain on and farm the land*. Serfs were not free to leave and become serfs for some other lord. Serfs were obligated to remain on the land, farm it, and serve their lord.

It was this system of duties, responsibilities, and obligations which governed the way the Feudal system operated. During the Feudal period, individuals were driven by these sentiments.

Whether or not the Feudal system was an exploitive system like the Slave systems before it, that is, whether or not serfs were forced to produce more than they consumed so that lords could consume more than they produced, can be debated. On one hand serfs received something in return for the duties they performed: initially protection and, later, the lords looking after the serfs' general welfare. Therefore, it can be argued serfs were not exploited. On the other hand, serfs were not free to leave and work somewhere else. They were obligated to remain on and farm the land and serve their lords. This obligation put serfs in a vulnerable position and, therefore, subject to exploitation. As result, for the most part, Feudalism is considered to have been an exploitive system.[iv]

[iv] For example, in his book *The Birth of the West*, Paul Collins states many lords were little more than thugs in their treatment of the serfs.

The most important economic entity during the Feudal period was the manor, which was the focal point of economic activity. The main economic activity of the manor was agriculture. The key to economic power, like in slave systems, was the control of land. The center of the manor was typically a castle where the lord and his soldiers were housed. The castle was surrounded by farm-land. The serfs lived in villages in the surrounding countryside.

The most important characteristic of the manor was that it was largely self-sufficient. Since there was a lack of trade during the Feudal period, it would be necessary for the main economic entity to be self-sufficient. Anything that was required to live and survive needed to be produced on the manor.

For the manor to be self-sufficient, another group of necessary people were freemen. Freemen were, for the most part, skilled craftsmen with such occupations as tailors, tanners, millers, blacksmiths, and shoemakers. As the name indicates, these craftsmen were freer than the serfs. The freemen were not obligated to remain on the manor; they were free to leave and practice their craft elsewhere if they so desired.

While cities and towns did exist during the Feudal period, it is crucial to understand they played a secondary role relative to the manors. Feudalism was an agriculturally based system, and manors were the focal point of economic activity. Lords, who controlled the land, were the most powerful group of people in the system.

The Catholic Church played an important role in governing how Feudalism operated and in the acceptance of the system of duties and obligations. During the Feudal period, Europe was Christian, and to be Christian was to be Catholic. The idea that god created individuals to fulfill a particular role in life was widely accepted. To some degree, salvation was determined by how well people fulfilled the particular role for which god created them. On judgment day, this would be factored into the ultimate fate of a person. This idea restrained the lords in the way they treated their serfs and caused the serfs to accept their role in the system.

It is important to recognize how different the Feudal system was from the Capitalist system which would replace it. In the Capitalist system there is an economic ladder which can be climbed. No matter how low or humble an individual's beginning, through hard work and commitment, an individual can rise in life and climb the economic ladder. The son of a custodian can strive to become a doctor, a wealthy industrialist, or whatever else he may desire.

In the Feudal system, there was no economic ladder to climb. The son of a serf was destined to be a serf. The son of a blacksmith was destined to be a blacksmith. The son of a lord would be a lord. For the most part, people accepted this and strove to do their best to fulfill the role god had created them for. The teachings of the Catholic Church re-enforced this idea. As a result, the Feudal system was a much less dynamic system than the Capitalist system.[v]

The growth of trade would eventually lead to the decline and collapse of Feudalism. As the lords solidified their power, Europe became less chaotic and more peaceful. Additionally, over time, the roads were gradually repaired by the lords. As Europe became less dangerous and travel became easier, merchants would come and trade would increase. The rise in trade, however, would create increasing problems for the Feudal system.

At first, the merchants were traveling merchants who went from manor to manor buying and selling goods. As trade continued to grow, the merchants would come in large groups, in caravans. It was no longer practical for the merchants to go from manor to manor buying and selling their goods. Instead, merchants began holding trade fairs. They would set up in a central location, typically in or near a city or town; and now the people from the manors would come to the trade fairs to buy and sell. This was a subtle but important transfer of power;

---

[v] The Protestant Reformation aided the development of the Capitalist system. Martin Luther's proclamation that people are "saved by faith alone" helped to diminish adherence to and free people from the old Feudal idea that people had to accept a particular role in life and the duties and obligations that were part of that role since salvation was no longer affected by what people did, .i.e., how well they fulfilled their roles.

rather than the merchants going to the people in the manor, the people in the manor now went to the merchants.

Eventually where the trade fairs were held, some merchants began setting up permanent shops. The traveling merchant was being transformed into a resident merchant. Now it was possible to buy and sell with the merchants year-round rather than just when the trade fairs were being held.

The permanent shops were usually located in or near towns or cities. With the establishment of permanent shops came the development of markets in the cities and towns. As markets grew, so did the cities and towns. As markets, cities, and towns became increasingly important and powerful, manors declined. The most important characteristic of the manor was its self-sufficiency; but in a market-oriented system, self-sufficiency is irrelevant. As a result, markets (and, therefore cities and towns) gradually began to supplant the manors as the focal point of economic activity. Markets, not manors, were becoming the main economic entity in the system.

As trade grew, merchants became increasingly wealthy and powerful. The wealth and power of the merchants were based on trade. However, Feudalism was based on a lack of trade, which created a fundamental challenge for the Feudal system. How does a power group (the merchants) whose power is based on trade fit into an economic system based on a lack of trade? The wealth and power of the merchants could not be accommodated in the Feudal system. Something had to give, and what gave was the Feudal system.

With the development of markets came the development of a money-wage system. Merchants in the cities and towns needed workers, and so they began offering a money-wage. Serfs began to desert the manors to work for a money-wage in the cities and towns. Merchants willingly accepted the serfs because they needed workers.

As time passed, the Feudal system came under increasing stress. Merchants became increasingly powerful, markets and cities grew in importance, and manors slowly declined. Belatedly, the lords attempted to re-establish their authority and power. They increased their efforts to force the serfs to remain on the manors and to reverse the changes that were occurring. The result was Peasant Revolts which shook Europe. This was a very brutal period that led to the slaughter of thousands of people as the peasants resisted the lords.

In the end, it was too late for the lords. They could not turn back the clock and re-institute the old ways. Feudalism would collapse and be replaced by a new economic system, Capitalism.

3

The Beginning of Capitalism

Early Capitalism

Capitalism, unlike Slave systems and the Feudal system before it, is a non-agriculturally based economic system. There was a gradual increase in the importance of industry relative to agriculture. Eventually, capital, rather than land, became the key to economic power. The first stage of Capitalism was Early Capitalism, which existed from approximately 1300 to 1500 ACE.

In the Capitalist system markets are the most important economic entity; the focal point of economic activity. Since markets are located primarily in cities and towns, cities and towns are an important part of the Capitalist system.

In Early Capitalism, there were three primary groups of people: merchants, petty capitalists, and workers. Merchants controlled trade. Petty capitalists controlled industry (and thus capital). Merchants would purchase goods from the petty capitalist shops to sell in markets. Workers sold their labor services to petty capitalists.

During Early Capitalism the key to economic power was trade. Thus, merchants were the most powerful group of people in the system. Overtime this would change, and eventually the control of capital would become the key to economic power.

It is important to appreciate the difference in the relationship between the capitalist and the worker relative to the old feudal relationship between the lord and the serf. Lords and serfs were driven by their mutual duties and obligations. The most important aspect of this relationship was the lords' obligation to look after the general welfare of the serfs. The teachings of the Catholic Church re-enforced this obligation. For the most part, lords accepted it. This obligation existed in both good times and bad. So, if there was a drought and a poor harvest, the lord had the responsibility to look after his people, to ensure they had something to eat. He was obligated to open up his storehouse and provide whatever grain was available.

In contrast, the relationship between the capitalist and worker is a *market-based relationship*. The worker is paid a money-wage. The capitalist owes the worker a day's pay for a day's work. If times are bad and the capitalist has to close his shop and there is no work to be had, the capitalist doesn't owe the worker anything. The fact the worker cannot pay their rent and cannot feed their family is not the capitalist's problem. The capitalist is not obligated, as the lord was, to provide for the worker during hard times.

This negative side of Capitalism, for the most part, was not apparent during the Early Capitalist period for two main reasons. First, a new economic system was being born, so the Early Capitalist period of time was largely a period of economic growth. This meant there were no long periods of time of widespread unemployment. Second, during the Early Capitalist period, production occurred in small shops. As a result, a personal relationship developed between the petty capitalist and the worker. They knew each other on a personal basis. In such a situation, most capitalists developed a sense of comradeship and responsibility to the worker. They were hesitant to just lay workers off when times became hard. Instead, they would tend to spread the work out the best they could to keep the worker employed. It would be later, during the Industrial Revolution, the darker side of Capitalism would appear.

Mercantilism

The second stage of Capitalism was Mercantilism, which existed from approximately 1500 to 1800 ACE. Mercantilism is a combination word, Merchant-Capitalism. During the Mercantilist period of time, merchants and petty capitalists would merge and become one group. As trade grew, merchants became increasingly wealthy and powerful. Eventually, they were able to take over the shops of the petty capitalists. As this occurred, the merchants became merchant-capitalists, thus the term Mercantilism.

During this period of time, trade remained the key to economic power. However, as time passed, industry (and the control of capital) became increasingly important relative to trade. This would culminate with the Industrial Revolution. Merchant-capitalists would then become known as simply capitalists.

The Mercantilist period coincided with the rise of nationalism and the development of nation-states. It was in the interest of merchant-capitalists to have governmental units that had authority over a broader area so the rules of trade (the laws governing trade) were more consistent over a wider area. It made trade easier. As a result, the merchant-capitalists increasingly threw their power behind a central authority which could consolidate power over a wider area and standardize the rules of trade.

Two other factors were major contributors to the development of nation-states. First, a distinction was increasingly made between the ruler and the state; they were seen as two distinct entities. Previously the state and the ruler were largely considered to be one and the same. Second, as Capitalism developed, there was a decline in religious authority over the state. The power of the Catholic Church over countries declined as the Protestant Reformation occurred.[i] Increasingly, the nation-state was seen as distinct and independent of religious authority.

Nation-states were larger and much more complex political/economic entities when compared to what had existed in the previous

---

[i]   The rise of Capitalism and the Protestant Reformation have been closely linked. See *The Protestant Ethic and the Spirit of Capitalism* by Max Weber.

Feudal system. There was a concern over how these larger entities could be controlled and held together, and how they could be made economically strong. *Mercantilists believed the key to a country being economically strong was gold.* Nation-states needed large amounts of wealth in the form of gold to be powerful. This enabled them to fund the needed militaries and state infrastructures to sustain the nation-states. Thus, the attainment of gold by the nation-state was a paramount concern in Mercantilism.

One way to obtain gold was to conquer and take it away from other countries, and European powers certainly did this. Cortez went to Mexico, conquered the Aztecs, and took their gold. Pizzaro did the same in Peru to the Incas. However, for our purposes we need to focus on the Mercantilist idea of how a country *economically* obtained gold.

For the mercantilist, the main economic way a nation-state obtained gold was through exports, i.e., by selling products to other countries. When a country sells products to other countries, the selling country receives gold and sends products. The main way a country lost gold was through imports, i.e., by buying products from other countries. When a country buys products from other countries, they send gold and receive products. *Exports result in an inflow of gold to a country and imports result in an outflow of gold.* For the mercantilist, the inflow of gold *must* be greater than the outflow of gold, so the value of exports *must* be greater than the value of imports. This will result in a country obtaining greater amounts of gold, which is the key to a nation-state being powerful. Thus, for Mercantilist countries:

Value of Exports > Value of Imports

To ensure that this occurred, Mercantilist countries adopted two policies. *The first was the establishment of trade monopolies. A trade monopoly is an exclusive trading privilege granted to a company by a country.* It was believed that such monopolies would enable the company to control prices for the benefit of the nation-state. For example, England granted a trade monopoly to the British East Indies Company for trade with India.

28

England wanted to sell cloth to India. If many English companies were allowed to go to India and compete against each other to sell cloth, the price of cloth would be driven down. Mercantilists believed that this lower price of cloth would drive the value of English exports to India down, resulting in less gold flowing into England from India. If, instead, a trade monopoly was granted to one English company, it would be able to keep the price of cloth higher, resulting in the value of the exported cloth rising and increasing the inflow of gold to England.

The opposite would be true on the import side. England wanted to buy tea from India. If many English companies were allowed to go to India and compete against each other to buy tea, the price of tea would be driven up. Mercantilists believed that this higher price of tea would drive the value of English imports from India up, resulting in more gold flowing out of England into India. If, instead, a trade monopoly was granted to one English company, it would be able to keep the price of tea lower, resulting in the value of the imported tea falling and decreasing the outflow of gold from England.

However, even if England granted trade monopolies, the policy would be undermined if other European countries were allowed to go to India and trade. As a result of the competition, the price of European cloth would be driven down, decreasing the inflow of gold and the value of exports, and the price of Indian tea would be driven up, increasing the outflow of gold and the value of imports.

This problem was solved by the second major policy of Mercantilism, the establishment of colonies. To circumvent the problem of competition from other European countries, England declared that India was their colony. *A colony is an exclusive trading territory claimed by a country.* England declared that they were the only country allowed to trade with India; no other countries would be allowed in.

To enforce this policy required that England have a strong military. Other European countries did the same. There was a scramble to build up the military might, particularly the navy, of the European powers.

The result were numerous wars fought among the European nations-states. Wars over colonies and trade routes. England emerged as the most victorious and powerful of the European countries. The English ended up with the most and some of the most lucrative colonies and trade routes, but they did not get them all. France, Spain, Portugal, and Holland all established colonial empires. The European countries essentially divided the world among themselves, establishing colonies across the globe where they granted trade monopolies and had exclusive trading privileges.

4

Free Market Capitalism

Adam Smith and the Wealth of Nations

The foundation for the creation of the Free Market Capitalist system was laid by one of the most important books about Economics ever written, *The Wealth of Nations*,[2] authored by Adam Smith in 1776. Smith is often referred to as the Father of Economics. He was not the first person to ever write about Economics, but he was the first to write an extensive book on the subject.

The Wealth of Nations is about exactly what the title indicates: how can a country be made wealthy, i.e., how can a country be made economically strong? Smith disagreed with the mercantilist idea that gold was the key to a nation-state being powerful. He believed that the focus of Mercantilism on obtaining gold was, in fact, counter-productive.

Smith believed that the key to economic strength for a country was the country's productive capabilities. Countries are economically powerful (wealthy) because they are very productive. Countries that are economically weak (poor) are not very productive.

Smith believed that the mercantilists confused the relationship between economic power and gold. It is true economically powerful (wealthy) countries have lots of gold. However, mercantilists were wrong in believing gold was the *cause* of economic power. For Smith, gold was the *result* of economic power. The cause of economic power (wealth) was a country's productive capabilities.

Smith argued that, rather than focusing on obtaining gold, a country should, instead, focus on increasing its productive capabilities. He contended one of the main ways a country could increase its productive capabilities was through trade, and so he advocated countries should establish a policy of allowing free trade. *Free trade means individuals should be free to trade with whomever they want.* He argued against Mercantilist polices. He believed countries should not establish trade monopolies and dictate whether or not someone is allowed to trade in a particular area. Countries should, instead, establish a *free market; a market where people are free to trade with whomever they want.*

Smith's argument that free trade and free markets increased the productive capabilities of a country is essentially the following:

Free Trade   ➝   Increases Trade   ➝   Larger Markets   ➝
Increases Division of Labor   ➝   Increases Use of Capital   ➝
Increases Productivity   ➝   Increases Consumption

For Smith, countries became economically stronger (wealthier) through trade, which increased production and, therefore, consumption (living standards) in the country.

Free trade increases trade. The fewer rules and regulations there are concerning trade, the easier trading is. The easier trading is, the more trade will occur. Increased trade, then, leads to larger markets.

Larger markets enable producers to increase the division of labor. *The division of labor is the way a job is broken down into parts.* There are many ways to do any job. Producers have to decide how a job should be done. Increased production increases the options a producer has in determining how work is done.

For example, historically shoe making was a skilled craft; shoemakers were skilled craftsmen who produced shoes. For the most part, a shoemaker did the entire job of making a pair of shoes. However, if more shoes are produced, the job of making a pair of shoes can be broken down into several different jobs.

There are several steps necessary to produce a pair of shoes: leather must be cut, the leather needs to be dyed, it must then be sewn together, soles and heels need to be made and attached to the shoe, holes need to be put in the leather, and laces inserted. A skilled shoemaker would do all the steps involved in producing a pair of shoes.

For Smith, if the market grew larger and the number of pairs of shoes being produced increased, rather than having one person do all the steps in producing a pair of shoes, the job could be broken down into several different jobs: cutting leather, dyeing leather, sewing leather, making soles or heels, attaching the sole or heel, putting holes in the leather, and lacing the shoe. According to Smith, breaking down the job of making shoes into several different jobs would increase productivity for three main reasons.

First, when workers focus on one part of doing a job they become more proficient, i.e., productive, in that one part. A worker who focuses only on cutting leather becomes faster and better at cutting leather. More leather will be cut and the cuts will be more precise.

Second, there is a natural inefficiency built in when a worker transitions from one task to another. Tools must be put aside and different tools need to be gathered. There also tends to be a natural pause as a worker moves from one task to another. This all takes time, time which could be spent on the task at hand, e.g., cutting leather. Focusing on one task eliminates this natural inefficiency that exists as the worker transitions from one step in the production process to another.

Finally, and most important for Smith, breaking down a job into several different jobs increases the opportunity to use capital (machines) to increase productivity. For example, in making a pair of shoes, a skilled shoemaker would use a pair of shears to cut the leather. Suppose there is a machine that exists that cuts leather more efficiently; it can cut much more leather than the shoemaker in the same amount of time and the cuts are more consistent. However, the machine is costly; so, the use of the machine can only be justified if enough pairs of shoes are being produced. If the market is too small, it is not worth it to buy the machine because there are not enough pairs of shoes being sold to pay for the machine. But if the market is bigger, more pairs of shoes are being sold; so, it pays to use the machine.

The use of the machine (capital) increases productivity, allowing more pairs of shoes to be produced (and consumed). Living standards rise. However, the market has to be large enough to absorb the additional pairs of shoes being produced. Free trade increases the size of the market enabling producers to use more capital. The adoption of a policy of free trade makes a country economically stronger and wealthier.

The fundamental argument Adam Smith made in favor of Free Market Capitalism was:

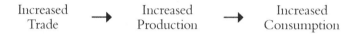

Increased Trade → Increased Production → Increased Consumption

Thus, the key to higher living standards in a country was the establishment of free trade, that is, a free market.

Smith argued that mercantilist policies were, in fact, counter-productive; they actually made countries economically weaker and poorer. By establishing trade monopolies and colonies, restricting who was allowed to trade where, the policies actually decreased trade, causing markets to be smaller, limiting the division of labor, and restricting the use of capital causing production and, therefore, consumption (living standards) to go down.

Smith contended the mercantilist idea of the government being heavily involved in the economic system by granting trade monopolies and establishing colonies was wrong. Instead, the government's role in economic matters should be very limited, getting out of the way and allowing the natural course of economic activity to flow on its own. This is the idea of "laissez-faire," a French phrase meaning "let it be." The government should just let the economy be.

Smith's ideas coincided with the movement in Western Europe at that time towards the belief that human beings should be freer. There was a movement towards the acceptance of the idea of political freedom. Human beings should have more say in who their rulers are. Political rule should not be hereditary, nor should it be based on military or financial strength. People should be able to choose their rulers by voting for them. Also, human beings should have the freedom to criticize those in power without fear of retribution or punishment. This is embodied in the freedom of the press, which is the ability to print or say whatever one wants about the government.

There was also a greater demand that human beings should be religiously free, free to practice whatever religion they choose. Rulers should not be determining what religious beliefs were allowed or not allowed and punishing those who practiced some other non-favored religion.

Just as there were movements towards greater political and religious freedom at the time, there was also a movement towards the idea that human beings should be more free economically. The government should not be granting trade monopolies and establishing colonies, dictating who was allowed to trade with whom. Free trade, a free market, should exist where human beings are free to trade with whomever they want. This is the importance of Adam Smith, the individual who first advocated for economic freedom.

Mercantilism Versus Free Market Capitalism

Mercantilism was the last major economic system to exist before the development of Free Market Capitalism[i], so it is important to understand the critical ways that Mercantilism and Free Market Capitalism differ. Additionally, there are countries in the world today that still practice mercantilist-type policies (e.g., China), so looking at the differences will help to understand why such policies are still practiced. There are four major comparisons that need to be made:

1. The view of trade
2. The economic well-being of a country versus the economic well-being of the people in the country
3. The economic basis of each system
4. The role of government.

---

[i] While Mercantilism as the dominant economic system would come to end, the appropriation, domination, and exploitation of colonies by Western Capitalist powers would continue until the mid-twentieth century.

35

First, the view of trade differs. In Mercantilism, trade is viewed as a win-lose situation. When trade between countries occurs, one country wins and the other country loses. If, for England, the value of exports (the inflow of gold) is greater than the value of imports (the outflow of gold), then the opposite must be true for India. So, as England becomes stronger from trade, India must become weaker. The mercantilist countries wanted to ensure that they were on the winning side of this arrangement.

In Free Market Capitalism, trade is viewed as a win-win situation. The critical difference is that one of the important principles of Free Market Capitalism is individual freedom. Whether or not trade occurs is up to each party (country) involved. Every country is free to trade or not trade. In this case, the only time trade would occur is if each country agreed to trade. A country would only agree to trade if it was beneficial to the country. Thus, trade would have to be win-win.

The problem in Mercantilism is that the colony is forced to trade with the mercantilist country—and only that country. If a country is forced to trade with another, even if they don't desire to trade, not surprisingly, trade could end up being win-lose.

The second important comparison is the concept of the economic well-being of the country versus the economic well-being of the people in the country. In Mercantilism, these are considered to be two different, distinct things. Mercantilism is focused on the economic well-being of the country over the economic well-being of the people in the country.

Mercantilist policies certainly were detrimental to the economic well-being of the people in the colonies. However, it is important to note not everyone in the mercantilist country benefited from mercantilist policies. Certainly, the company granted a trade monopoly, like the British East Indies company, benefited. This would primarily be the owners of the company and employees of the company. Their living standards rose as a result of the trade monopoly. However, other people in the mercantilist country would be harmed, i.e., their living standards would go down. This mainly involved two groups of people.

The first group were other English companies who would have liked to trade in the colony where the trade monopoly existed. However,

36

they were prohibited from directly doing so. The only way an English company selling cloth could sell its cloth in India was to go through the British East Indies Company. Therefore, the British East Indies Company was in a position to dictate the price it paid the other company for cloth. The British East Indies Company could hold down the price of cloth, hurting the owners and employees of the company selling the cloth and enriching the owners and employees of the British East Indies Company. The other company could have obtained a higher price for its cloth if it were allowed to go directly to India and sell their cloth.

In addition to paying a lower price for the cloth it bought from other English companies, the British East Indies Company was also able to charge a higher price for the cloth in India due to the lack of competition. Thus, the living standards of the owners and employees of the British East Indies Company increased while the living standards of the owners and employees of other cloth-producing English companies, who otherwise would have obtained the higher price, went down.

The second, and more important group, were consumers in England who would see their living standards (consumption) go down. As a result of the trade monopoly, the British East Indies Company was able to pay a lower price for the tea it bought in India. However, since the company was the only one selling Indian tea in England, the company was able to charge a higher price for the tea. The living standards of the owners and employees of the British East Indies Company would go up while the living standards of people who bought tea in England (consumers) went down.

The English government was willing to accept the fact that the living standards of some people in England would go down because it was believed there was a distinction between the economic well-being of the country versus the economic well-being of the people in the country. Mercantilist governments were focused on increasing the well-being (economic strength) of the country. If this meant some of the people in the country had to make economic sacrifices (have their living standards, i.e., well-being, go down), so be it. What was important was the economic strength (well-being) of the country.

In Free Market Capitalism, on the other hand, the economic well-being of a country and the economic well-being of the people in the country are considered to be one and the same. For advocates of Free Market Capitalism, it is absurd to think that a country can be made economically stronger while the people in the country are made economically weaker. Advocates of Free Market Capitalism believe the way to increase a country's economic well-being (strength) is to increase the economic well-being (strength) of the people in the country. Again, mercantilist policies are counter-productive.

The third important comparison between Mercantilism and Free Market Capitalism is the economic basis for the two systems. Mercantilism is based on the existence of monopolies. The economic basis of Free Market Capitalism, on the other hand, is competition. Mercantilists believe the path to economic strength was through the granting of monopolies. Advocates of Free Market Capitalism believe the path to economic strength is through competition.

The last important comparison between Mercantilism and Free Market Capitalism is the role of the government. Mercantilists believe the government should be heavily involved in the economic system, granting trade monopolies and determining who should be able to trade with whom. Advocates of Free Market Capitalism believe in laissez-faire; the government should have limited involvement in the economic system and should adopt a policy of free trade, allowing the market to work.

Mercantilism as the dominant economic system in the world would largely come to end in the late 1700s. Increasingly, Adam Smith's ideas of the benefits of free trade and a free market would be accepted and adopted. However, it must be noted, even though Mercantilism as the dominant economic system in the world would end, there still would be countries in the world adopting mercantilist-type policies. That is still true to the present day.

The United States and Free Market Capitalism

The publication of *The Wealth of Nations* in 1776 coincided with the beginning of the American Revolution. The United States was initially a colony of England and, as such, a part of the Mercantilist system. The revolution was, in some part, a revolt against mercantilist policies. While the revolution was primarily caused for political reasons, certainly economic concerns also played a role.

After the American colonists won the revolution, they established their new country based largely on the ideas of freedom: political, religious, and economic. These tenets of freedom would drive the development of the country.

When the United States was first established, it was governed by the Articles of Confederation. Under the Articles, the states were very loosely tied together and were able to establish policies largely independent of each other. This included economic policies. As a result, states put up barriers against other states' products in the form of tariffs, reducing trade between states and lowering living standards. They did so to protect producers within a state from outside competition.

The Articles of Confederation proved to be defective in a number of ways in establishing the necessary unity among the states. As it became increasingly clear the Articles would never lead to the needed cohesion to create an effective union, there were calls to create a new governing document. This resulted in the Constitutional Convention and the adoption of the United States Constitution in 1788. As the preamble to the Constitution states, the purpose was to create "a more perfect union." This relates to both political and economic unity.

The Commerce Clause, Article 1 Section 8, of the Constitution, addresses the economic issue of trade. It gives the Federal government the authority "to regulate Commerce with foreign Nations, and among the several States, and with the Indian Tribes." No longer would states be allowed to put up barriers, i.e., tariffs against other states. This resulted in the creation of a large free trade zone within the boundaries of the country. *The result was exactly what Adam Smith asserted: an increase in trade, production, and consumption (living standards) within the country.* It has been argued the key to the United States becoming the economically powerful and wealthy country it became was this adoption of free trade within the boundaries of the country stipulated by the Constitution.

No other country in the world is more associated with the ideas of economic freedom, free trade, and free markets than the United States. It has been, perhaps, the chief proponent of the adoption of such policies across the globe. While there have been periods of time when protectionist, anti-trade policies have been adopted, such as during the Great Depression, the long-run trajectory of the country has been towards the establishment of freer trade and freer markets.

Trade has become a particularly important issue at the end of the twentieth and beginning of the twenty-first century. There has been a concerted movement towards signing trade agreements to increase global trade over the last thirty years with a promise that rising living standards would result. However, the proliferation of trade agreements has been a very contentious issue, with many questioning whether the benefits Adam Smith asserted would result have really occurred. We turn to this in the next chapter.

5

The Expansion of Free Trade

The North American Free Trade Agreement

Towards the end of the twentieth century, more and more governments accepted the ideas of Adam Smith: increased trade leads to increased production, and, therefore, increased consumption (living standards). As governments strove to increase the living standards of their people, they turned to freer trade and freer markets as the key.

The first step in this direction was the signing of regional free trade agreements creating free trade zones among countries in a specific area. One of the first and most important was the North American Free Trade Agreement (NAFTA) between the United States, Canada, and Mexico signed in January 1994. This agreement has been the source of a great deal of controversy. It has been a frequent target of President Donald Trump as being particularly harmful to the United States economy.

> "NAFTA, signed by her [Hillary Clinton's] husband, is perhaps the greatest disaster trade deal in the history of the world."

> "NAFTA is the worst trade deal maybe ever signed anywhere, but certainly ever signed in this country."

"[Bill Clinton] approved NAFTA, which is the single worst trade deal ever approved in this country."

"NAFTA is a horrible agreement, one of the worst trade deals ever. It's just one of the worst."

"America has lost one-third of its manufacturing jobs since NAFTA, a deal signed by Bill Clinton and supported strongly by Hillary Clinton. And by the way, the single worst trade deal ever made in history anywhere."

"America has lost nearly one-third of its manufacturing jobs since 1997 following the enactment of disastrous trade deals supported by Bill and Hillary Clinton."

—AZ QUOTES, AZQUOTES.COM,
DONALD TRUMP QUOTES ABOUT TRADE

It is important to review the actual impact of NAFTA.

The NAFTA agreement clearly increased trade in North America, that is, between the United States, Canada, and Mexico. Freer trade leads to increased trade. The fewer rules and regulations there are concerning trade, the more trade will result. Trade in North America *had* to increase as a result of NAFTA. As a result of increased trade, production and, therefore, consumption in North America *had* to increase. This is the basic lesson of Adam Smith. *In other words, NAFTA had to result in higher living standards in North America.*

Whether or not NAFTA benefited the United States (increased living standards) is a more complicated issue. It is possible living standards in Canada and Mexico increased while living standards in the United States fell as a result of the trade deal. However, for this to have happened, the increases in living standards in Canada and Mexico would have to outweigh the decrease in living standards in the United States since, overall, living standards in North America *had* to go up:

Canada & Mexico   >   United States
Living Standards Rise   Living Standards Fall

Freer trade *must* lead to more trade, which leads to higher levels of production and consumption. *So, again, living standards in North America had to go up.* Therefore, falling living standards in the United States *would have to be outweighed by* rising living standards in Canada and/or Mexico. Higher living standards in Mexico and/or Canada would come at the expense of the United States. So, *theoretically*, it is possible the United States was made worse off (lower living standards) as a result of NAFTA.

However, when looking at the actual economic situation for the three countries, it would have been virtually impossible for NAFTA to result in living standards in the United States going down. This is due to the size of the economies of each country, which is measured by Gross Domestic Product (GDP).[i]

In 2018 the GDP of the United States was over $20 trillion. At the same time, the GDP of Canada was $1.7 trillion and the GDP of Mexico was $1.2 trillion, a combined total of $2.9 trillion.[3] In other words, the U.S. economy by itself is approximately eight times as big as the economies of Canada and Mexico combined. For living standards in the United States to go down while living standards overall in North America increase, living standards in Canada and Mexico would need to increase at totally unrealistic rates. *The United States economy is simply too big relative to the combined economies of Canada and Mexico to have living standards in the United States go down while overall living standards in North America go up.* The combined economies of Canada and Mexico are simply too small to offset declines in the economy of the United States, so that, overall, the economy of North America rises. Whichever direction the United States economy goes, so goes the overall economy of North America. *We know that trade, production, and living standards in North America had to go up as a result of NAFTA; therefore, trade, production, and living standards had to go up in the United States as well.*

Why then is the NAFTA deal so thoroughly denigrated and attacked? Why is there a belief among so many Americans that NAFTA was a bad deal for the United States, causing living standards in the United States to go down?

---

[i]   Gross Domestic Product is the total value of a country's production over a period of time.

The key is the distribution of the benefits from the NAFTA deal. While NAFTA resulted in the living standards of many Americans to rise, it also resulted in the living standards of many Americans to fall. Not everyone in the United States saw their living standard rise as result of NAFTA. It is very important to understand whose living standard in the United States went up and whose went down and the reasons why this happened. We will explore this below.

The European Union

NAFTA was one of the first important regional free trade agreements. Other areas of the world were also working on the creation of regional free trade agreements of their own. One of the most important was the European Union, which was signed in November 1993.

European countries increasingly recognized they were ill-equipped to compete economically in the twenty-first century. The world was quickly becoming dominated by two economic behemoths, the United States and China. The United States has the biggest economy in the world with a GDP in 2018 of over $20 trillion. China is second with a GDP of $14 trillion. Germany has the largest economy in Europe at $4.2 trillion.[4] Germany by itself, and the other European countries on their own, had little chance of being able to effectively compete with the gigantic economies of the United States and China.

European countries soon realized their best opportunity to become globally competitive was to unite. The result was the creation of a regional free trade zone across Europe, the European Union. The agreement also allowed the free movement of citizens among the member states.

The European Union consisted of 27 countries in Europe. The agreement created free trade, a free market, across the 27 countries. The result would be, as Adam Smith asserted, increased trade leading to increased production and consumption (living standards) across Europe.

Another important aspect of the European Union agreement, which made it distinct from other regional free trade agreements, was the creation of a single currency, the Euro. The purpose was to increase economic ties among the countries and unify the market. Creation of a single currency would increase trade, production, and living standards across Europe. A single currency makes trade easier and cheaper. No longer is it necessary to pay the cost of exchanging currencies in order to trade. With trade being easier and cheaper, more trade occurs, leading to higher production and consumption just as Adam Smith asserted.

The United Kingdom (U.K.) joined the European Union (it was the 28th member at the time) but did not participate in the common currency. Instead, the U.K. retained the pound as its form of money. The U.K. wanted to ensure London remained one of the leading financial centers in the world, and it was felt this role would be compromised if the Euro were adopted. Also, the U.K. wanted to maintain more economic flexibility and independence of action by having its own monetary system. The U.K. believed these considerations outweighed the benefits of joining the common currency.

Like the NAFTA agreement, the European Union has been marked by controversy. The European economic crisis of 2009, primarily involving Greece, Spain, and Italy, was a result of imperfections in the European Union agreement. The crisis resulted in the possibility that Greece, in particular, would withdraw from the European Union. Doing so proved extremely difficult for both Greece and the Union itself. In the end, the crisis was weathered; and Greece remained in the Union.

In 2016 the United Kingdom voted to withdraw from the European Union in what has become to be known as Brexit. Many in the U.K. did not believe the agreement had resulted in higher living standards. There was also a great deal of dissatisfaction with the free movement of other European people into the United Kingdom.

The U.K. and the European Union had a little over two years to work out how the exit would occur, with a target date of March 29, 2019. As with Greece's potential exit, leaving the European Union proved to be extremely difficult and contentious. When the target date arrived, no agreement had been reached. United Kingdom Prime

Minister Theresa May negotiated an extension with the European Union of the exit date to October 30, 2019.

Boris Johnson's Conservative Party won the Parliamentary elections in July 2019 and he took office as Prime Minister. He vowed to meet the October 30 deadline with or without a withdrawal deal in place with the European Union. However, opposition members of Parliament along with members of his own party blocked a withdrawal from the European Union unless there was an exit agreement in place.

Johnson was forced to seek an extension with the European Union, and an exit date of January 31, 2020 was agreed to. Johnson then called for a new election in December 2019. His Conservative Party won a resounding majority and the United Kingdom left the European Union on January 31, 2020. However, a transition period for finalizing exactly how the U.K. would accomplish leaving the Union was needed and negotiated. The final deadline date is December 31, 2020. Many matters remained unresolved. Unless agreement is reached, the U.K. will be forced to leave without an agreement which creates a great deal of uncertainty and the potential for significant economic and political disorder.

Even if the United Kingdom is able to negotiate an agreement that enables them to fully exit the European Union, substantial challenges will remain. The United Kingdom's GDP is just $2.7 trillion.[5] Many economists doubt the United Kingdom on its own has the capability to effectively compete with the economies of the United States, China, and the European Union. It appears the United Kingdom will strive to establish a stronger economic bond with the United States to compensate for what it loses with Brexit. How that might be accomplished remains to be seen.

The World Trade Agreement

Regional free trade agreements were the initial step taken in trying to increase trade (and raise living standards) across the globe. Ultimately, however, the target was a trade agreement which would encompass most of the world. The resulting World Trade Agreement (WTA) was established in January 1995. It was created to increase trade across the globe and, thus, increase production and consumption (living standards). Currently 164 countries are members of the WTA.

The predecessor to the WTA was the General Agreement on Trade and Tariffs (GATT) agreement. The GATT agreement was created in 1947 in the aftermath of World War II. It was believed contributors to the war were the protectionist policies (tariffs and quotas on goods), which countries adopted in response to the Great Depression. These policies had aggravated the impact of the Depression by reducing trade among countries, further reducing production and living standards across the world. It was believed increased living standards would result from reducing protectionist policies like tariffs; and increasing trade would decrease economic conflict among countries. Additionally, it was felt creating greater economic ties among countries would make it less likely they would engage in destructive wars.

Beginning in the late 1980s, there was an increasing belief the GATT agreement should be expanded and strengthened. The result was the adoption of the World Trade Agreement. The agreement established the World Trade Organization (WTO) to oversee the WTA. Since the WTA was instituted, trade across the globe has exploded. Global GDP in 1995 was approximately $50 trillion. By 2017, global GDP had reached $75 trillion, an increase of 50%.[6]

GDP per capita (per person) is the main measure of living standards used by economists. The change in global GDP per capita from 1995 and 2017 is shown in Table 5A. In nominal terms, global living standards increased by 95% between 1995 and 2017. In real terms, the increase was 44%.[ii]

[ii]   Nominal GDP ignores the impact of inflation on the value of the dollar. Nominal GDP is measured in current dollars, the value of the dollar in the year of measurement. Nominal GDP in the year 1995 is based on the value of the dollar in the year 1995. Real GDP takes into consideration the impact of inflation on the value of the dollar. Real GDP is measured in constant dollars, which keeps the value of the dollar constant over time. A base year, such as 2011, is selected. Real GDP in the year 1995 would then be based on the value of the dollar in the year 2011. Doing so makes comparisons of production between years more accurate in terms of the actual impact of any changes.

Table 5A   Nominal and Real GDP per Capita 1995 & 2017[7]

Year	Nominal GDP per Capita	Increase	Real GDP per Capita	Increase
1995	$5,500		$7,394	
2017	$10,722	95%	$10,636	44%

Real GDP measured in 2011 Dollars

So, economically the WTA has been a resounding success. Just as Adam Smith asserted, increased trade resulted in increased production and, therefore, increased living standards.[iii] However, despite the impressive increases in global GDP and living standards, there are many critics of the WTA and the WTO (and trade agreements in general).

The Economic Impact of Trade Agreements

Trade agreements have come under a great deal of scrutiny and criticism in recent years. There has been no greater critic of trade agreements than President Donald Trump. It is important to fully appreciate the unrelenting nature and severity of his attacks on America's trade agreements.

> "We have been ripped off by China. We've been ripped off by — excuse me, Mr. President — the European Union, of which you're a part of. We've been ripped off by everybody."

> "Our country is in serious trouble. We don't win anymore. We don't beat China in trade. We don't beat Japan, with their millions and millions of cars coming into this country, in trade. We can't beat Mexico, at the border or in trade. We can't do anything right."

> "This country is in big trouble. We don't win anymore We lose to China. We lose to Mexico both in trade and at the border. We lose to everybody."

[iii]   Of course, it could be argued that the increases would have occurred even if the WTA had never been adopted. However, economists nearly universally agree that the WTA was a major contributor to rising global GDP and living standards.

"You look at what the world is doing to us at every level, whether it's militarily, or in trade, or in so many other levels, the world is taking advantage of the United States and it's driving us into literally being a third world nation."

"Mexico continues to make billions on not only our bad trade deals but also relies heavily on the billions of dollars in remittances sent from illegal immigrants in the United States."

"The economy is very sick. We're losing our jobs to China, to Japan, to every country. We're making horrible trade deals. We are losing jobs in this country…"

"America is being absolutely devastated with bad trade deals."

"With our trade deals we are always second. You can pick any country and they're eating our lunch and making us look bad and so we're going to change that."

"We have the most incompetently worked trade deals ever negotiated probably in the history of the world…"

"We have to renegotiate our trade deals, and we have to stop these countries from stealing our companies and our jobs."

"America has hundreds of billions of dollars of losses on a yearly basis – hundreds of billions with China on trade and trade imbalance, with Japan, with Mexico, with just about everybody. We don't make good deals anymore."

—AZ QUOTES, AZQUOTES.COM,
DONALD TRUMP QUOTES ABOUT TRADE

With the litany of statements like those above being made by the President of the United States, it is little wonder many Americans have come to believe the source of their problems are the trade deals themselves; the United States is being victimized by our trading partners. Other countries are "stealing our jobs," driving American living standards down.

But the fundamental lesson from Adam Smith is trade increases production and, therefore, consumption (living standards). An increase in production means

an increase the number of jobs.[iv] *It is inarguable that trade agreements have increased trade across the globe, resulting in the creation of jobs and an increase in living standards around the world.*

So, as with NAFTA, the argument *must* be that whereas jobs and living standards have risen in the world as a result of trade agreements, the United States has actually seen a decrease while the rest of the world has seen an increase. Again, for this to have happened, increases in jobs and living standards in the rest of the world would have to have increased by a great-enough amount to offset the decreases in jobs and living standards which occurred in the United States.

As with NAFTA, this is virtually impossible to have happened. As Table 5B shows, the United States has the largest Gross Domestic Product in the world.

Table 5B   GDP and % Global GDP by Country 2017[8]

Country	GDP (Trillions)	% Global GDP
United States	$20.49	25.4%
China	$13.41	16.6%
Japan	$4.97	6.2%
Germany	$4.00	5.0%
United Kingdom	$2.83	3.5%
Italy	$2.78	3.4%
India	$2.72	3.4%
Barzil	$2.07	2.6%
Canada	$1.71	2.1%
European Union	$18.88	23.4%
Global GDA	$80.70	

[iv] There are two reasons why it may be possible for production to increase without an increase in jobs. First, the increase in production could be the result of an increased use of capital rather than labor, i.e., a substitution of capital for labor, increasing productivity. Second, production could increase due to increases in productivity that could occur for two other reasons. First, workers could become more productive due to such factors as better training, education, health, or nutrition. Second, new technology could result in the creation of more productive capital or production techniques.

The GDP of the United States is 53.8% bigger than the second biggest country, China. It is just slightly smaller than the economies of the next three biggest economies, China, Japan, and Germany, combined. It is bigger than the economy of the entire European Union. The United States economy is the engine that drives the global economy. It is virtually impossible for the United States' economy to experience fewer jobs and falling living standards at the same time the overall global economy is experiencing job growth and rising living standards.

The statistics bear this out. Between 1995 and 2018, the United States GDP rose from $7.6 trillion to $20.5 trillion in nominal terms, an increase of 169%. In terms of real GDP, it increased by 74%.[9] These are enormous increases. While it could be argued GDP growth would have been even higher if not for the trade agreements, this is a highly unrealistic argument. The trade agreements clearly *contributed* to growth of production in the United States; they did not *detract* from it. Adam Smith's fundamental premise, increased trade increases production and consumption, *had* to hold true for the largest economy in the world between 1995 and 2018.

As with the NAFTA agreement, it is not possible to both accept Adam Smith's argument that increased trade increases production and living standards and, at the same time, accept overall production and living standards have fallen in the United States and risen in the overall global economy as a result of the agreements. From a common-sense perspective, one can just look at how well people overall in the United States still live relative to people in other parts of the world like China and Mexico.

It also must be kept in mind the United States has been the leading advocate for freer trade in the world. Over the years the United States has continually asked for, pressured for, insisted on, and pleaded for more open trade across the globe. Our leaders, both political and economic, both Democrat and Republican, have widely recognized, as the largest economy in the world, we would benefit from more open markets. We are the most powerful country in the world on a number of fronts, including economically. It is difficult to fathom how less-powerful countries like Mexico, Japan, the countries in the European Union, China, and others could have possibly continually out-negotiated and taken advantage of us on trade over the last 40 years given our country's advocacy of it.

But that is exactly the argument that President Trump makes. He paints a picture of the United States as a weak country being victimized by its global trading partners. And he argues the reason for this is the incompetence and stupidity of the leaders of the United States over the last forty years.

"We're being taken advantage of because we have leaders who are incompetent."

"I love free trade, but we need great leadership to have real free trade. And we don't have good leadership. We have leadership that doesn't know what it's doing."

"I love trade. I'm a free trader, 100 percent. But we [the USA] need smart people making the deals, and we don't have smart people making the deals."

"We have people that are political hacks negotiating our trade deals."

"In America, we've had people that are political hacks making the biggest deals in the world, bigger than companies."

"On trade, our country is a disaster. We have political hacks. People that give money to politicians. That's how they get their jobs. We have the worst people negotiating our trade deals."

"Mexico with the United States has out negotiated us and beat us to a pulp through our past leaders. They've made us look foolish."

"We have the greatest negotiators in the world, we have the greatest business people in the world, we don't use them. We use political hacks."

—AZ QUOTES, AZQUOTES.COM,
DONALD TRUMP QUOTES ABOUT TRADE

This perception of the United States of America having been out-negotiated, out-smarted, and just plain incompetent and stupid in the trade deals which have been negotiated by Presidential administration after administration, both Democrat and Republican, over the last 40 years is both absurd and wrong. As former chief economist at the World Bank Joseph Stiglitz stated,

> From my perch as chief economist at the World Bank, it was obvious that the global rules of the game were tilted— not against, but in *favor* of the United States…The idea that our trade negotiators got snookered is laughable: we got almost everything we wanted in late twentieth-century trade negotiations.
>
> —STIGLITZ, 2019, P. 80

Certainly, governmental officials can be incompetent, perhaps stupid, and can make mistakes. But the United States would not still be the greatest economic power in the world, demonstrated by the size of our economy and the overall living standards of its citizens if, for the last 40 years, we have continually followed disastrous trade policies negotiated by incompetent leaders. The movement towards freer trade has been negotiated and implemented by both Democrat and Republican Administrations resulting in significant increases in production (jobs) and consumption (living standards) across the globe as well as in the United States. The basic lesson Adam Smith taught over two hundred years ago holds true today.

Then, why is it that so many Americans accept Trump's arguments and feel that these trade agreements have worsened their lives? What is the reason for the tremendous dissatisfaction with our trade policies? This is one of the most important questions we face today.

While the overall economic effect of the trade agreements has been beneficial by increasing trade, production, and living standards, in the United States, the distribution of the benefits has been too unequal. The gains from these agreements have, for the most part, disproportionately benefited higher-income/higher-wealth households while the vast majority of lower-income/middle-income/lower-wealth households have seen small, if any, increases in their living standards. Changes in the distribution of incomes and wealth in the country since the adoption of the trade agreements demonstrate how much higher-income/higher-wealth households have seen their living standards rise, while lower-income/middle-income/lower-wealth households have seen their living standards fall. This is shown in Table 5C.

Table 5C   *Share of Income by Income Group in the United States 1995 &*
             2017[10]

Income Group	1995	2017	% Change
Top .01%	2%	5%	150%
Top .1%	6%	10%	66%
Top 1%	15%	21%	40%
Bottom 99%	85%	79%	–7%

As shown in the table, since the adoption of the trade agreements, the share of income at the top of the scale has increased dramatically while the share of income for the vast majority of Americans has declined. While this trend has been in place since the early 1980s, it has been exacerbated since 1995 with the income gap significantly increasing.

A similar picture is shown with wealth as seen in Table 5D. Share of wealth has increased for those with the most wealth while it has actually decreased for most Americans.

Table 5D   *Share of Wealth by Wealth Group in the United States 1995 &*
             2016[11]

Wealth Group	1995	2016	% Change
Top 1%	38.5%	39.6%	2.85%
Top 5%	60.3%	66.7%	10.61%
Top 10%	71.8%	78.8%	9.74%
Bottom 90%	28.2%	21.2%	–24.82%

Since the adoption of the recent trade agreements, the vast majority of Americans have seen little, if any, rise in their standard of living. Additionally, the soaring incomes and wealth of the highest-income and highest-wealth households have created an even greater sense for most Americans that they are falling further behind and that there is a lack of opportunity for them and their children to get ahead.

The idea trade that agreements have caused overall living standards in the United States to fall is flawed. It is not the trade agreements which have been harmful to the United States, causing living standards to go down. On the contrary, the trade agreements have caused living standards, on average, to go up in the United States. The problem is the distribution of the gains from the agreements has caused the living standards for higher-income/higher-wealth households to soar and living standards for lower-income/middle-income/lower-wealth households to stagnate or go down. There are two main reasons why this has occurred.

First, trade agreements have enormously improved the environment for corporations to make profits. Never before in the history of the world has the global economy been so open for corporations to do business. As markets opened up, it has become increasingly easy for corporations to sell their products anywhere in the world. Additionally, trade agreements made it increasingly easy for corporations to set up the production of products in the least costly countries. As a result, corporate profits have skyrocketed. In 1995 corporate profits were approximately $500 billion. By 2018 they were over $2 trillion, a four-fold increase.[12]

However, the distribution of these increased profits among the United States population has been very skewed. As of 2016, just 10% of households owned 84% of the stock in the country. [13] As a result, soaring corporate profits have resulted in the wealth and incomes of higher-income/higher-wealth households, the ones who own most of the stock, to dramatically increase relative to the wealth and incomes of lower-income/middle-income/lower-wealth households who own a relatively small proportion of stock.

The second reason for the unequal distribution of the benefits of trade is the fact the jobs and incomes of more-educated/

higher-income/higher-wealth households have been little impacted by the trade agreements. On the other hand, it has been the jobs and incomes of less-educated/lower-income/middle-income/lower-wealth households which have been mostly negatively impacted by the trade agreements.

The transfer of production to other countries, e.g., the closing of factories in the United States, has negatively impacted the jobs and incomes of many less-educated/lower-income/middle-income/lower-wealth households. Their jobs have gone overseas and their wages have been lowered due to the increased competition from lower-wage countries.

Meanwhile, the negative impact on the wages of more-educated/higher-income/higher-wealth households has been negligible. High-ranking corporate executives have not lost their jobs. Rather, their incomes have soared with corporate profits since much of their compensation is bonus based. Incomes of high-tech employees of Silicon Valley-type companies have risen. Scientists working in fields like pharmaceuticals, agri-business, and telecommunications have benefited. Additionally, occupations of higher-income service providers, like doctors, has remained largely unscathed.

Another reason why the public at large tends to view trade agreements negatively is because job losses from trade agreements receive much greater publicity than job gains. Job losses are much easier to identify and quantify. When a factory closes and moves to Mexico, we see it, know it happened, and count the job losses. On the other hand, job gains from trade agreements are much more difficult to identify and quantify. The fact businesses in the United States hire more people because they are selling more computer software, banking services, or medical technology/hardware overseas is difficult to precisely identify and quantify and doesn't receive the press coverage a factory closing does.

One of the main benefits from trade agreements is that all Americans, lower-income, middle-income, and higher-income, have benefited as consumers from the lower prices resulting from trade agreements. *Thus, trade agreements end up being a win-win situation for more-educated/higher-income/higher-wealth households.* Their incomes have largely not been negatively impacted but often positively impacted, and they are paying lower prices for the products they buy. *On the other hand, for less-educated/lower-income/middle-income/lower-wealth households, trade agreements typically end up being win-lose.* They benefit from the lower prices, but they lose because of the lost jobs and/or lower wages resulting from competition from lower-wage countries. For the vast majority of these households, the loss of income/jobs far outweighs the benefit of lower prices.

Summary

Adam Smith's basic proposition that increased trade increases production and consumption has been true for the United States over the last 40 years. Trade agreements have caused overall living standards in the United States to rise.

The criticism that trade agreements have come at the expense of the United States and to the benefit of our trading partners is wrong. Blaming trade agreements for our economic woes is counterproductive to actually solving the economic problems confronting our country. Advocating the idea that the United States is a weak country being victimized by its trading partners and blaming them for our economic problems is divisive and dangerous to the interests and economic well-being of the country.

The main problem has been that the distribution of the benefits from the trade agreements have disproportionately gone to higher-income/higher-wealth households at the expense of everyone else. This is where the solution to the problems with trade agreements lies. It indicates the American economic system has evolved into a particular type of Capitalism, Oligarchic Capitalism, which ensures a small group of higher-income/higher-wealth households will end up with a disproportionately large percentage of income and wealth.

We will discuss this more fully in later chapters. But first, we need to look at the economic system which was the main competitor to

Capitalism for many years, an economic system that many people in the United States are increasingly interested in and intrigued by. That economic system is Socialism.

6

Socialism

The Industrial Revolution

The primary impetus for the development of Socialist ideas was the Industrial Revolution which occurred in Europe during the late 1700s and early 1800s. Adam Smith wrote *The Wealth of Nations* in 1776 just as the Industrial Revolution was beginning. The Industrial Revolution would occur a little later in the United States, during the early to mid-1800s.

The Industrial Revolution was a period of great technological innovation; innovations which would transform the way production occurred. It would complete the transition in Capitalism whereby industry (capital), rather than trade, would become the key to economic power.

Perhaps the single most important piece of new technology developed during the Industrial Revolution was the steam engine. It would lead to dramatic changes in how production was organized.

Prior to the development of the steam engine, machines in production facilities were powered using water-wheel technology. With water-wheel technology, production facilities were located next to rivers or streams. A water wheel was extended into the river or stream. As the river or stream flowed, the water wheel would turn, powering the machinery.

There are two important limitations to water-wheel technology. First, the size of the machinery that can be powered tends to be small. Second, the number of machines that can be operated is very limited. This is why, prior to the Industrial Revolution, production facilities tended to be small in size.

As a result of the steam engine, both the size and the amount of machinery which could be used greatly increased. The consequence was the size of production facilities grew enormously. This new method of huge production facilities became known as the *Factory System of Production*.

To a large extent, the new Factory System of Production had a negative impact on the lives of working people for several reasons. First, the new factories were dangerous places to work. Industrial machinery at the time was not designed with safety in mind. Workers were frequently injured or killed on the job.

Second, the personal relationship which had existed between the owner and the worker when production facilities were small ended. The owner was now removed to an office, where he had little contact with the workers. He did not know their names or anything about them; they became faces in a crowd. Direct contact with the workers was delegated to an overseer. As a result, workers could no longer take their problems or concerns to an owner they had a relationship with and personally knew. As the workers became strangers to the owner, the owner naturally developed less concern for the workers' well-being.

Third, with the advent of mass production, the swings, i.e., the natural ups and downs which occur in economic activity in the economy, became more pronounced. During downswings in activity (recessions), owners would not hesitate to lay off workers. The fact that workers could not support themselves or their families was of little concern to most factory owners. They no longer knew the workers personally, so the owners' concern for the workers' well-being was naturally reduced. The owners no longer saw up close the devastating effect on the workers of losing their jobs.

Fourth, the lives of the workers became very disrupted from what had previously existed. Factory hours were long and the work was dirty and dangerous. Workers needed to live close to the factories, virtually in their shadows, so they could get to work. Slums developed around the factories to house the workers. Pollution from the factories was significant, so the slums were unhealthy and often dangerous places in which to live.

Finally, there were virtually no governmental laws, regulations, or social programs to protect or help workers. The government had no role in workplace safety or the prohibition of child labor. Government programs such as food assistance, housing assistance, health-care assistance, compensation for injuries on the job, and unemployment assistance did not exist. Workers had to depend on private charities or family members when they became unemployed or injured. Both became overwhelmed and proved to be totally inadequate for the assistance needed, especially during times of widespread unemployment.

Increasingly, society was divided into two primary groups of people. There existed a small group of extremely wealthy capitalists who lived very, very well. Meanwhile, the vast majority of people were very poor workers struggling to survive.

It was in this environment the ideas of Socialism took hold. Increasingly, the Capitalist system was seen as a system benefiting a very small minority of people at the expense of everyone else. Increasingly, there were calls for a new type of economic system, one ensuring all people had the opportunity to meet their needs. That system was Socialism.

Socialism

According to advocates of Socialism, the primary problem in Capitalism is the private ownership of resources (especially capital). They argue that, as a result of private ownership, production only occurs for private gain.

The only reason the capitalists run their factories is to make a profit for themselves. If there is no profit to be had, the capitalists will shut down their factories. The fact workers who lose their jobs cannot pay their rent or feed their families is not the responsibility of the capitalists. The capitalists owed the workers a day's pay for a day's work. If there was no work to be had, the capitalists owed the workers nothing. The capitalists are only concerned with their own benefit. They are not concerned with the benefit of the workers or society at large; their only concern is their own profit.

Advocates of Socialism believe the solution to this problem is public owner-ship of resources; the resources of society should be owned by everyone, not just a small group of capitalists. The government would then manage and control resources for the public.[i] *Advocates of Socialism argue that, as a result of public ownership, production occurs for the public benefit.* Factories will be run for the benefit of the public at large, i.e., for society as a whole, not just for a small group of capitalists.

Capitalism Versus Socialism

Advocates of Capitalism respond that the advocates of Socialism make a fundamental error. *According to the advocates of Capitalism, in a Free Market Capitalist system, production for private gain and production for public benefit are actually one and the same.* The reason why this is so is due to two important principles of Free Market Capitalism: individual free-dom and competition.

Advocates of Capitalism agree that in Capitalism, capitalists are only concerned with their own private gain (profit). But because of individual freedom and competition, when capitalists act in their own interest, they necessarily act in the public's interest too. As stated by Adam Smith in *The Wealth of Nations*:

> It is not from the benevolence of the butcher, the brewer, or the baker that we expect our dinner, but from their regard to their own interest. We address ourselves, not to their humanity but to their self-love, and never talk to them of our own necessities but of their advantages.

—SMITH, 1776/1937, P. 14

---

[i] Socialism sometimes is said to call for government ownership. I believe this is somewhat misleading. Again, Socialism actually calls for public ownership with the government managing and controlling resources for the benefit of the public (society).

As every individual, therefore, endeavours as much as he can both to employ his capital…and so to direct that industry that its produce may be of the greatest value, every individual necessarily labours to render the annual revenue of the society as great as he can. He generally, indeed, neither intends to promote the public interest, nor knows how much he is promoting it…he intends only his own security; and by directing that industry in such a manner as its produce may be of the greatest value, he intends only his own gain, and he is in this, as in many other cases, led by an invisible hand to promote an end which was not part of his intention. Nor is it always the worse for the society that it was not part of it. By pursuing his own interest he frequently promotes that of the society more effectually than when he really intends to promote it.

—SMITH, 1776/1937, P. 423

This is Smith's famous statement about the "invisible hand."

For example, the owner of a shoe factory is only interested in making as much profit as they can. They are not interested in the well-being of the consumer or the benefit of society. Perhaps they believe the way they can make the most profit is by selling low-quality shoes at high prices. What prevents them from doing so? The principles of individual freedom and competition are the keys.

If individual freedom exists in society, consumers are free to buy whatever shoes they want from whomever they want. If a shoe factory owner attempts to sell low-quality shoes at high prices, consumers won't buy those shoes; they will, instead, buy higher-quality, lower-priced shoes from other companies. The owner of the factory, then, won't make any profit.

However, if the owner of a shoe factory has a monopoly, i.e., they are the only one selling shoes so consumers have no other choice but to buy from them, the factory owner could succeed in selling low-quality shoes at high prices. Competition prevents this from happening. As long as monopolies are prevented and shoe companies are required to compete, no shoe company can succeed by selling low-quality shoes at high prices. Other companies will sell higher-quality shoes at lower prices, forcing the shoe company to do the same or go out of business.

For advocates of Free Market Capitalism, as long as individual freedom and competition exist, production for private gain and production for public benefit are one and the same. Therefore, private ownership is not the problem socialists believe it is; and public ownership is unnecessary.

Capitalism, Socialism, and Living Standards

The debate between advocates of Capitalism and advocates of Socialism can go back and forth, as they each respond to the other's arguments. Ultimately what matters, however, is the issue of what determines a person's living standard, i.e. their consumption. What determines how well a human being lives in this world? Why is it that some people in the world have so much and live so well (very high consumption) and others have so little and live so poorly (very low consumption)? Why are the needs and desires of so many people in the world not met? Why are there poor people? These are, perhaps, the most important questions in Economics. The different answers that advocates of Capitalism and advocates of Socialism give to these questions is critical to understand.

According to advocates of Capitalism, the primary determinant of an individual's consumption (their living standard) is their production. The reason some people have so much and live so well is because they are highly productive individuals. Their high level of consumption is a reward for their high level of production. The reason others live so poorly and have so little is due to their lack of productivity. Their low level of consumption is a consequence of their low productivity.

For advocates of Free Market Capitalism, on an individual basis:

Value of Production[ii] = Income = Amount of Consumption.[iii]

[ii] The value of production is the combination of the individual's productivity and the amount that the product can be sold for. This is referred to as Marginal Revenue Product and is discussed in more detail in Appendix 1.

[iii] Allowances may be made for individuals such as children, the elderly, and the sick or disabled.

How much income a person receives is determined by the value of what they produce.[iv] The more productive a person is, the more money they make. Their level of income then determines their level of consumption, i.e., how well they live. Therefore, the more productive you are, the more money you make and the better you live. The less productive you are, the less money you make and the worse you live.

High-income, wealthy individuals have high incomes and are wealthy due to their high levels of productivity. Low income, poor people have low incomes and are poor due to their low levels of productivity. For advocates of Free Market Capitalism, it is a just system. An individual's standard of living is a reflection of their productivity.

According to advocates of Free Market Capitalism, the existence of the principles of individual freedom and competition assures companies will be forced to pay people according to their productivity. If a company attempts to underpay workers, i.e., pay workers less than their productivity, the company will be unable to retain workers as long as workers are free to work for whomever they want and companies are forced to compete against each other to hire workers.

Assume the following situation exists for a company's workers:

Value of Production > Income = Amount of Consumption

In this case, the company is underpaying its workers. In such scenario, it will be worthwhile for other companies to pay these workers more money. If a company can pay workers less than their productivity, the company can increase their profits. As companies compete against each other to hire these workers, the wages of the workers will be bid up until their production and income are equal.

---

iv For Free Market capitalists, a person's productivity includes the capital they own, i.e., they receive the income from their capital's productivity. Their ownership and control of capital is a further reflection of their productivity because it was through their productivity that they obtained ownership and control of capital. Also, the income a capitalist receives from engaging their capital in productive is due to the risk they incur in doing so.

Assume the following situation exists for a company's workers:

Value of Production < Income = Amount of Consumption

In this case, the company is overpaying its workers. In such a scenario, the company will lose money and be unable to survive. Companies cannot pay workers more than their productivity and make profits. These companies will be driven out of business. As these workers lose their jobs and compete for new ones, the wages of the worker will be bid down until their production and income are equal.

So, according to advocates of Free Market Capitalism, workers are paid according to their productivity due to individual freedom and competition. The fact that some people have high incomes, are very wealthy, and live very well and others have low incomes, are very poor, and live very poorly is justified.

For advocates of Free Market Capitalism, how well a person lives is primarily their personal responsibility. People have high incomes and are wealthy due to their levels of high productivity. People have low incomes and are poor due to their low levels of productivity. The responsibility for their low productivity is primarily their own.

Advocates of Socialism disagree with the above interpretation of how the Free Market Capitalist system works. Advocates of Socialism argue that there is no necessary connection between the value of person's production, their income, and their consumption (standard of living). Advocates of Socialism contend it is a myth to believe this is true.

For advocates of Socialism, the main determinant of an individual's income and consumption is not their production but, rather, the power the person has in the system. High income, wealthy people have high incomes and are wealthy because they have power in the system. Low income, poor people have low incomes and are poor because they lack power in the system.

Advocates of Socialism believe that the Free Market Capitalist system is controlled by the capitalists. As a result, capitalists control the government. Because capitalists control the government, capitalists write the laws. Therefore, laws are written for the benefit of the cap-italist and at the expense of workers. The laws reward and favor the ownership and control of capital over labor.

As a result, for the capitalist:

Value of Production < Income = Amount of Consumption

Meanwhile for workers:

Value of Production > Income = Amount of Consumption

Advocates of Socialism believe the Capitalist System is funda-mentally no different from the Slave and Feudal systems that came before it. Capitalism, like Slave systems and the Feudal system, is an exploitive system. In Slave systems, masters exploited slaves. In the Feudal system, lords exploited serfs. And in the Capitalist system, capitalists exploit workers.

For advocates of Socialism, how well a person lives is primarily a result of the system. People have high incomes and are wealthy because they have power in the system and, as a result, are able to exploit others. People have low incomes and are poor because they have little power in the system and are exploited. The responsibility for their low incomes and poverty lies not with them, but with the exploitive system they live in.

The main advocate for Socialist ideas was one of the most important economists to ever live, Karl Marx. Marx wrote during the mid-1800s as he witnessed the detrimental impact of the Industrial Revolution on workers' lives. He published the book *Capital* in 1867. He had planned to publish two additional volumes but died before they were completed. His friend and partner, Frederich Engels, used Marx's notes to write and publish the second two volumes.

Capital, Productivity, and Income

Capital is productive in its own right and increases the productivity of the worker who uses it. A worker can dig more dirt using a shovel than with their bare hands. A worker can move more dirt with a bulldozer than with a shovel. Who has a claim to the additional productivity (and resulting income) from using capital?

Advocates of Free Market Capitalism argue the claim to the additional productivity (and income) from capital belongs to the owner of the capital, the capitalist. The ownership of capital is a productive act in itself. Capitalists take risks in employing their capital. The reward for taking the risk, and the income resulting from the productivity of the capital, belongs to the capitalist.

Advocates of Socialism disagree. Marx's Labor Theory of Value states that labor is the only productive resource; capital merely "embodies" the labor of the workers who made it. The productivity of capital, and the income resulting from it, belongs to the workers who produced the capital. According to Marx:

> Capital is dead labor, which, vampire-like, lives only by sucking living labor, and lives the more, the more labor it sucks.
>
> —MARX, 1867/1990, P. 342

Capitalism is, therefore, an exploitive system whereby capitalists, through their ownership and control of capital, are able to expropriate the income resulting from the productivity of the capital. This income rightfully belongs to the workers.

The Incentive to Be Productive

In Free Market Capitalism, an important connection is supposed to exist between production and consumption; the level of an individual's consumption is determined by the level of their production. The more a person produces, the more they consume. The less a person produces, the less they consume. This connection between production and consumption is what gives a person the incentive to put in the effort required to be productive.

Individuals put in the effort to increase their productivity by doing such things as attending school, getting training, and obtaining a college degree, because doing so will result in them being more productive which will result in a higher living standard. Individuals put in the effort of showing up for work and performing well because they are rewarded for their productivity with higher income and higher consumption.

People may enjoy their work, but such enjoyment is not the primary reason they work (produce); they work (produce) because of the resulting consumption. The main reason a person puts in the effort to become a doctor is because as a doctor they will be more productive, have a higher income, and, therefore, a higher living standard. Perhaps they may enjoy being a doctor; but that is not the primary reason for becoming one.

Marx believed the acts of production and consumption were corrupted by the Capitalist system. He believed the connection between an individual's production and consumption was an artificial one created by the Capitalist system. He did not believe there was necessarily any need to tie a person's level of consumption to their level of production. This connection was, in fact, unnatural.

For Marx, the incentive to produce should not be driven by the desire to consume. Rather, Marx believed work, itself, was naturally a pleasurable, creative activity all human beings, because of their very nature, were incentivized to do. All human beings had an innate desire to develop their natural talents to become all they could become.

A person would put in the effort to become a doctor, not to make money so they can consume more but, rather, because becoming a doctor accomplishes their natural desire to fulfill themself. *Therefore, according to Marx, a person should naturally produce according to their ability.* The Capitalist system, with its emphasis on profits and on connecting individual production to individual consumption, corrupted this natural desire of human beings to be productive. As a result of the capitalistic production process with its emphasis on profits, workers become *alienated* from their work. What should be a natural, creative, enjoyable endeavor for workers instead, becomes onerous and disagreeable, connected only to the need to consume.

For Marx, the act of consumption should be independent from the act of production. *A person should consume according to their need.* And since human beings, for the most part, all have the same needs, everyone's level of consumption should be about the same. No one needs three homes, a 30-room mansion, 10 cars, or a private airplane. There is no reason or justification anyone should consume at that level. All human beings should consume according to their need.

For Marx, it may well be a custodian should consume more than a doctor. If the doctor is single while the custodian is married with three children, the custodian's needs are actually higher than the doctor's needs. Therefore, the custodian should get to consume more; the custodian needs a bigger house, a bigger car, and more food. The doctor's higher level of production should not result in a higher level of consumption.

The Capitalist system allowed some individuals to have extra-ordinary levels of income and consumption not because of their productivity but because the Capitalist system is an exploitive one. Because capitalists control the government, they make the laws which sanction their ownership and control of capital, which enables them to expropriate income that rightfully belongs to the worker.

Summary

There are important fundamental differences of opinion between advocates of Socialism and advocates of Capitalism. Ultimately what is important, however, is how the two systems end up working in practice. We turn to this in the following chapters.

7

The Experience of Socialism

The Parable of the Well-Intentioned Teacher

There was a teacher who wanted all the students in his class to learn more and get higher grades. To accomplish this, he thought it would be beneficial if the more capable (productive) students in his class would work with and help the less capable (productive) students so all students would learn more and get higher grades. To incentivize the more capable student to work with the less capable, he adopted a policy all the students in the class would receive the same grade. He would average all the grades in the class together, and every student in the class would receive the average grade. For any one student to get an A, all the students would need to earn an A. This would give the more capable students the incentive to work with the less capable.

As the first test approached, the more capable students began encouraging the whole class to work and study together so they could all get higher grades. They organized a study group that met on the Saturday and Sunday before the test in the library to go over the material.

The problem was, however, some students cared less about the grade they received than others. It didn't matter to them whether or not they received an A; they would be satisfied with a C. They did not want to spend their Saturday and Sunday in the library studying. In fact, since everybody in the class would receive the same grade determined by the average grade, these students could actually do less studying (work) than if their grade was solely based on what they did.

The results from the first test were disappointing. The average grade in the class was lower than the teacher expected because the grades of the students who didn't show up for the study sessions pulled the average grade down.

As the second test approached, the more capable students redoubled their efforts to get everybody together on the Saturday and Sunday before the test to study. The students who had not shown up previously still had no interest in showing up; they had done little studying but had received the same grade as everyone who did study, which, for them, was a satisfactory grade. However, now there were other students who weren't interested in spending their Saturday and Sunday studying. Other students hadn't shown up and had gotten the same grade as everyone else. Why should they spend their time studying when, regardless of how much they studied and how well they did, they would receive the same grade as students who did no studying at all? As a result, even fewer students participated in the study sessions.

The results from the second test were even more disappointing than the first. Since so many more students had not shown up to study, the average grade in the class was even lower than the first test.

As the third test approached, the more capable students tried even harder to persuade the others to participate in the Saturday and Sunday study sessions. Those who previously had not participated still did not want to join in; they were still satisfied with the grade they received. However, now even more of the students who had participated were not interested. Why should they spend their Saturday and Sunday studying when others, who did no studying, received the same grade as they did? Even fewer students showed up for the study sessions.

As the more capable students saw their grade go down, they began questioning why how well they did in the class was dependent on how

THE EXPERIENCE OF SOCIALISM

well everyone else did. They no longer wanted to be in a class where the grade they got depended on the grade everyone else got. They wanted to be in a class where the grade they got depended on how much they studied and how they personally did.

The teacher did not want to lose his students, especially the more capable ones. He informed the class they were prohibited from leaving his class and enrolling in a different one. They were required to remain in his class for the entire year.

By the end of the year, no one showed up for the study sessions and all the students flunked the class.

Russia and China

The first country to implement Marx's socialist ideas was Russia. The Russian Revolution occurred in 1917 during World War I. Eastern Europe would be incorporated into the Russian socialist orbit after World War II. China would be the second major country to adopt Socialism after World War II and the Chinese Civil War in 1947. The experiences of Russian and China illustrate the problems Socialism presents in practice.

In accordance with the ideas of Marx, Russia and China created an economic system on the premise individuals should produce according to their ability and consume according to their need. The intent was, for the most part, everyone would consume the same amount since everyone's needs were about the same. Everyone would have the same living standard. The connection between an individual's production and their consumption would be broken. Like in the Parable of the Well-Intentioned Teacher, the results were not as intended.

With the connection between individual production and consumption severed, the incentive to produce was reduced. If how much a person produces has little or no relationship to how much the person consumes, people produce less. There was no longer an economic ladder to climb. Why should a person strive to be more productive if it has little effect on how well they personally live? The idea people would be more productive to simply fulfill their potential as a human being was flawed. Additionally, regardless of how much a person produced, they were only able to consume the same as everyone else. There was no need to be productive to be able to consume. *This lack of incentive to be productive was the main reason Socialism failed in Russia and China.*

The result was productivity growth in Russia and China lagged behind other countries. As total productivity stagnated, total consumption (living standards) stagnated as well, just like the grades in the Parable of the Well-Intentioned Teacher.

So, as in the Parable of the Well-Intentioned Teacher, the more productive individuals no longer wanted to be part of this system. They wanted to go to a place where how well they lived (their living standard) was determined by their own productivity. They wanted to leave countries like Russia and China and go to places, like Western Europe or the United States. where a person's level of consumption is more connected to their level of production.

This is where the most troubling problem in Socialism is revealed. Any country which loses its most productive citizens will become a country in decline. So, Socialist countries like Russia and China denied their citizens the freedom to leave. *This was the ultimate problem with Socialism in practice: denying people individual freedom.* Russia and China built walls and put up barbed-wire fences. These countries had armed guards and guard dogs at their borders, the purpose being to keep their citizens from leaving. Anyone who attempted to leave could be shot, killed, or imprisoned. Despite steps like these, many individuals were desperate to leave and risked their lives to escape.

Despite Russia and China forcing their most productive people to remain, over time productivity and living standards continually lagged far behind those in Capitalist countries. Eventually these Socialist systems collapsed. In Russia, Socialism lasted about 70 years, symbolized by the falling of the Berlin Wall in 1989. Socialism lasted in China for about 45 years, the end signified by the events of Tiananmen Square, also in 1989. With this collapse of Socialism, Capitalism became the dominant economic system in the world.

Capitalist or Socialist?

It is an oversimplification to describe countries as being either Capitalist or Socialist. A better way to think about it is the extent of government involvement in the economic system of a country. Countries having less government involvement tend to be more capitalistic; countries having more government involvement tend to be more socialistic. It is helpful to think of it as a continuum as shown in Table 7A.

Table 7A   Government Involvement in Economic System

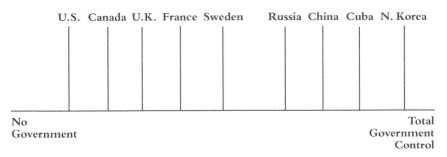

The extreme situations would be on the far left, with no government, and the far right, with the government in total control. No country falls at either extreme; it is a matter of how much government involvement exists.

The United States is to the left of Canada; government is less involved in the economic system in the United States than in Canada. It could be said Canada is more socialistic than the United States. That does not mean Canada is a socialist country; Canada is a capitalistic country. For the most part, it follows the principles of Capitalism. Likewise, Sweden is more socialistic than France. Again, Sweden is not a socialist country. It is more socialistic, adopting more socialistic policies. However, it is a capitalistic country.

Capitalism, Socialism, and Communism

Communism can be thought of as the most extreme form of Socialism. However, for Marx, it was more accurately thought of as the final step in the evolution of economic systems.

Marx argued over time economic systems had evolved from Primitive systems to Slave systems to Feudalism to Capitalism. These systems were characterized by "class struggles"; between masters and slaves, between lords and serfs, and between capitalists and workers. Marx believed the next step in the evolution would be Socialism replacing Capitalism, which would eventually evolve into Communism.

For Marx, Socialism was a necessary intermediary step to prepare workers for the final step into Communism. This final stage in the development of economic systems would end class struggles and result in a classless society. Private property would be abolished. It would operate on the basis of "From each according to their ability, to each according to their need." Workers would no longer be exploited and would be in control of the system.

Marx predicted socialist revolutions would lead to the collapse of Capitalism. Many believed (or feared) the first step in the process was the Russian Revolution of 1917. This resulted in the "Red Scare" of the early and middle twentieth century, whereby capitalist countries were continually on guard against socialist revolutions.

Whether or not Russia or China ever became truly Communist countries, though subject to debate, is very doubtful. Whether the attainment of such a state is even possible is highly questionable in itself. Nevertheless, it is very apparent neither Russia nor China ever attained Marx's vision of a classless society run and controlled by workers for the benefit of workers. Instead, Communist party leaders became the elites, controlling resources and production. They had very high living standards relative to the vast majority of households.

The Great Depression of the 1930s was the greatest crisis Capitalism ever faced. Some thought it was the beginning of the final collapse of Capitalism and the establishment of a world-wide Socialist system. Capitalism, however, did not collapse. A major contribution to solving the problems of the Great Depression was made by one of greatest economists of all time, John Maynard Keynes. The ideas he developed, now called Keynesian Economics, laid the foundation for the policies eventually adopted by governments to enable capitalist countries to recover from the Great Depression.[62]

To a large extent, the twentieth century can be seen as the era of a great struggle between Capitalism and Socialism. The struggle began in 1917 with the Russian Revolution and ended in 1989 with the collapse of the Soviet Union and the near revolution in China. These former socialist countries would now begin to plug into the Capitalist system and transform themselves into more market-oriented, capitalist countries.

Crony Capitalism and Mercantilist Policies

The transformation of former socialist countries, like Russia and China, into capitalist countries has proven to be difficult and challenging. What has developed is a form of Capitalism that is very problematic, Crony Capitalism.

The basis of Free Market Capitalism is individuals should be rewarded for their productivity, on merit. More productive individuals should have higher incomes and, therefore, higher levels of consumption (higher living standards). Individual freedom and competition assure this should happen. Who should be hired or promoted when a company has a job to fill? According to the Free Market Capitalist theory, it should be the most productive individual who applies for the job.

When individuals apply for a job, they submit a resume. When a company reviews a resume, what is it the company should be looking for? What is it that a company should be trying to discern? According to Free Market Capitalism, it should be a person's productivity.

The two main attributes an applicant includes in a resume are the person's education and previous experience. These are important because they are supposed to be indicators of an individual's productivity. A person with a higher level of education is believed to be more productive than a person with less education. Likewise, a person with more experience is believed to be more productive than a person with less experience. This does not always hold true; but other things being equal, individuals with more education and more experience are expected to be more productive.

During an interview what is it a company should be trying to discern about the interviewee? Again, the objective should be to try figure out the person's productivity. Characteristics like communication skills, attitudes, ability to work in teams, and personality are all traits a company looks at during an interview. Individuals with superior traits such as communication skills, better attitudes, greater ability to work in teams, and more cooperative personalities are believed to be more productive.

Companies doing a better job of identifying and hiring the most productive individuals will be more successful than companies doing a poorer job that end up hiring less productive individuals. The successful companies will be more profitable. Companies which are less successful in this process will be less profitable and eventually go out of business. As a result, in a competitive Free Market Capitalist system, more productive individuals are supposed to be rewarded with higher pay and higher living standards.

The basis of a system of Crony Capitalism is that individuals are rewarded not for their productivity but, instead, for their connections. Whom a person knows (their connections) is more important than a person's productivity.

In Crony Capitalism companies hire and promote individuals who have connections: connections in a company, in government, or in a political party. Relatives, friends, neighbors, and acquaintances of people in power are given preferential treatment in getting hired and promoted. Productivity is of secondary or of little importance.

Countries practicing Crony Capitalism are at a disadvantage relative to countries practicing Free Market Capitalism. An economic system which fosters and rewards the hiring and promotion of more productive individuals will prosper relative to an economic system which fosters and rewards the hiring and promotion of individuals who have connections. Over time, production and living standards in Crony Capitalist countries will lag further and further behind production and living standards in Free Market Capitalist countries.

Crony Capitalism has plagued many of the former socialist countries, although former socialist countries were not the first countries to be Crony Capitalist. Many countries which were never socialist have also been crippled by Crony Capitalism: countries in Central and South America, in Africa, Asia, and Eastern Europe. The result has been economic underperformance and lower living standards in these countries

Again, it is not a question of whether or not a country is Crony Capitalist but rather a matter of degree. Certainly, the United States has problems of Crony Capitalism. However, the problem of Crony Capitalism is relatively less pronounced in the United States than in most countries in the world. More than most countries, the United States tends to reward the most productive individuals with access to jobs, higher incomes, and higher living standards rather than the well connected. It is one of the main reasons so many individuals from across the globe strive to emigrate to the United States.

A second problem besetting former socialist countries in their transition to more market-oriented capitalist systems is the adoption of mercantilist policies. This has been a particular issue in China. In order to protect government-controlled large industries with large numbers of worker such as the steel industry, China has reverted to mercantilist protection policies like tariffs. Such industries in these countries are very inefficient and are ill-equipped to compete globally. The result would be the closing of plants and high rates of unemployment. This could cause widespread discontent among the population and undermine support of and the monopoly on political power of the Communist party in China. However, mercantilist protectionist policies raise the living standards of the individuals who are connected (are employed) in the industries while lowering the living standards of the majority of the Chinese population, reducing overall living standards in the country.

Summary

The main problem that plagued Socialist systems and eventually caused them to collapse was a lack of incentive to be productive. The socialist belief that the primary incentive for an individual to be productive is the desire for human beings to fulfill themselves proved to be faulty in practice. Breaking the connection between an individual's production and their level of consumption resulted in less incentive to be productive, lower productivity, and lower living standards. The idea that people should produce according to their ability and consume according to their need did not work well in practice.

8

The First Era of
Oligarchic Capitalism

The End of the Era of Free Market Capitalism

The period of Free Market Capitalism was relatively short-lived. By 1870 it rapidly began evolving into an Oligarchic Capitalist system. *Oligarchy is a system in which a small group of people have power and control. Oligarchic Capitalism is an economic system in which a small group of high-income, high-wealth individuals control the economic system, and the protection of wealth, income, and inheritance is prioritized. It is governed by a Plutarchic political system. Plutocracy is a political system controlled by individuals of great income or wealth.*

There is a natural trajectory in Free Market Capitalism for a small group of individuals who are slightly better at "playing the game" (slightly more productive) to accumulate greater and greater shares of the income and wealth in the system.[i] As this occurs, fewer and fewer individuals accumulate more and more wealth, resulting in great concentrations of wealth in a few hands.

Prior to 1870 business in the United States tended to be relatively small, family affairs. Fathers, brothers, sons, uncles, and nephews were

---

[i]   Why this happens will be discussed in detail in Chapter 13.

bound together in the extended family business enterprise. Birthright, loyalty, and trust among family members held the firm together and assured its long-term existence. Since businesses were relatively small, they had little economic or political power.

The dominance of the family business enterprise would begin to diminish after the Civil War. First, the needs of supplying the military with the goods necessary for fighting the war contributed to greater business opportunities and a general increase in the size of many businesses. Also, the turmoil and destruction created by the war led to a re-ordering of American society on new grounds. This began a transformation of how business was structured in the country, a transformation accelerated by technological advancements in transportation and communication, and the development of a new source of energy.

Railroads, the Telegraph, and Oil

Revolutions in transportation, communication, and energy would transform the American economic system and bring an end to the era of Free Market Capitalism. Railroads, the telegraph, and oil would be the vanguards of change for the American economic system.

Railroads

Transportation was revolutionized with the development of railroad technology. Railroads were the first big business in the country. There were two reasons big business developed in the railroad industry.

First was the consolidation of the railroads in the East. Initially, many small, independent companies built railroad lines between cities. These lines were not connected; so, goods often needed to be unloaded from one line, hauled across town, and then loaded onto another line to continue to their destination. For example, in 1850 rail service from Albany to Buffalo in New York consisted of eight independent, companies operating lines along the route.[14] This was a costly and inefficient system.

From 1850 to 1870 these independent railroad lines were consolidated into "trunk lines"; lines handling long distance, through traffic.

These included companies like the New York Central Railroad and the Pennsylvania Railroad. While such companies improved efficiency and lowered the cost of rail service, their monopoly power meant the full benefits of cost reduction of a more efficient railway system were not passed on to consumers. The result was the owners of these companies, men like Cornelius (Commodore) Vanderbilt of the New York Central Railroad, became enormously wealthy.

The second reason for the growth of big business in the railroad industry was the building of the Transcontinental Railroad. In 1862 two companies, the Union Pacific Railroad and the Central Pacific Railroad, were formed and tasked with building a railroad line that would connect the East with the West. It was a huge undertaking requiring enormous amounts of money and two huge companies to complete the endeavor.

Prior to the development of railroads, businesses largely served a local or regional market. With the creation of trunk lines and the Transcontinental Railroad, a larger national market developed. This contributed to the spread of big business to other industries.

The Telegraph

Samuel Morse received a patent for the electromagnetic telegraph in 1841. He built the first telegraph line in the country between Baltimore and Washington in 1844. By 1851 there were 75 telegraph companies operating over 21,000 miles of line.[15]

Consolidation in the industry began in the late 1840s. By 1857 there existed six regional monopolies in the industry. By 1864 the regional monopolies had further combined to form two larger companies, Western Union and the American Telegraph Company. Finally, in 1866 Western Union took over any remaining competitors, including the American Telegraph Company, and formed a national monopoly.[16]

The creation of the telegraph industry further enhanced the growth of big business. Due to this revolution in communication technology, it was now possible to control a wide-ranging business enterprise from a central location. The telegraph further enabled big business to spread to other industries.

The Oil Industry

In 1859 Edwin Drake drilled the first American oil well in Titus, Pennsylvania. This began a revolution in energy production. Oil would be used to produce kerosene, which became the primary source of light in American homes.

Western Pennsylvania became a hotbed of oil drilling. Thousands went there to drill wells and discover oil in an attempt to become rich. The oil needed be shipped east. Due to its location on the Great Lakes, Cleveland became a center of the oil processing and shipping industries.

John D. Rockefeller was a partner in a business in Cleveland, acting as a middleman selling dry goods and produce. In 1863 Rockefeller entered the oil refining business. It soon become apparent the oil business offered far more opportunity than produce or dry goods, so Rockefeller left that business. By 1864 Rockefeller owned the largest oil refinery in Cleveland, one of the largest in the world.

As the largest oil refiner in Cleveland, Rockefeller was able to negotiate secret, discounted shipping rates from the railroads, giving him an advantage over other refiners. Eventually, he was able to buy out or drive out of business other refiners in Cleveland. In 1870 the partnership of Rockefeller, Andrews, and Flager was abolished and replaced with a joint-stock company, the Standard Oil Company of Ohio. In 1882 Rockefeller re-organized the company in a combination with other refiners to form the Standard Oil Trust. By 1890 the Standard Oil Trust controlled over 90% of the refined oil in the United States and Rockefeller was its primary shareholder.[17] The Standard Oil Trust became the model for many of the large business enterprises formed during this period.

The Rise of Finance and Spread of Big Business

The rise of big business necessitated a change in the way businesses were organized. Increasingly, the corporate form of business organization was adopted for these big business enterprises. As a result of the limited liability provision for corporations, it became easier to raise money to build businesses and protect the owners of the businesses from liability.

The rise of big business required the growth of finance to help build the giant enterprises being created. Communication and transportation technology better enabled financiers in New York to connect with business leaders across the country and provide the required funds.

John Pierpont (J.P.) Morgan was the son of financier Junius Spencer Morgan. Through his father's connections, Morgan partnered with Anthony Drexel and formed Drexel, Morgan & Company. Upon the death of Drexel in 1895, the firm was renamed J. P. Morgan & Company. Morgan became the leading financier in the country and was the financing agent for most of the large business enterprises formed at the time. More and more, it was control of finance, not direct control of capital, leading to economic power. This began the period of Financial Capitalism, which quickly evolved into an Oligarchic Capitalist System.

Big business rapidly spread across the country. During the period 1895 to 1904, business mergers in the country skyrocketed, with huge conglomerations being formed. In 1890 James Duke merged the five largest tobacco firms together to form the American Tobacco Company, which produced 90% of the cigarettes manufactured in the country. By 1900 the firm controlled 80% of cigarettes, smoking tobacco, plug tobacco, and snuff. The largest meat-packing companies including Swift, Armour, and Morris formed the National Packing Company in 1902. The Shoe Machinery Corporation was formed in 1899 and by 1910 controlled 80% of the shoe machinery market. The peak of the mergers was in 1899 with over 1,200 mergers that year.[18]

One of the most important combinations formed was in the steel industry. The building of the railroads had created a tremendous demand for steel rails. A new technology for producing steel, the Bessemer Process, had been developed by Henry Bessemer in England.[ii] The Bessemer process dramatically reduced the cost of pro-

---

[ii] Bessemer was issued a patent for the process in 1856. William Kelly is actually credited with the invention of the process, but Bessemer was the first to patent it.

ducing steel. However, the expense of building a Bessemer steel mill and the resulting quantities of steel produced required a market large enough to absorb all the steel produced. The steel rails required for the building of railroads provided the necessary demand.

The first Bessemer steel mill was built in the United States in 1865. One of the partners in the enterprise was Andrew Carnegie. In 1875 Carnegie built his own steel mill, Carnegie Steel. The price of steel dropped by over 80% by 1890.

By 1901 Carnegie was one of the wealthiest men in the country and wanted to retire. J. P. Morgan saw an opportunity, bought out Carnegie, and merged Carnegie Steel with the two other largest steel producers to form the U.S. Steel Corporation, the largest business enterprise in the country up to that time.

The First Era of Oligarchic Capitalism

The first era of Oligarchic Capitalism can be divided into two periods: the Gilded Era from 1870 to 1900 and the period during and after the Progressive Era, 1900 to 1930.

The Gilded Era 1870–1900

During the Gilded Era, there was little action by the government to modify the Oligarchic Capitalist system. It was largely a period of unbridled Capitalism.

The only significant act of government to limit the power of business at the time was the passage of the Sherman Anti-Trust Act of 1890. *Anti-trust policy prohibits anti-competitive behavior by business and prohibits the formation of monopolies.* A better term would be anti-monopoly policy. The term anti-trust was adopted because, during the Gilded Age, the legal device used to form monopolies was the trust. As a result, for the public at large at the time, trusts were the equivalent of monopolies.

Trusts were used to monopolize because state incorporation laws prohibited corporations from owning the stock of other corporations. This greatly inhibited the ability of companies to join together. The trust was used to get around this inhibition.

The use of the trust was pioneered by Rockefeller and the Standard Oil Company. As discussed above, it was a tremendous success and was soon modeled by businesses in other industries. Trusts came to dominate the business landscape.

In 1896 New Jersey amended its corporate chartering laws legalizing the creation of holding companies. A holding company is a corporation which is allowed to own the stock of other corporations. The holding company proved to be a more efficient device to form monopolies. As a result, most trusts were converted to New Jersey holding companies; and the trust was no longer utilized. However, the term "anti-trust" is used to this day to describe anti-monopoly policy.

The Sherman Act did little to restrain business behavior in forming monopolies during the Gilded Age. There were two main reasons. First, Presidents tended to be pro-business and did not enforce the law. Second, court interpretation of the law rendered it ineffective.

As in all Oligarchic Capitalist systems, there was an increasing inequality in wealth and income during the Gilded Age. The actual extent of inequality is difficult to ascertain due to the dearth of accurate economic data. It has been estimated that by 1890 the top 1% of the population owned 51% of wealth. The top 12% is estimated to have owned 86%. Meanwhile, the bottom 44% of the population owned only 1.2%.[19]

The Progressive Era and After, 1900-1930

A second revolution in technology would again transform the transportation, communication, and energy industries during the second period of the first era of Oligarchic Capitalism. In transportation the automobile industry both supplanted and supplemented railroads; in communication, the telephone supplanted the telegraph and the radio was invented; and in energy, electric power largely supplanted kerosene.[iii] As during the earlier revolution in these sectors, the birth of the new industries transformed the American economy, fueled economic growth, and created enormous opportunities for bankers and financiers.

[iii] With electric power replacing kerosene as the energy source for lighting, the oil industry turned its attention to the production of gasoline to fuel the internal-combustion engines powering automobiles.

The Progressive Era began when Theodore Roosevelt assumed the Presidency in 1901. William McKinley had been re-elected President in 1900, backed by the wealthy and the trusts. During his administration little had been done to enforce the Sherman Act or limit income and wealth inequality. After McKinley's assassination, Roosevelt became President and would embark on a new course of action.

Under Roosevelt the Sherman Act would be enforced. Court interpretation of the law would change, too. In the landmark court case *Northern Securities Company v. United States* in 1904, the Northern Securities Company was declared an illegal monopoly and ordered dissolved. The company had been put together by J.P. Morgan and monopolized the railroad industry in the northwestern United States. It was the first major victory for the government over big business.

Roosevelt also initiated action against Standard Oil. The case would be decided in 1911, after Roosevelt had left office. In another landmark decision in *Standard Oil Company of New Jersey v. United States*, the company was declared an illegal monopoly and broken up.

The Progressive Era limited the actions of business in other ways. Regulation such as the Pure Food and Drug Act was passed in 1906, creating the Food and Drug Administration (FDA) to regulate the food and drug industries. In 1901 Roosevelt created the United States Forest Service to limit business appropriation and exploitation of public lands and resources. Protection of public lands and resources would be expanded with the creation of the National Parks Service in 1916.

The Progressive Era issued in the passage of taxes on income and wealth. The first income tax had been passed in 1862 to finance the Civil War, but was repealed in 1872 eight years after the war ended. The modern income tax was established with the passage of the Revenue Act of 1913. The initial highest rate was relatively low at 7%. The United States entry into World War I led to the tax being increased in 1916 and again in 1917. In 1918 it reached its highest level in this period, 77%. It began to be reduced in 1919 and was further reduced in the 1920's reaching a low of 25% in 1925. Table 8A shows the history of the Income Tax at the time.

Table 8A   ***Marginal Income Tax Rates*[iv] *1913–1931*[20]**

	Number of Tax Brackets	Lowest Rate	Highest Rate
1913–15	7	1%	7%
1916	14	2%	15%
1917	21	2%	67%
1918	56	6%	77%
1919–21	56	4%	73%
1922–23	50	4%	58%
1924	43	2%	46%
1925–31	23	1.5%	25%

The estate tax had also been first instituted in 1862. It was repealed in 1870, six years after the Civil War ended. The modern estate tax began with the passage of the Revenue Act of 1916. Initially, the first $50,000 of an estate's value was exempted from estate taxes, increased to $100,000 in 1926, and then reduced to $50,000 in 1927. The starting rate was set at 1% with a top rate of 10%. The rates were increased in 1917 to 2% and 25%, respectively. In 1924 the initial rate was reduced to 1%; and the top rate increased to 40%, reducing the tax on smaller estates while increasing it on larger ones. In 1926 the top rate was reduced to 20%. Table 8B shows the history of the estate tax from 1916 to 1931.

The Federal Gift Tax was passed in 1924 in response to individuals transferring their wealth while they were still alive to avoid the estate tax. Due to strong opposition, it was repealed in 1926. The top rate was set at 25% with amounts above $10 million subject to this rate.[21]

A capital gains tax[v] and a corporate income tax were also adopted. The capital gains rate was set at 12.5%.[22] The rate on corporate income was initially set at 1%. It would reach a peak of 14% in 1926 and reduced to 11% by 1929.[23]

[iv]   The marginal rate is the tax rate on an additional dollar of income. It is discussed in more detail in Appendix 2.

[v]   A capital gains tax is a tax on the profit from the sale of a capital asset, such as property or an investment.

Table 8B   Federal Estate Tax 1916 to 1931[24]

	Amount Exempted	In 2003 Dollars	Initial Rate	Top Rate
1916	$50,000	$625,713	1%	10%
1917–23	$50,000	$503,930	2%	25%
1924–25	$50,000	$447,826	1%	40%
1926–31	$100,000	$881,630	1%	20%
1932–33	$50,000	$584,244	1%	45%
1934	$50,000	$568,518	1%	60%
1935–39	$50,000	$557,940	1%	70%
1940	$50,000	$543,350	2%	70%
1941	$60,000	$611,076	2%	77%
1942–76	$60,000	$566,608	3%	77%

Wealth and Income Concentration

There is a widely held belief that the Progressive Era brought an end to the Oligarchic Capitalist period. This is a misconception. Despite Progressive Era policies, the Oligarchic Capitalist period would continue for another ten years, until 1930. Implementation of income, estate, and gift taxes did little to change the extent of concentration of wealth and income.

Income inequality is shown in Table 8C. From 1917 to 1929, the highest income households saw the biggest increases. The share of income for the top .01% of households increased nearly a 50%; the top .1%, over a 30%; and the top 1%, over 25%. The top 10% share of income rose over 16% while the bottom 90% of households had a drop of over 10%.

Table 8C   Share of Income by Fractile Selected Years 1917–1929[25]

	1917	1925	1929	% Change
Top .01%	3.37%	3.33%	5.03%	49.25%
Top .1%	8.41%	8.57%	10.99%	30.67%
Top 1%	17.75%	20.36%	22.51%	26.81%
Top 10%	40.54%	46.61%	47.05%	16.05%
Bottom 90%	59.46%	53.39%	52.95%	-10.94%

Table 8D shows wealth inequality during this period. It paints a similar picture. Between 1917 and 1929, wealth share of the top .1% of wealthiest households rose 8.69%. The top 1% saw an increase of 18.51; and the top 10%, 7.79%. Meanwhile, the wealth share of the bottom 90% of least wealthy households fell over 28%.

Table 8D   Share of Wealth by Fractile Selected Years 1917–1929[26, 27]

	1917	1925	1929	% Change
Top .1%	23.0%	18.0%	25.0%	8.69%
Top 1%	40.5%	40.9%	48.0%	18.51%
Top 10%	78.3%	82.2%	84.4%	7.79%
Bottom 90%	21.7%	17.8%	15.6%	-28.11%

Wall Street

Communication technology played an important role in creating greater opportunities for the public at large to have access to financial markets on Wall Street in New York. Radio news programs regularly covered the enormous fortunes being made in companies such as General Electric, General Motors, Ford Motor, and Radio Corporation of American. The telephone made it easier for individuals to contact brokers in New York or for the brokers to contact clients to sell securities. The result was increasing numbers of upper-income and even some middle-income individuals being drawn into the stock market.

During the Oligarchic Capitalist period, government regulation of financial markets was virtually non-existent. Despite the occurrence of the Progressive Era, it was still left to the financial industry to regulate itself. The result was an arena where questionable and unethical behavior flourished. Insider trading, manipulation of securities prices, and self-dealing are examples of common and accepted practices at the time. This put millions of unsophisticated individuals who were new to investing at great risk.

The Collapse of Oligarchic Capitalism

The first era of Oligarchic Capitalism would end with the Stock Market Crash in 1929 and the Great Depression of the 1930s. The extreme inequality in wealth and income would finally become too much, and the system would collapse. The excessive, unregulated behavior of business firms, especially in finance, would contribute to the collapse of the system.

It has been argued the government could have taken stronger action when the market crashed to avert the worst consequences of the Great Depression. This is particularly true of the monetary authorities of the Federal Reserve System who should have engaged in a monetary expansion to prevent the collapse of the banking system. While this stop-gap measure would have lessened the effect of the crash, it would not have solved the core problems of wealth and income inequality, the central flaws of an Oligarchic Capitalist system. Fundamental changes were needed to deal with these foundational problems in Oligarchic Capitalism.

The election of Franklin Roosevelt as President in 1932 and the launching of the New Deal would usher in a new era of Democratic Capitalism. This is the subject of the next chapter.

9

The Birth of
Democratic Capitalism

An Economic Bill of Rights

Democratic Capitalism is an economic system where the distribution of wealth and income is more equalized, the incentive to be productive is prioritized, and economic support is provided. It is governed by a Democratic political system.

The initial era of Democratic Capitalism was created by Franklin Roosevelt from the collapse of Oligarchic Capitalism and the ashes of the Great Depression. It would be enhanced and strengthened with Lyndon Johnson's Great Society programs in the 1960s.

The principles of Democratic Capitalism are best expressed in Roosevelt's last inaugural address in 1944 when he advocated for a Second Bill of Rights, also known as The Economic Bill of Rights.

We have come to a clear realization of the fact that true individual freedom cannot exist without economic security and independence. "Necessitous men are not free men." People who are hungry and out of a job are the stuff of which dictatorships are made.

In our day these economic truths have become accepted as self-evident. We have accepted, so to speak, a second Bill of Rights under which a new basis of security and prosperity can be established for all — regardless of station, race, or creed. Among these are:

- The right to a useful and remunerative job in the industries or shops or farms or mines of the nation;
- The right to earn enough to provide adequate food and clothing and recreation;
- The right of every farmer to raise and sell his products at a return which will give him and his family a decent living;
- The right of every businessman, large and small, to trade in an atmosphere of freedom from unfair competition and domination by monopolies at home or abroad;
- The right of every family to a decent home;
- The right to adequate medical care and the opportunity to achieve and enjoy good health;
- The right to adequate protection from the economic fears of old age, sickness, accident, and unemployment;
- The right to a good education.

All of these rights spell security. And after this war is won we must be prepared to move forward, in the implementation of these rights, to new goals of human happiness and well-being.

—US HISTORY.ORG, *HISTORIC DOCUMENTS: THE ECONOMIC BILL OF RIGHTS*

Advocates of Democratic Capitalism have been fighting for these ideals ever since.

The New Deal

Toward the end of his acceptance speech at the 1932 Democratic Convention, Roosevelt used a phrase which would come to epitomize his program of reform for the American economic system,

"I pledge you, I pledge myself, to a new deal for the American people."

—TEACHING AMERICAN HISTORY,
TEACHINGAMERICANHISTORY.ORG, *ACCEPTANCE
SPEECH AT THE DEMOCRATIC CONVENTION 1932*

This New Deal would encompass programs establishing the foundations of a Democratic Capitalist system. It ensured the dismantling of the Oligarchic Capitalist system, which had existed since 1870.

The core policies of the New Deal were to provide Americans with economic support and security. It enabled the government to take responsibility for job creation if the private sector proved incapable of creating the necessary employment opportunities.

Prior to the Great Depression, Americans accepted the idea that unemployment and poverty were the responsibility of the individual; being unemployed and/or poor was caused by some personal failing. In such a situation, it was felt society or the government had no responsibility to assist the unemployed or the poor.

The advent of the Great Depression demonstrated unemployment and poverty may not always occur due to any personal short-comings of the individual. Instead, unemployment and poverty could be caused by a failure of the economic system. The system itself could break down and fail to provide job opportunities for all the population. If unemployment and poverty were not the personal responsibility of the individual but, rather, due to a failing of the system, then society and the government had some responsibility to assist the citizen.

Supporters of Oligarchic Capitalism refused to accept the idea the system could so utterly fail. They believed the government had no duty or responsibility to protect its citizens economically; it was the citizens' own responsibility to find work and support themselves. Government assistance would only repress and delay this from happening.

The extent of unemployment during the Great Depression discredited the Oligarchic Capitalist idea unemployment and poverty were necessarily due to the personal failings of the individual. There were just too many unemployed individuals who were clearly desperate to work who could not find jobs. The system had failed.

The unemployment rate rose from 3.14% in 1929 to 24.75% in 1933, the depth of the Depression.[28] Statistics for the underemployed (individuals involuntarily working part-time rather than working full-time) and discouraged workers (individuals who have given up looking for work though they want to work) were not calculated during the Depression. It has been estimated if these groups had been included, the total of workers negatively impacted by the Depression would have approached 50%. In such a situation, Roosevelt received a mandate from the American public to act.

Keynesian Economics

John Maynard Keynes was the economist who laid the theoretical foundation for the creation of Democratic Capitalism. His book, *The General Theory of Employment, Interest, and Money*,[29] published in 1936, dealt with the causes of and solutions for the Great Depression and the failure of the Oligarchic Capitalist system. It was the most important and influential book written about economics since *The Wealth of Nations*.

Keynes disagreed with the laissez-faire belief the macro economy was self-regulating; that the self-correcting mechanisms of lower prices and lower interest rates built into the system would ensure problems like recessions and unemployment would be resolved in a short time on their own. He contended that during a severe economic crisis, these self-correcting mechanisms could be overwhelmed and the system could enter a protracted period of high unemployment.

His key insight was that during an economic crisis like the Great Depression, expectations and confidence would be so damaged companies and individuals would be unwilling to spend and would, instead, hoard money. Lower prices and lower interest rates, the typical mechanisms leading to a rebound in spending, would be overwhelmed by worsening expectations and confidence. The fundamental problem in the crisis was this lack of confidence, which resulted in a lack of demand (spending).

His solution was that, in such a situation, the government must intervene in the system by increasing demand (spending) by increasing government spending. The increased government spending would begin to reverse the economic downturn, improve expectations and confidence, and spur increased spending in the private sector. This would lead to economic recovery.

Laissez-faire economists' solution for the Great Depression was to wait it out. They believed in the long run the economy would self-correct and the Depression would end. Keynes' thoughts on this reveal his disdain for the laissez-faire line of thinking.

> The long run is a misleading guide to current affairs. In the long run we are all dead. Economists set themselves too easy, too useless a task if in tempestuous seasons they can only tell us that when the storm is past the ocean is flat again.
>
> —KEYNES, 1923/2000, PP. 80-82

Keynes' call for increased government spending was largely ignored by politicians. The increased spending of the New Deal was not enough to end the Depression. It was the occurrence of World War II, and the enormous increases in government borrowing and spending to finance the war, which resulted in the Great Depression ending.

The Policies of the New Deal

New Deal policies can be broken into four basic categories:

- Job Creation and Public Infrastructure Projects
- Economic Support
- Financial Regulation
- Tax Policy.

Job Creation and Public Infrastructure

Prior to the Great Depression, job creation was seen as the responsibility of the private sector. The government had no role in ensuring adequate job opportunities existed. As discussed earlier, unemployment and poverty were seen as an individual failure. The Great Depression changed the public view so unemployment and poverty were seen as, perhaps, the result of a failure of the system. In such a circumstance, the public accepted the need for government to play a role in ensuring sufficient employment opportunities existed.

There were two primary job creation programs initiated during the New Deal. The Civilian Conservation Corps (CCC) operated from 1933 to 1942. It employed single, unemployed men in public works projects involving conservation. These projects involved projects such as planting trees, building roads, working on soil-conservation projects, building wild-life refuges, and building public parks in wilderness areas. Participants were directly employed and paid by the Federal government. Participants were housed in camps and provided three meals a day, work clothes, and recreational activities. A portion of their pay was sent home to help support their families. The program included educational and job training components. Thousands of the participants were taught to read, write, and do basic math. Job training included skills such as carpentry, plumbing, welding, typing, and basic electronics. Over three million individuals were eventually employed, trained, and educated by the CCC.

The second job creation program of the New Deal was the Works Progress Administration (WPA) created in 1935 (renamed the Work Projects Administration in 1939). The program employed workers in a broad range of areas.

A major part of the WPA was public infrastructure construction projects. WPA construction projects included the building of over 4,000 school buildings, 130 hospitals, 9,000 miles of storm drains and sewer lines, 29,000 bridges, 150 airfields and the paving and repair of over 280,000 miles of road.[30] These projects created jobs in the short-run and provided much-needed infrastructure repair and expansion that laid the foundation for economic growth in the long-run. Participants were hired and paid by the government. At its peak, over 3.3 million individuals worked for and were paid by the WPA.[31]

There were five, other principal WPA projects:

- Federal Writers' Project to employ writers
- Historical Records Survey to create historical records
- Federal Theater Project to employ actors and other theater workers
- Federal Music Project to employ musicians
- Federal Artist Project to employ artists.

Another large infrastructure project of the New Deal was the creation of the Tennessee Valley Authority (TVA). The TVA was charged with building infrastructure that would enhance navigation, flood control, and electricity generation in the Tennessee Valley area. The TVA was faced with fierce opposition from private utility companies who saw it as a threat. Lawsuits were filed to prevent the government from encroaching in what utility companies considered their turf. However, widespread dissatisfaction and distrust of the motives of public utilities and the high prices the private utilities charged resulted in the TVA project moving forward with broad public support. The TVA covered an eight-state area in the south and led to improved navigability of the Tennessee River and better flood control. Over 9,000 individuals were employed by the TVA and 16 hydroelectric dams were constructed.[32]

Two other major infrastructure projects undertaken to improve navigation, flood control, and develop hydroelectric energy generation were the construction of the Hoover Dam on the Colorado River and the Grand Coulee Dam on the Columbia River. Like the projects of the TVA and WPA, the construction of the Hoover Dam and Grand Coulee Dams provided much needed employment in the short-run while laying the foundation for economic expansion and growth in the long-run. Over 21,000 jobs were created in the construction of the Hoover Dam,[33] while the building of the Grand Coulee Dam project employed over 8,000.[34]

Another important New Deal public infrastructure program was created by the Rural Electrification Act passed in 1936 and the creation of the Rural Electrification Administration (REA). In 1935 only 11% of homes in rural areas were hooked up to electrical power.[35] Rural areas were largely still using kerosene as their main source of lighting. Private power companies were not willing to run power lines long distances in rural areas to connect scattered households to the power grid. The power companies estimated it would cost $1,500 to $2,000 for each mile of power lines constructed.[36]

The initial purpose of the REA was to incentivize private utility companies to construct the lines despite the cost so electric service could be provided to rural communities. However, due to the lack of interest on the part of these private companies, the REA quickly turned to making loans to state governments, local governments, and private groups to create non-profit cooperatives to provide electric power to rural communities. Loans were made to construct generating plants, transmission and distribution lines, and for the installation of electrical and plumbing appliances in homes. The electric cooperatives became a center piece of the program, with 80% of the land mass of the country (rural areas) now provided with electricity through such co-ops.[37] These groups were able to build power lines for less than $825 per mile in contrast to the cost estimates of $1,500 to $2,000 of the private utility companies.[38] By 1936 over 380,000 miles of lines had been built with over one million households now able to receive electricity. By 1960 the REA would provide electricity to over 97% of rural communities.[39]

Economic Support

The most important economic support program of the New Deal was Social Security, created by the Social Security Act of 1935. The act provided economic support to four primary groups:

- the elderly (retirement insurance)
- the unemployed (unemployment insurance)
- widows and orphans (survivor benefits)
- the disabled (disability benefits)

As with job creation, prior to the Great Depression these types of activities were believed to be the responsibility of the individual. Citizens were obligated to provide for their own economic support or rely on family members or private charities to assist them. The Great Depression overwhelmed the capability of families and private charities to provide relief. Since the Depression was seen as a failure of the economic system and not the individual, the public readily accepted the government had a role in providing such support.

Financial Regulation

Another major area of government intervention was financial regulation. The collapse of the financial system had exacerbated the severity and length of the Depression. No longer was it seen as being sufficient that the financial system should regulate itself. There were two major pieces of financial regulation passed during the New Deal.

The first was the Glass-Steagall Act in 1933. There were two main components of the act. First, it established a prohibition on Investment Banks from owning and operating Commercial Banks. An Investment Bank is a bank which assists companies in raising money by underwriting and/or selling the issuance of new shares of stock or bonds. They are often referred to as Wall Street Banks. A Commercial Bank is a bank which provides services such as accepting deposits, making loans, and offering basic banking services to the general public.

Prior to the passage of the Glass-Steagall Act, Investment Banks were allowed to own and operate Commercial Banks. As a result, Investment Banks had an incentive to sell stocks and bonds to the public through the Commercial Banks they owned. Investment Banks would act in their own self-interest by advising and guiding their Commercial Bank customers to invest in securities of questionable value and entirely inappropriate investments for those individuals. They would put the interests of the Investment Bank corporate clients (to sell new issues of stocks and bonds) ahead of the interests of their Commercial Bank customers. They also encouraged their customers to use borrowed money (buying on margin) to purchase securities, dramatically increasing the risk to the client. Typically, the money was borrowed from the bank itself. It was widely believed this contributed to the severity of the financial devastation following the stock market crash in 1929.

The Glass-Steagall Act also created the Federal Deposit Insurance Corporation (FDIC) to provide insurance for depositors' money in a Commercial Bank. The collapse of the banking system was largely caused by depositors desperately trying to withdraw their funds from banks as the system collapsed, which aggravated the problem. The provision of deposit insurance would assure depositors their deposits were safe so there would be no need to rush to the bank to withdraw funds.

The second piece of financial reform passed was the Securities and Exchange Act in 1934. The act created the Securities and Exchange Commission (SEC) tasked with overseeing and enforcing securities laws and regulating the securities industry. This includes all major stock and bond markets. Practices like insider trading, security price manipulation, and self-dealing which occurred with regularity in the lead up to the stock market crash, were now illegal and laws prohibiting such activities enforced.

Tax Policy

Prior to Roosevelt's election, the Revenue Act of 1932 had been passed during the Hoover Administration. Hoover was focused on the Federal government deficit that had dramatically increased as a result of falling tax receipts due to high levels of unemployment. Hoover and the Republican controlled Congress mistakenly thought that increasing tax rates would solve the deficit problem. Instead, the higher tax rates drove the economy deeper into depression, reducing tax revenues.

The Revenue Act of 1932 increased the highest marginal tax rate from 25% to 63%. The Revenue Act of 1935 raised it further to 79%. Later legislation raised it to a maximum of 94% in 1944 as shown in Table 9A. As a result of the war, the lowest rate was raised from 4% to 23%. This rate reflected the need to raise funds to finance World War II.

Table 9A   *Marginal Income Tax Rates 1932–1945*[40]

	Number of Tax Brackets	Lowest Rate	Highest Rate
1932–33	54	4%	63%
1934–35	30	4%	63%
1936–40	33	4%	79%
1941	32	10%	81%
1942–43	24	19%	88%
1944–45	24	23%	94%

Federal estate taxes were also increased. In 1932 the top rate was raised from 20% to 45%. The amount exempted dropped from $100,000 to $50,000. They would reach their maximum of 77% in 1941, with a slight increase in the exempted amount to $60,000. Estate tax rates are shown in Table 9B.

Table 9B   *U.S. Federal Estate Tax 1932 to 1945*[41]

	Amount Exempted	Initial Rate	Top Rate
1932–33	$50,000	1%	45%
1934	$50,000	1%	60%
1935–39	$50,000	1%	70%
1940	$50,000	2%	70%
1941	$60,000	2%	77%
1942–45	$60,000	3%	77%

The gift tax was re-instituted in 1932 with the top rate gradually increasing to 57.75% in 1941. The lifetime exemption, the total amount that can be gifted by an individual during the course of their life, dropped from $50,000 to $30,000. The annual exclusion, the maximum that can be given in any year, was gradually lowered from $5,000 to $3,000. The amount subject to the top rate initially was any amount over $10,000,000 and would be increased to $50,000,000 in 1938 and lowered back to $10,000,000 in 1942. Gift tax rates are shown in Table 9C.

Table 9C   U.S. Federal Gift Tax 1932 to 1945[42]

	Annual Exclusion	Lifetime Exemption	Top Rate	Subject to Top Rate (Above)
1932–33	$5,000	$50,000	33.5%	$10,000,000
1934	$5,000	$50,000	45.0%	$10,000,000
1935–37	$5,000	$40,000	52.5%	$10,000,000
1938–40	$4,000	$40,000	52.5%	$50,000,000
1941	$4,000	$40,000	57.75%	$50,000,000
1942–45	$3,000	$30,000	57.75%	$10,000,000

The capital gains rate was also increased during the New Deal. Initially it was more than doubled to 31.5% in 1934 and then raised further to 39% in 1936. In 1938 it was reduced to 30% and then again in 1943 to 25%. Capital gains tax rates are shown in Table 9D.

Table 9D   U.S. Capital Gains Tax Rate 1932–1945[43]

Year	Rate
1932–33	12.5%
1934–35	31.5%
1936–37	39.0%
1938–41	30.0%
1942–45	25%–27.5%

The top corporate income tax rate was increased from 12% to 14% in 1930, to 19% in 1939, and to 53% in 1942 due to the war.[44]

Results of New Deal Policies

Economic Recovery

While New Deal policies mitigated the worst effects of the Great Depression, they did not result in full recovery. The problem was the ideas of Keynes were not fully implemented. The policies adopted were inadequate to achieve full recovery.

Keynesian policies required the government to engage in an extensive program of spending to revive demand and reduce unemployment.

104

The spending levels required were unprecedented, so government officials were unprepared to implement the level of spending required to end the Depression. Instead, half-hearted measures were undertaken that eased the crisis but did not resolve it.

Keynesian policies required the government to engage in a massive program of deficit spending; spending financed through borrowing which would dramatically increase the government deficit. At this time, government officials were as concerned about balancing government budgets as they were about ending the economic crisis. Many believed government deficits were part of the problem, not part of the solution. They viewed government deficits as evidence the government could not get its own house in order; they believed government deficits reduced the confidence of the public in the government being able to resolve the crisis. How could the public trust a government that couldn't even balance its own budget?

Keynesian Economics was revolutionary because it viewed economic recovery, not government deficits, as the priority. The increased government spending required to resolve the crisis would require the government to increase, not decrease, deficits. Once recovery was accomplished, government deficits could be dealt with.

Roosevelt's implementation of Keynesian deficit spending policies resulted in the economic recovery beginning in 1933. Table 9E shows the government deficit, GDP growth rate, and the unemployment rate during the initial years of the New Deal.

The Depression began in earnest in 1930. GDP shrank 8.5%. It contracted by 6.4% in 1931 and 12.9% in 1932. Unemployment rose to 8.7% in 1930 and to 24.9% by 1933.

Measuring the impact of deficits on the economy requires comparing the amount of the deficit relative to the size of the economy, i.e., GDP. A larger deficit has less impact on a bigger economy than a smaller economy. Likewise, a smaller deficit has more effect on a smaller economy than a larger economy. To gauge the impact of deficit spending on the economy, economists look at the deficit as a percentage of GDP.

Table 9E   *Government Deficit, GDP Growth Rate, & Unemployment*
1930–1937[45, 46]

	Government Deficit (Billions)	Percent of GDP	GDP Growth Rate	Unemployment Rate
1930	-$1	-0.8%	-8.5%	8.7%
1931	$0	0.6%	-6.4%	15.9%
1932	$3	4.5%	-12.9%	23.6%
1933	$3	4.5%	-1.2%	24.9%
1934	$4	5.4%	10.8%	21.7%
1935	$3	3.8%	8.9%	20.1%
1936	$4	5.1%	12.9%	16.9%
1937	$2	2.4%	5.1%	14.3%

Keynesian deficit spending policies were implemented in 1932 and 1933 with the deficit increasing to 4.5% of GDP as shown above in Table 9E. The crisis lessened, with GDP contracting only 1.2%. With the deficit increasing to 5.4% of GDP in 1936, the recovery accelerated, with GDP growing by 12.9%. The unemployment rate fell to 14.3% by 1937.

With recovery underway, the Roosevelt Administration turned to reducing the government deficit by cutting expenditures. Table 9F shows the results of this on the deficit, the growth rate of GDP, and unemployment.

Table 9F   *Government Deficit, GDP Growth Rate, & Unemployment*
1936–1940[47, 48]

	Government Deficit (Billions)	Percent of GDP	GDP Growth Rate	Unemployment Rate
1936	$4	5.1%	12.9%	16.9%
1937	$2	2.4%	5.1%	14.3%
1938	$0	0.1%	-3.3%	19.0%
1939	$3	3.0%	8.0%	17.2%
1940	$3	2.8%	8.8%	14.6%

The deficit fell to 2.4% of GDP in 1937 and 0.1% in 1938. As Keynesian Economics predicted, this short-circuited the recovery;

and a second phase of the Great Depression began. GDP growth fell to 5.1% in 1937 and to -3.3% in 1938. Unemployment rose to 19% by 1938.

Seeing these results, the Roosevelt Administration reversed course and resumed deficit spending in 1939, causing the deficit to rise as a percent of GDP. GDP growth rebounded to 8%. Unemployment fell to 17.2% in 1939 and 14.6% in 1940.

Income and Wealth Concentration

Income inequality increased during the New Deal as shown in Table 9G. Highest income households had an increase of over 3%. The top 1% saw an increase of over 6%. The bottom 90% had an increase of less than 2%

Table 9G   Share of Income by Income Fractile Selected Years 1932–1940[49]

	1932	1935	1940	% Change
Top .01%	1.99%	2.19%	2.05%	**3.01%**
Top .1%	5.97%	6.41%	6.01%	**0.67%**
Top 1%	15.56%	16.71%	16.50%	**6.04%**
Top 10%	46.39%	44.58%	45.35%	**-2.24%**
Bottom 90%	53.61%	55.42%	54.65%	**1.93%**

On the other hand, there was a significant decrease in wealth inequality during the New Deal as shown in Table 9H.

Table 9H   Share of Wealth by Wealth Fractile Selected Years 1932–1940[50, 51]

	1932	1935	1940	% Change
Top .1%	23%	21%	15%	**-34.70%**
Top 1%	38.1%	40.5%	37.7%	**-1.04%**
Top 10%	84.8%	81.7%	77.1%	**-9.08%**
Bottom 90%	15.2%	18.3%	22.9%	**50.65%**

Decreasing wealth concentration was not really due to New Deal policies but, rather, due to the stock market crash and the

Depression itself. The value of assets had been greatly reduced. Table 9I shows the peaks and troughs of the rallies and downturns of the Dow Jones Industrial Average from August 1929 to January 1940.

Table 9I   Dow Jones Industrial Average Selected Dates August 1929–
January 1940[52]

	Dow Jones Industrial	Percent Change from August 1929
Aug 1929	372	
July 1932	44	-88.1%
Jan 1940	150	-59.6%

The market peaked in August 1929 at 372. By 1944, it had fallen over 88% to 44. It then recovered but in January 1940 was still less than half its value from over ten years earlier. This had a devasting impact on wealth, which was primarily held by a small fraction of the population. As a result, the impact on high-income, wealthier families tended to be greater than on lower-income/middle-income/lower-wealth families who were not as invested in the market, so the stock market crash on had a greater effect on decreasing wealth concentration than New Deal policies.

World War II and the End of Depression

New Deal policies did not fully apply Keynesian policies, which inhibited full recovery from the Depression. The government needed to be much more aggressive in expanding spending and deficits if the economy was to fully recover.

Table 9J shows the record of government deficits, GDP growth, and unemployment during World War II.

The war led to the government expanding deficits and spending enough to bring about the end of the Great Depression. The economy fully recovered as a result of these unprecedented levels of government spending and deficits to fight the war.

Table 9J   *Government Deficit, GDP Growth Rate, & Unemployment*
             1940–1945[53]

	Government Deficit (Billions)	Percent of GDP	GDP Growth Rate	Unemployment Rate
1940	$3	2.8%	8.8%	14.6%
1941	$5	3.8%	17.7%	9.9%
1942	$21	12.3%	18.9%	4.7%
1943	$55	26.9%	17.0%	1.9%
1944	$48	21.2%	8.0%	1.2%
1945	$48	20.0%	-1.0%	1.9%

Keynes recognized the problem:

"It is, it seems, politically impossible for a capitalistic democracy to organize expenditure on the scale necessary to make the grand experiments which would prove my case – except in war conditions."

—KUTTNER, 2018, THE AMERICAN
PROSPECT, PROSPECT.ORG

Summary

The Great Depression and World War II transformed Americans' view of how the economic system operated and the role of government. It became accepted that unemployment and poverty were not necessarily the fault of the individual; the economic system itself could collapse and fail to provide adequate job opportunities. Keynesian Economics provided the prescription for solving the crisis. Franklin Roosevelt's New Deal and the financing of World War II demonstrated that Keynesian policies worked.

World War II also changed the American's public perception of the role and functions of government. The war had been successfully prosecuted; fascism defeated; and economic recovery achieved. Going forward, Americans would trust, have confidence in, and expect the government to play an active and effective role in ensuring economic stability. A Democratic Capitalist economic system had been established.

10

The Expansion of
Democratic Capitalism

Post War America 1945-1960

The post–World War II period was a time of prosperity and economic opportunity for many American families. During the decade of the 1950's, economic growth averaged 4.3%. Unemployment throughout the period averaged 4.5%. This was a dramatic departure from the experience of the Depression during the 1930s. Income and wealth inequality also lessened as shown in Tables 10A and 10B.

Table 10A   Share of Income by Income Fractile Selected Years 1946–1959[54]

	1946	1955	1959	% Change
Top .01%	1.49%	1.32%	1.20%	**–19.46%**
Top .1%	4.44%	3.73%	3.48%	**–21.60%**
Top 1%	13.41%	11.11%	10.74%	**–19.91%**
Top 10%	37.08%	34.09%	34.31%	**–7.47%**
Bottom 90%	62.92%	65.91%	65.69%	**4.40%**

Table 10B   Share of Wealth by Wealth Fractile Selected Years 1946–1959[55, 56]

	1946	1955	1959	% Change
Top .1%	11%	10%	10%	-10.0%
Top 1%	29.9%	27.5%	27.8%	-7.55%
Top 10%	71.5%	68.1%	69.6%	-2.65%
Bottom 90%	28.5%	31.9%	30.4%	6.67%

Both share of income and share of wealth fell for higher-income/higher-wealth households. For the bottom 90%, income share and wealth share increased.

Estate tax and gift tax rates would not be changed from the rates established in 1942. The capital gains tax would remain relatively flat. However, income tax rates would be increased, as shown in Table 10C.

Table 10C   Marginal Income Tax Rates 1946–1960[57]

	Number of Tax Brackets	Lowest Rate	Highest Rate
1946–50	24	20%	91%
1951	24	20.4%	91%
1952–53	24	22.2%	92%
1954–60	24	20%	91%

Government oversight of the macro economy and Keynesian economic policies were practiced and widely accepted. It was perceived that the government should be active and could be effective in ensuring economic stability and creating opportunity in the country.

Building on the success of the public infrastructure projects that had been undertaken during the New Deal, the government embarked on one of the most ambitious public infrastructure projects in the country's history. An Interstate Highway system would be constructed, enhancing and improving the transportation system across the country. In the short run, the building of the system created tens of thousands of well-paying construction jobs. In the long run, the system would dramatically improve the transportation system; expanding markets and fueling economic growth. Additionally, the building of the Interstate Highway system further cemented the public's belief and confidence in the capability of government to improve people's lives. The stage was set for further implementation of Democratic Capitalist policies.

Lyndon Johnson and the Great Society

The day after the assassination of President John Kennedy, Lyndon Johnson told an aide: "I am a Roosevelt New Dealer" (Woods, 2016, p. 15). Several months later the new President stated to his aide Bill Moyer, "I really intend to finish Roosevelt's revolution" (Woods, 2016, p. 35).

The program he embarked on was The Great Society, a term Johnson coined in his commencement address to graduates at the University of Michigan in May 1964.

"Your imagination, your initiative, and your indignation will determine whether we build a society where progress is the servant of our needs, or a society where old values and new visions are buried under unbridled growth. For in your time we have the opportunity to move not only toward the rich society and the powerful society, but upward to the Great Society.

The Great Society rests on abundance and liberty for all. It demands an end to poverty and racial injustice, to which we are totally committed in our time. But that is just the beginning.

The Great Society is a place where every child can find knowledge to enrich his mind and to enlarge his talents. It is a place where leisure is a welcome chance to build and reflect, not a feared cause of boredom and restlessness."

—TEACHING AMERICAN HISTORY,
TEACHINGAMERICANHISTORY.ORG,
GREAT SOCIETY SPEECH

Three areas of concern would be addressed by Johnson's programs: economic support, economic opportunity, and protection of public resources.

Economic Support

The economic support programs of the Great Society were part of Johnson's War on Poverty. In his State of the Union address on January 8, 1964, Johnson stated, "This administration today, here and now, declares an unconditional war on poverty in America." (Woods, 2016, p. 62)[58].

Health Care

The Social Security Act of 1965 created the Medicare and Medicaid Programs. Medicare provides economic support for health care to people over age 65 and individuals with disabilities. Elderly and disabled individuals were at risk of being unable to afford needed medical services. Medicare has two parts. Part A provides insurance for inpatient hospital care, skilled nursing care, and hospice care. Part B provides insurance for outpatient care, preventive services, ambulance services, and medical equipment.

Medicaid provides health insurance to qualifying low-income individuals who do not qualify for Medicare, many of whom are children. Like the elderly and disabled, these individuals are at risk of being unable to afford needed medical services. Unlike Medicare, Medicaid is administered by the States, which have broad authority to determine the income requirements necessary to qualify for the program.

Food Assistance

The first food assistance program in the country was created during the Roosevelt Administration in 1939 and discontinued in 1943. The Food Stamp Act of 1964 provided economic support for low-income individuals to buy food. A pilot program operated from 1961 to 1964. Criteria for qualifying for the program and the operation of the program have changed frequently over the years. The program was renamed the Supplemental Nutrition Assistance Program (SNAP) in 2008.

Housing Assistance

The Housing and Urban Development Act was passed in 1965, creating the Department of Housing and Urban Development (HUD). Local housing authorities were created to oversee the program.

The program provided for two types of economic support for qualifying low-income individuals, the elderly, and individuals with disabilities to obtain adequate housing. The first is public housing, which is housing built and operated by the government. The local housing authority is charged with overseeing and operating public housing.

The second is a program of housing vouchers provided to qualifying low-income individuals to go into the private market and obtain housing. Housing vouchers are a rent subsidy. It is typically referred to as Section 8 because it is part of Section 8 of the Housing Act of 1937 when rental assistance was first provided for low-income individuals as part of the New Deal.

Economic Opportunity

The Great Society dealt with three areas of economic opportunity: job training, education, and civil rights. These areas were addressed in the Economic Opportunity Act of 1964, the Elementary and Secondary Education Act of 1965, the Higher Education Act of 1965, and the Civil Rights Act of 1964.

Job Training

The main job training program of the Great Society was the Job Corps. Its mission was to provide job and vocational training, primarily to low-income and disadvantaged individuals aged 16 to 24. It provided assistance to 100,000 men, half who were employed in conservation projects and half who received training in job centers.[59] The program was modeled after the Civilian Conservation Corps of the New Deal.

Education

The Head Start program was created by the Office of Economic Opportunity. It provided pre-school opportunities for children of low-income families, which included emotional, social, health, and psychological support programs.

The Elementary and Secondary Education Act of 1965 provided federal funding to schools serving children from low-income families. It included support for instructional materials and professional development of teachers. Since elementary and secondary education is primarily funded through local property taxes, higher-income/higher-wealth areas provided greater educational opportunity for students than lower-income/lower-wealth areas. The act attempted to create more equalized funding among schools in higher-income/higher-wealth areas and lower-income/lower-wealth areas.

The Higher Education Act of 1965 increased resources to colleges and universities and established expanded financial resources for students to obtain post-secondary education. The most important provisions of the act created a system of scholarships, low-interest loans, and work-study programs, particularly for students from low-income and middle-income families.

Civil Rights Act of 1964

The primary beneficiaries of the post-World War II economic expansion had been white males and those connected to them (primarily their families). Large swaths of the American public were effectively prohibited from participating. These included minority groups, women, and the gay community. Discrimination, institutionalized by laws in the American South, effected by action in the rest of the country, and embedded in corporate business practices, ensured many were denied economic opportunity.

The Equal Pay Act of 1963 had been passed during the Kennedy Administration to address the issue of pay discrimination based on gender. It stated:

No employer…shall discriminate…between employees on the basis of sex by paying wages to employees…at a rate less than at the rate he pays wages to employees of the opposite sex…for equal work on jobs."

—EQUAL EMPLOYMENT OPPORTUNITY COMMISSION, EEOC.GOV, *THE EQUAL PAY ACT OF 1963*

The Civil Rights Act of 1964 further addressed the problem of discrimination in the workplace. It stated:

It shall be an unlawful employment practice for an employer

1. to fail or refuse to hire or to discharge any individual, or otherwise to discriminate against any individual with respect to his compensation, terms, conditions, or privileges of employment, because of such individual's race, color, religion, sex, or national origin; or

2. to limit, segregate, or classify his employees or applicants for employment in any way which would deprive or tend to deprive any individual of employment opportunities or otherwise adversely affect his status as an employee, because of such individual's race, color, religion, sex, or national origin.

—EQUAL EMPLOYMENT OPPORTUNITY COMMISSION, EEOC.GOV, *TITLE VII OF THE CIVIL RIGHTS ACT OF 1964*

The law also applied to employment agencies and labor organizations. The Equal Employment Opportunity Commission (EEOC) was created to enforce the law.

Protection of Public Resources

Theodore Roosevelt recognized the problem of business and private citizens appropriating and exploiting public resources for their own benefit. He created the National Forestry Service to address the problem. In many ways, the Civilian Conservation Corps created by Franklin Roosevelt furthered the idea the government needed to be more assertive in protecting and caring for public resources.

Lyndon Johnson would become the first President to aggressively attempt to protect public resources from private appropriation and exploitation. He would expand the idea of public resources to include not only land but to air, water, and species protection as well.

The extent of environmental legislation passed during the Great Society is not well recognized. It greatly strengthened and expanded the Federal government's efforts to advance the public interest by protecting public resources. Legislation included:

- Clean Air Act 1963
- Pesticide Control Bill 1964
- Wilderness Act 1964
- Water Quality Act 1965
- Water Resource Planning Act 1965
- Water and Sanitation Systems in Rural Areas Bill 1965
- Solid Waste Disposal Bill 1965
- Sale Water Conservation Act 1965
- Endangered Species Act 1966
- Air Quality Act 1966
- Air Quality Act 1967
- Wetlands Preservation Bill 1967
- National Parks Foundation 1967

—NATIONAL PARK SERVICE, NPS.ORG,
LYNDON B. JOHNSON AND THE ENVIRONMENT

Never before had there been such commitment to, and success in, passing legislation protecting public resources and the environment.

The Johnson Administration's efforts to protect public resources would culminate after he left office when a Democratic Congress passed the Environmental Protection Act in 1970, establishing the Environmental Protection Agency (EPA) to oversee and enforce the enacted laws. Republican President Richard Nixon would sign the bill and ultimately receive most of the credit for the environmental legislation first passed during the Johnson Administration.

Results of Great Society Programs

Economic Performance

Economic performance during the years of the Johnson Administration was among the best in the history of the country. GDP growth averaged 4.45%, the unemployment rate averaged 4.41%, and the rate of inflation averaged 2.53%. The inflation rate had begun to rise during the end of the decade due to inflationary monetary policies practiced by the Federal Reserve, which will be discussed below. Table 10D shows economic performance during the Johnson years.

Table 10D   Growth, Unemployment, & Inflation 1960–1969[60]

	GDP Growth Rate	Unemployment Rate	Rate of Inflation
1960	2.6%	6.6%	1.4%
1961	2.3%	6.0%	0.7%
1962	6.1%	5.5%	1.3%
1963	4.4%	5.5%	1.6%
1964	5.8%	5.0%	1.0%
1965	6.4%	4.0%	1.9%
1966	6.5%	3.8%	3.5%
1967	2.5%	3.8%	3.0%
1968	4.8%	3.4%	4.7%
1969	3.1%	3.5%	6.2%

Tax Policy

The highest marginal income tax rate was reduced, for the most part, with the exception of an increase in 1968 as shown in Table 10E.

Estate and gift taxes would remain unchanged from the rates adopted in 1942. The capital gains tax rate and corporate income tax rates were slightly increased in 1968, from 25% to 26.9% in the capital gains rate and from 48% to 52.8% for corporate income.[61, 62]

Table 10E   Marginal Income Tax Rates 1960–1968[63]

	Number of Tax Brackets	Lowest Rate	Highest Rate
1960–63	24	20%	91%
1964	26	16%	77%
1965–68★	25	14%	70%

★A 7.5% Surtax increased the effective highest rate to 75.25% in 1968.

Income and Wealth Concentration

Income inequality fell to its lowest level in history during this period. By 1970 the bottom 90% of the population received an unprecedented 67.13% of income. Wealth inequality was also reduced, with the top .1% wealth share falling by 10% while the bottom 90% had an increase of nearly 5%. Income and wealth inequality for the period are shown in Tables 10F and 10G.

Table 10F   Share of Income by Income Fractile Selected Years 1960–1970[64]

	1960	1965	1970	% Change
Top .01%	1.18%	1.50%	1.00%	-15.25%
Top .1%	3.27%	3.67%	2.80%	-14.37%
Top 1%	10.10%	10.95%	9.09%	-10.00%
Top 10%	33.69%	34.96%	32.87%	-2.43%
Bottom 90%	66.31%	65.04%	67.13%	1.23%

Table 10G   Share of Wealth by Wealth Fractile Selected Years 1960–1970[65, 66]

	1960	1965	1970	% Change
Top .1%	10%	10%	9%	-10.0%
Top 1%	27.8%	26.9%	28.1%	1.07%
Top 10%	69.8%	69.8%	68.3%	-2.14%
Bottom 90%	30.2%	30.2%	31.7%	4.96%

Economic Support Programs

Expansion of New Deal policies by the Johnson Administration was met by great resistance from opponents of Democratic Capitalism. Leading Republicans spoke out against economic support programs like Medicare.

> "If you don't (stop Medicare) and I don't do it, one of these days you and I are going to spend our sunset years telling our children's children what it once was like in America when men were free."
>
> —RONALD REAGAN 1961

> "Having given our pensioners their medical care in kind, why not food baskets, why not public housing accommodations, why not vacation resorts, why not a ration of cigarettes for those who smoke and of beer for those who drink?"
>
> —BARRY GOLDWATER 1964

> "I was there, fighting the fight, voting against Medicare… because we knew it wouldn't work."
>
> —BOB DOLE 1965 VOLSKY, 2009, THINKPROGRESS.ORG

Despite this opposition, most Americans recognized the need to provide health care for the elderly; many had parents and grandparents who received inadequate, substandard care and, therefore, supported the program.

Other programs such as Food Stamps, were more broadly supported by politicians. This was because the Food Stamp program was structured and presented as a program to aid farmers by increasing the demand for and, thus, the price of food. Reflecting this, the program was managed by the Agricultural Department.

Economic Opportunity

The legislation which created the greatest opposition and divisiveness in the country was the Civil Rights Act. As discussed earlier, white males and those connected to them (primarily their families) had been the primary beneficiaries of the economic expansion of the 1950s. These individuals were not prepared, nor willing, to see their economic privileged position challenged and put at risk by other groups.

Federal actions and aid to provide greater equality for education for students in primary and secondary education were also perceived as a threat to higher-income, higher-wealth, mostly white, privileged groups. The system of local property tax funding for public schools ensured individuals living in higher-income, wealthier communities had more than adequate resources to fund their schools and educate their children. It ensured local control of the funds and, therefore, of the schools. However, families living in lower-income, poorer communities suffered from inadequate funding and substandard schools. As long as local property taxes were the primary source of funding for schools, it would be difficult to provide sufficient funding to improve the schools in these areas.

Federal funding to lower-income, poorer districts was seen as a threat to the property tax model of funding schools. It was feared there would be increasing Federal encroachment in public education, threatening the ability of higher-income, wealthier areas to control and fund their schools.

Opposition became violent when Federal Courts declared that schools within the same district, mostly in large cities, needed to provide more equalized funding among schools. Schools attended by whites in a school district were better funded and better maintained than schools attended by minorities in the same district. This ultimately resulted in the courts ordering that students be bussed out of neighborhood schools to other schools in the same district. This led to demonstrations and violence by whites who saw minorities bussed into their neighborhood schools and saw their children bussed out of their neighborhood schools to schools in other neighborhoods with a majority of minority students.

Protection of Public Resources

The business community was opposed to the public resource protection laws of the Great Society. Legislation concerning air quality, water quality, waste disposal, the protection of wildlife, wildlife habitat, and waterways was seen as an infringement on their rights, restricting their freedom of action and ability to expand and make profits. They began a systematic campaign to discredit and undermine the protection of public resources.

The Great Society and the Vietnam War

Under the best of circumstances, the Johnson Administration would face stiff opposition and challenges from supporters of Oligarchic Capitalism in strengthening and expanding the New Deal of Franklin Roosevelt. An unanticipated event made the task even more difficult. Escalation of the War in Vietnam would divert attention and resources away from Great Society programs and create even greater divisiveness in the country.

Johnson wanted to avoid the costs of the war from undermining the financing of the Great Society. He feared raising taxes would further undermine support for the war. He pressured monetary authorities (the Federal Reserve) to expand the money supply. For the most part, they accommodated him. This laid the foundation for the inflationary problems that would plague the country in the 1970s.

The practice of granting deferments from the military draft to college students also created divisiveness. The deferments primarily went to middle-income and upper-income white males. Lower-income white males and minority males were left subject to the draft, creating increasing dissatisfaction and protests against the draft and the war.

The impossibility of both fighting the war and implementing Great Society programs became increasingly evident to Johnson. The war had become the primary political concern in the country. On March 31, 1968 Johnson addressed the nation and made a startling announcement:

"Accordingly, I shall not seek, and I will not accept, the nomination of my party for another term as your President."

—ELVING, 2018, NPR.ORG

The era of Democratic Capitalism was coming to an end.

Summary

The Johnson Administration's Great Society program was intended to continue the policies of the New Deal, strengthening and expanding the system of Democratic Capitalism created by Franklin Roosevelt. Programs promoting economic support, creating economic opportunity, and protecting public resources were aggressively pursued and implemented.

Opponents of Democratic Capitalism tried to prevent the passage of these programs; but public opinion was, for the most part, favorable. Also, the public at large continued to have trust and confidence in the government playing an active role in moving the country forward.

Supporters of Oligarchic Capitalism would need to undermine public trust and confidence in government if they were to reverse the advances of Democratic Capitalism and re-institute an Oligarchic Capitalist system. The events of the 1970s would provide them with just such an opportunity.

11

The Rebirth of Oligarchic Capitalism

Political and Economic Challenges of the 1970's

Three events would set the stage for the re-institution of Oligarchic Capitalism in 1980. They were:

- the Vietnam War
- the impeachment and resignation of Richard Nixon
- the occurrence of stagflation.

The Vietnam War and the Resignation of Richard Nixon

As discussed previously, the Vietnam War created a great deal of divisiveness and conflict in the country. The riots at the 1968 Democratic Convention in Chicago illustrate the extent the war divided the nation. With the Democratic Party torn apart, Richard Nixon was elected President in 1968.[i] It was anticipated by many that Nixon, as he had promised, would get the U.S. out of the war. Instead, he followed a policy of escalation which created even greater divisions in the country.

---

[i] The third-party candidacy of George Wallace also affected the election.

The war also created economic stresses. In an attempt to mitigate the economic impact of the war on the public, Nixon continued to finance the war effort with expansionary monetary policies rather than increases in taxes. This further laid the foundation for the inflationary problems that would plague the country in the 1970s.

The break-in of Democratic Headquarters at the Watergate complex in 1972 and subsequent cover-up would lead to the impeachment and resignation of Nixon. Eventually, even Republicans in Congress recognized that Nixon had committed crimes and would need to be impeached. Gerald Ford replaced Nixon as President and one of his first acts was to pardon Nixon. This created even greater divisiveness in the country.

The Vietnam War ended with the defeat of the United States. Combined with the resignation of Nixon, this created a mounting paralysis in government. A sense that the government and political system were incapable of dealing with our problems also began to infect the nation. It made the government increasingly incapable of dealing with any problems that arose. This included the economic problems that would plague the country in the 1970s.

Supporters of Oligarchic Capitalism would use the failure in Vietnam and the resignation of Nixon to foster destruction of public confidence, trust, and belief in the government's ability to play an active role in promoting economic well-being. This would better enable them to work towards reducing the role of government and re-instituting an Oligarchic Capitalist System.

Stagflation

Stagflation is the occurrence of high unemployment and high inflation at the same time. Historically, unemployment and inflation had been inversely related; when one was high, the other was low. Initially, stagflation perplexed both economists and politicians who were ill-prepared to deal with it. Combined with the political paralysis resulting from the defeat in the Vietnam War and the resignation of Nixon, the economic system experienced its worse crisis since the Great Depression.

Stagflation was caused by the oil embargos of the 1970s. The first embargo was the result of the Arab-Israeli War in 1973. In October Egypt and Syria invaded Israel, initially with great success. However, with U.S. military aid, the Israeli's were able to recover and turn back the Egyptian and Syrian offensives.

In retaliation for the U.S. support of Israel during the war, the Organization of Petroleum Exporting Countries (OPEC), which was dominated by the oil-producing Arabic countries of the Middle East, voted to initiate an oil embargo, cutting the production and export of oil. The result was a dramatic increase in the price of oil.

Table 11A   *Price of a Barrel of West Texas Intermediate Crude Oil July 1973–February 1974*[67]

Month	Year	Price	% Increase
July	1973	$20.63	
February	1974	$55.00	**166.5%**

Adjusted for Inflation

A second oil embargo occurred in 1979 in response to the Iranian revolution. Production of Iranian oil fell driving world oil production down 7%.[68] This created a second dramatic increase in oil prices.

Table 11B   *Price of Barrel of West Texas Intermediate Crude Oil January 1979–June 1980*[69]

Month	Year	Price	% Increase
January	1979	$55.82	
July	1980	$122.65	**119.7%**

Adjusted for Inflation

Between July 1973 and July 1980, the price of a barrel of oil had increased an unimaginable 495%.

The oil embargoes resulted in the cost of production rising dramatically since oil is a major source of energy across all segments of the economy. Companies responded by cutting production and laying off workers. At the same time, the increased cost of production caused prices to rise. The result was stagflation, a combination of high unemployment and high inflation. Table 11C shows the relationship between unemployment and inflation during this time.

Table 11C   Unemployment and Inflation Selected Years 1968–1980[70]

Year	Unemployment Rate	Inflation Rate
1968	3.4%	4.7%
1972	5.2%	3.4%
1974	7.2%	12.3%
1978	6.0%	13.3%
1980	7.2%	12.5%

An unemployment rate of 7.2% combined with an inflation rate of 12.3%, as occurred in 1974, was unprecedented. This combination of high unemployment and high inflation would continue throughout the 1970s, creating economic problems across the economy. Economists and politicians searched for a solution.

Taxes, Income, and Wealth in the 1970s

Tax Policy

With the policies of Democratic Capitalism in flux and the economic crisis of stagflation, the government searched for answers. Tax policies were reviewed and modified.

In 1979 the number of tax brackets was reduced from 25 to 15, reducing the progressivity of the system. This would be a pattern that would continue throughout the 1980s.

In 1976 both the estate tax rate and the gift tax rate were finally changed from what they had been set at in 1942. The amount exempted from the estate tax was decreased while the initial rate was raised and the top rate reduced. The lifetime exemption from the gift tax was increased; the top rate increased; and the amount subject to the top rate reduced. These changes are shown in Tables 11D, 11E, and 11F.

Table 11D   Marginal Income Tax Rates 1969–1980[71]

	Number of Tax Brackets	Lowest Rate	Highest Rate
1969-78★	25	14%	70%
1979-81	15	14%	70%

★Surtaxes increased the effective highest rate in some years:
1969: Surtax 10%, Effective rate 77%
1970: Surtax 2.5%, Effective rate 71.25%

Table 11E   U.S. Federal Estate Tax 1970 to 1980[72]

	Amount Exempted	Initial Rate	Top Rate
1970-76	$60,000	3%	77%
1977	$120,000	18%	70%
1978	**$134,000**	**18%**	**70%**
1979	$147,000	18%	70%
1980	$161,000	18%	70%

Table 11F   U.S. Federal Gift Tax 1970 to 1980[73]

	Annual Exclusion	Lifetime Exemption	Top Rate	Subject to Top Rate (Above)
1970-76	$3,000	$30,000	57.75%	$10,000,000
1977	$3,000	$120,000	70%	$5,000,000
1978	$3,000	$134,000	70%	$5,000,000
1979	$3,000	$147,000	70%	$5,000,000
1980	$3,000	$161,000	70%	$5,000,000

Income and Wealth Inequality

There was an improvement in wealth inequality. The bottom 90% saw more than a 13% increase in their share of wealth. The wealthiest households had a drop: the top .1%, over 10%; the top 1%, almost 20%; and the top 10%, 4.68% as shown in Table 11G.

129

Table 11G   Share of Wealth by Wealth Fractile Selected Years 1970–1980[74, 75]

	1970	1975	1980	% Change
Top .1%	9%	7%	8%	**-11.11%**
Top 1%	28.1%	22.8%	22.5%	**-19.92%**
Top 10%	68.3%	67.3%	65.1%	**-4.68%**
Bottom 90%	31.7%	32.7%	35.9%	**13.24%**

The decline in wealth inequality was largely due to the performance of the stock market during this period, which gyrated between highs and lows as shown in Table 11H.

Table 11H   Dow Jones Industrial Average Selected Dates
May 1969–November 1980[76]

	Dow Jones Industrial	Percent Change	Percent Change May 1969–Nov 1980
May 1969	961		
June 1970	710	-26.1%	
Jan 1973	1046	47.3%	
Dec 1974	577	-44.8%	
Sept 1976	1014	75.7%	
Mar 1978	746	-26.4%	
Nov 1980	991	32.8%	3%

Such volatility makes investing decisions difficult. However, during the entire period the market essentially remained flat. In May 1969 the Dow Jones Industrial Average stood at 961. At the end of the period, in November 1980, it stood at just 991, an increase of just 3.1%. Meanwhile, inflation averaged 7.41% per year during the decade of the 70s. In real terms investors had lost over 4%. Since stock ownership is concentrated with the wealthiest, their share of wealth had fallen.

Income inequality worsened during the 1970s. The top .01% saw the biggest increase in share of income, a rise of nearly 30%. Increases went down from there. The top .1% had an increase of 23% while the top 10% increased by 6.6%. Share of income for the top 10% rose only .6%. The bottom 90%'s share of income fell 1.2%. Rising income inequality was brought on by the increase in unemployment, which was largely borne by middle-income and lower-income groups. These changes are shown in Table 11I.

Table 11I   Share of Income by Income Fractile Selected Years 1970–1980[77]

	1970	1975	1980	% Change
Top .01%	1.00%	0.86%	1.29%	29.00%
Top .1%	2.80%	2.59%	3.45%	23.21%
Top 1%	9.09%	8.97%	10.15%	11.66%
Top 10%	32.87%	33.79%	35.07%	6.69%
Bottom 90%	67.13%	66.21%	65.93%	-1.78%

Ronald Reagan and the Rebirth of Oligarchic Capitalism

Opponents of Democratic Capitalism used the economic crisis of the 1970s to reinstitute policies promoting Oligarchic Capitalism. The election of Ronald Reagan as President in 1980 began the process of re-establishing an Oligarchic Capitalist system.

The policies entailed the ideas of Supply-Side Economics. *Supply-Side Economics is the belief that the key to macro-economic performance lies with supply, i.e., production.*[ii] Advocates of Supply-Side Economics contend the key to increasing production and living standards is to increase the incentives for people to be productive. Advocates of Supply-Side Economics oppose the policies of Democratic Capitalism and the ideas of Keynesian Economics, which believes the key to macro-economic performance is demand, i.e., spending. Reagan's support of Supply-Side Economics led to it becoming known as Reaganomics in the popular press.

Stagflation and Supply-Side Economics

Advocates of Supply-Side Economics contended the problem of stagflation was not caused by the oil crises of the 1970s but, instead, by the policies of Democratic Capitalism. There were five basic criticisms:

[ii]   Macro-economics deals with the performance of the overall economy. It involves dealing with issues such as unemployment, inflation, and economic growth. It can be contrasted with micro-economics which involves the study of the performance of individual markets.

131

- High marginal tax rates reduced the incentive for high-er-wealth/higher-income individuals to invest and expand their businesses.

- High marginal tax rates reduced the incentive for low-er-income/middle-income/lower-wealth individuals to work and be productive.

- Economic support programs reduced the incentive to work and were being abused.

- Economic opportunity programs hindered the ability of businesses to hire and promote the most qualified individuals.

- Programs protecting public resources were too costly and inefficient, hindering the ability of businesses to be productive and profitable, and hampered their ability to be competitive.

As a result, the Supply-Side solution to stagflation was to cut tax rates, cut economic support programs, reduce programs to promote economic opportunity, and reduce programs protecting public resources.

Supply-Side Policies

Tax Cuts, Incentives, and Deficits

The Economic Recovery Tax Act of 1981 cut tax rates across the board. The highest marginal income tax rate was cut from 70% to 50%. Importantly, the number of brackets was decreased from 15 to 12, though the number would be increased to 13 from 1983 to 1986.

The Tax Reform Act of 1986 was even more draconian in reducing the taxes that the highest-income households paid. Rates were further lowered on the highest marginal tax rate being reduced to 28% in 1988, the lowest it had been since 1931. Most importantly, the number of brackets was reduced greatly reduced from thirteen to six and, eventually, to just two. *This reduction in the number of tax brackets was the most significant cause of the great increases in income and wealth inequality that would plague the nation during this second era of Oligarchic Capitalism.* Changes are shown in Table 11J.

Table 11J   Marginal Income Tax Rates 1980–1990[78]

	Number of Tax Brackets	Lowest Rate	Highest Rate
1982	12	12%	50%
1983–86	13	11%	50%
1987	6	11%	38.5%
1988–90	2	15%	28%

The top rate for the estate tax was lowered from 70% to 55%, the lowest since 1933. The amount exempted from the tax was increased from $161,000 to $660,000. Changes are shown in Table 11K.

Table 11K   U.S. Federal Estate Tax 1980–1990[79]

	Amount Exempted	Initial Rate	Top Rate
1980	$161,000	18%	70%
1981	$175,000	18%	70%
1982	$225,000	18%	65%
1983	$275,000	18%	60%
1984	$325,000	18%	55%
1985	$400,000	18%	55%
1986	$500,000	18%	55%
1987–1990	$600,000	18%	55%

The top rate for the gift tax was lowered from 70% to 55%; and the amount exempted from the tax increased from $161,000 to $660,000. The annual exclusion was increased from $3,000 to $10,000. These changes are shown in Table 11L.

The capital gains tax rate was reduced from 28% to 20% in 1981 but then raised back to 28% in 1987.[80] The top corporate income tax rate was reduced, falling from 51% to 39% in 1987.[81]

Table 11L   U.S. Federal Gift Tax 1980–1990[82]

	Annual Exclusion	Lifetime Exemption	Top Rate	Subject to Top Rate (Above)
1980	$3,000	$161,000	70%	$5,000,000
1981	$3,000	$175,000	70%	$4,000,000
1982	$10,000	$225,000	65%	$3,500,000
1983	$10,000	$275,000	60%	$3,000,000
1984	$10,000	$325,000	55%	$3,000,000
1985	$10,000	$400,000	55%	$3,000,000
1986	$10,000	$500,000	55%	$3,000,000
1987–90	$10,000	$600,000	55%	$3,000,000

A core principle of Supply-Side Economics is that high marginal tax rates create disincentives to be productive. Advocates contended that higher-income/higher-wealth individuals were not investing and expanding their businesses. They also asserted that lower-income/middle-income/lower-wealth individuals were not working all they wanted due to high tax rates. It was alleged workers in places like automobile plants were turning down the opportunity to work overtime because of the high percentage of their overtime wages that went to taxes. Advocates of Supply-Side Economics contended reducing marginal tax rates would re-incentivize people to invest and work, which would increase productivity and result in economic recovery.

Tied in with the idea a greater incentive to work would be created was the contention government deficits would be reduced. Government deficits had increased significantly in the 1970s as shown in Table 11M.

Advocates of Supply-Side Economics contended that lower tax rates would increase the incentive to work (to be productive). They asserted that the incentive to work which would increase so much that even though *tax rates went down, tax revenues would increase*. Productivity would increase so much that increases in income would result in higher tax receipts, even with lower tax rates. This was the idea of the Laffer Curve developed by Supply-Side economist Arthur Laffer.[iii]

[iii] President Donald Trump awarded Laffer the Presidential Medal of Freedom in 2019 for his development of the Laffer Curve.

Table 11M   U.S. Government Deficit 1970–1979[83]

Year	Deficit (Billions)	Percent of GDP
1970	$3	0.3%
1971	$23	2.0%
1972	$23	1.8%
1973	$15	1.0%
1974	$6	0.4%
1975	$53	3.1%
1976	$74	3.9%
1977	$54	2.5%
1978	$59	2.5%
1979	$41	1.5%

Reduction in Economic Support Programs

Advocates of Supply-Side Economics and Oligarchic Capitalism contended economic support programs in health care, food assistance, and housing assistance also reduced the incentive to be productive and work. Advocates argued reductions in these programs would result in individuals being forced back into the workforce to become productive. They contended many recipients were not really in need of assistance and there was wide-spread fraud in the programs. They sought to discredit the programs and undermine public support for the programs due to the extent of alleged fraud.

In his 1976 presidential campaign, Ronald Reagan created the image of the "welfare queen," an individual fraudulently living a life of excess from government support programs. He would frequently return to this theme throughout the rest of his political career. An example is a speech he gave in Gilford, New Hampshire, in February 1976:

"There's a woman in Chicago. She has 80 names, 30 addresses, 12 Social Security cards and is collecting veterans' benefits on four non-existing deceased husbands. And she's collecting

Social Security on her cards. She's got Medicaid, getting food stamps and she is collecting welfare under each of her names. Her tax-free cash income alone is over $150,000".

—NEW YORK TIMES, 1976, FEB 15

Reagan did not mention the woman's name. The press was not allowed to ask Reagan questions about the woman since he would only take questions from the local audience attending the rally.[84] State authorities in Illinois believed Reagan based his story on a woman by the name of Linda Taylor in Chicago, who was a recipient of economic support from the state. Her case had been widely publicized when a state senator from Illinois referenced her during a state investigation of fraud in economic support programs. During hearings, it had been alleged that she made between $100,000 and $150,000 from fraud. The facts were much less alarming. In the end, the Illinois state attorney who prosecuted the case charged Taylor with using four different aliases to fraudulently obtain $3,000 in aid.[85]

When Reagan became President in 1980, he began to systematically dismantle economic support programs.

Combined with the cuts announced Feb. 18, President Reagan has now axed these amounts from the 1982 budget proposed by President Jimmy Carter; jobs and unemployment benefits, $5.8 billion; food, $4.9 billion; education, $2.4 billion; health, $1.2 billion; legal and juvenile justice, $500 million; housing, $200 million; other welfare, $3.4 billion;…

—PIPPERT, 1981, UPI ARCHIVES, UPI.COM

The results were harsh for low-income individuals. More than one million individuals lost food-stamp benefits.[86] Six hundred thousand lost Medicaid.[87] The Department of Housing and Urban Development budget for subsidized housing assistance was cut from $26.6 billion in 1980 to $13.2 billion in 1982 to $7.3 billion by 1987.[88]

Reduction in Economic Opportunity Programs

Supporters of Oligarchic Capitalism portrayed the greater equality of economic opportunity afforded for minorities by the Civil Rights Act as providing them with unfair, preferential treatment. The long history of the discriminatory denial of economic opportunity to minority groups was downplayed. Supporters of Oligarchic Capitalism strove to create greater divisiveness between whites and the rest of the population. Providing access to the benefits of Democratic Capitalism to minorities, women, and the gay community was represented as unfairly compromising the benefits of the system to white males and resulting in "reverse discrimination." The divisiveness and animosity created was used to further undermine the Democratic Capitalist system.

Ronald Reagan had publicly opposed the Civil Rights Act of 1964 and the Voting Rights Act of 1965. In 1988 he vetoed the Civil Rights Restoration Act, but his veto was overridden by Congress. He opposed the Equal Rights Amendment for women.

Reduction in Programs Protecting Public Resources

Reagan was opposed to programs protecting public resources. He famously stated, "A tree's a tree. How many more do you need to look at?" (Brainy Quotes, brainyquote.com, *Ronald Reagan Quotes*). Also, "If you've seen one redwood, you've seen them all." (AZ Quotes, azquotes.com, *Ronald Reagan*).

Reagan appointed Anne Gorsuch as the Administrator of the Environmental Protection Agency (EPA) and James Watt as the Secretary of the Interior. Both had backgrounds opposing programs protecting public resources and supporting efforts to give corporate interests more access to exploiting and appropriating public resources.

Between 1980 and 1983 under Gorsuch's leadership, the budget of the EPA was cut 27%. Between 1981 and 1983, the EPA's staff was cut 21%.[89] Gorsuch was eventually forced to resign while under Congressional investigation for the mishandling of the $1.6 trillion toxic waste Superfund program.[90]

The Watt legacy is similar.

New Secretary Watt soon announced his intention to change the way Interior conducted its business. He believed that the new environmental laws and regulations were standing in the way of necessary development, and that federal public land policy should favor more resource utilization.

—COGGINS & NAGEL, 1990, P. 489

At the heart of Secretary Watt's new policies was the plan for outright disposal of large tracts of public lands. The debate began when President Reagan announced in February, 1982 that the government intended to sell approximately 35 million acres of federal land. While some of the tracts were in the national forests or under the jurisdiction of various other agencies, the bulk of the lands proposed for sale were managed by Interior's Bureau of Land Management.

—COGGINS & NAGEL, 1990, P. 492

Many believed that the groups most vocally supporting privatization were the powerful ranching, mining, logging, and land speculation interests who stood to benefit the most…

—COGGINS & NAGEL, 1990, P. 496-497

The public nationwide did not support the proposed sale of lands…The plan to privatize the public lands was halted primarily by political resistance…

—COGGINS & NAGEL, 1990, P. 496

Watt was forced to resign in 1983 after defending the composition of his Coal Advisory Board by stating, "We have every kind of mixture you can have. I have a Black, I have a woman, two Jews, and a cripple. And I have talent." (Bullinger, 2017, Outside, outsideonline.com)

Results of Supply-Side Policies

Economic Recovery

As shown in Table 11N, the economy recovered during Reagan's years in office. Economic growth averaged 2.76%, the unemployment rate averaged 6.73%, and the rate of inflation averaged 4.66%.

Table 11N   Growth, Unemployment, & Inflation 1980–1988[91]

	GDP Growth Rate	Unemployment Rate	Rate of Inflation
1980	-0.3%	7.5%	12.5%
1981	2.5%	8.8%	8.9%
1982	-1.8%	10.8%	3.8%
1983	4.6%	8.3%	3.8%
1984	7.2%	7.3%	3.9%
1985	4.2%	7.0%	3.8%
1986	3.5%	6.6%	1.1%
1987	3.5%	5.7%	4.4%
1988	4.2%	5.3%	4.4%

Supporters of Oligarchic Capitalism credit Supply-Side policies with the economic recovery of the 1980s. Such claims are very dubious for two reasons.

In August 1979 President Jimmy Carter had appointed Paul Volker Chairperson of the Federal Reserve with a mandate to fight inflation. Volker began restricting the growth of the money supply, driving interest rates higher. A major gauge of interest rates is the Federal Funds Rate, the interest rates banks charge each other for an overnight loan.[iv] Table 11O shows the Federal Funds rate during this period.

[iv] By law, banks having insufficient reserves (funds) to back their deposits must obtain adequate reserves. They do so by either borrowing from the Federal Reserve or borrowing from banks that have excess reserves in the Federal Funds Market.

Table 11O   Federal Funds Rate Selected Dates August 1979–September 1986[92]

Month	Year	Federal Funds Rate
January	1979	9.94%
August	1979	11.05%
February	1980	14.46%
June	1981	19.83%
April	1982	15.27%
December	1982	8.58%
September	1986	5.75%

The restrictive monetary policy and increase in interest rates led to a recession, which contributed to Reagan defeating Carter in the Presidential election of 1980. It is also the reason inflation fell from 12.5% in 1980, to 8.9% in 1981 and eventually to 3.8% in 1982. When rates began to be lowered after June 1981, economic recovery began.

The second reason for the recovery was the decrease in oil prices that occurred throughout the 1980s. The increases in oil prices were the primary cause of the economic problems of the 1970s; so, not surprisingly, the reversal in oil prices resulted in economic recovery.

Table 11P   Price of Barrel of West Texas Intermediate Crude Oil July 1980–March 1986[93]

Month	Year	Price	% Decrease
July	1980	$122.65	
August	1985	$66.75	–45.6%
March	1986	$24.59	–63.2%
TOTAL (7/1980–3/1986)			–80.0%

While the Supply-Side tax cuts did contribute to economic recovery, it is a myth to believe they were the primary cause. *The real fuel that re-ignited economic growth in the 1980s were falling interest rates and falling oil prices.*

Incentives, Tax Cuts, and Deficits

The result of the Supply-Side tax cuts on government deficits is shown in Table 11Q.

Table 11Q   U.S. Government Deficit 1979–1988[94]

Year	Deficit (Billions)	Percent of GDP
1979	$ 40.7	1.5%
1980	$ 73.8	2.6%
1981	$ 79.0	2.4%
1982	$ 128.0	3.8%
1983	$ 207.8	5.6%
1984	$ 185.5	4.5%
1985	$ 212.3	4.8%
1986	$ 221.2	4.8%
1987	$ 149.7	3.1%
1988	$ 155.2	2.9%
1989	$ 152.6	2.7%
1990	$ 221.0	3.7%

In response to the tax cuts, government deficits soared; Supply-Side tax cuts did not lead to the predicted reduction in government deficits. *Even though tax rates can affect the incentive to work, the rates existing in the United States had virtually no effect for most Americans on the incentive to work.* Lower-income/lower-wealth individuals already work as much as they can just to make ends meet, often working two or three jobs. Additionally, the picture painted by advocates of Supply-Side Economics of middle-class blue-collar workers in places like automobile assembly plants declining to work overtime due to high income tax rates was entirely fictional. Most of these individuals were working as much overtime as was offered to them. As a result, lowering tax rates had no real impact on the willingness of people to work and, instead, increased government deficits to record levels, disproving a fundamental tenet of Supply-Side Economics.

Wealth and Income Inequality

The top .1% also experienced an enormous increase of 50% in share of wealth. The top 1% had an increase of nearly 18%. Wealth share of the top 10% actually fell 3.68%. The bottom 90% of households had an increase of nearly 7%, but changes in income share would inevitably lead to a decrease in wealth share going forward. Changes in share of wealth are shown in Table 11R.

Table 11R   *Share of Wealth by Wealth Fractile Selected Years 1980–1988*[95, 96]

	1980	1984	1988	% Change
Top .1%	8%	9%	12%	**50.0%**
Top 1%	22.5%	23.9%	26.5%	**17.8%**
Top 10%	65.1%	61.4%	62.7%	**-3.68%**
Bottom 90%	34.9%	38.6%	37.3%	**6.87%**

Changes in income inequality were even more pronounced. The share of income of the highest-income households skyrocketed as a result of Supply-Side policies. The top .01% experienced an increase of over 123% in their share of income. The top .1% had an increase of over 98%. The top 1% had an increase of nearly 54%. The top 10% had a much smaller increase of 16.48%. For the bottom 90% of households, share of income sank over 10%. It was their lowest share of income since 1940. This bode very badly for the future. Changes are shown in Table 11S.

Table 11S   *Share of Income by Income Fractile Selected Years 1980–1988*[97]

	1980	1984	1988	% Change
Top .01%	1.29%	2.18%	2.88%	**123.25%**
Top .1%	3.45%	5.04%	6.84%	**98.26%**
Top 1%	10.15%	12.14%	15.58%	**53.49%**
Top 10%	35.07%	37.20%	40.85%	**16.48%**
Bottom 90%	65.93%	62.80%	59.15%	**-10.28%**

Summary

Supporters of Oligarchic Capitalism used the economic problems of the 1970s to re-establish an Oligarchic Capitalist System. By blaming the government for the economic problems and fomenting divisiveness in the country, they were able to destroy public belief, trust, and confidence the government could act to enhance economic well-being. The election of Ronald Reagan in 1980 created the opportunity to undo the policies of Democratic Capitalism and laid the foundation for a second era of Oligarchic Capitalism. The era of Democratic Capitalism had ended, and a new era of Oligarchic Capitalism was in full swing.

12

Oligarchic Capitalism in the Post-Reagan Era

The First Bush Administration

George H. Bush succeeded Ronald Reagan as President in 1988. Previously Bush had served as Reagan's Vice President. He had run against Reagan for the Republican nomination in 1980. He famously had derided the ideas of Supply-Side Economics as "voodoo economics". He was particularly critical of the idea cuts in tax rates would lead to increases in tax revenues which would decrease the government deficit.

When Bush ran for President in 1988, he presented himself as a convert. To demonstrate his commitment to Reaganomics, in his acceptance speech during the Republican convention that year he stated,

> "And my opponent won't rule out raising taxes. But I will. And the Congress will push me to raise taxes, and I'll say no, and they'll push, and I'll say no, and they'll push again. And I'll say to them: Read my lips. No new taxes."

> —THE GUARDIAN, 2018, THEGUARDIAN. COM, *READ MY LIPS. NO NEW TAXES*

Economic performance during the Bush Administration was poor as shown in Table 12A. Growth slowed and unemployment rose. Despite this, inflation increased. It was the 1970s all over again. In August 1990 the Gulf War was launched. Combined with the recession, the government deficit increased to record levels as shown in Table 12B.

Table 12A   Growth, Unemployment, & Inflation 1988–1992[98]

	GDP Growth Rate	Unemployment Rate	Rate of Inflation
1988	4.2%	5.3%	4.4%
1989	3.7%	5.4%	4.6%
1990	1.9%	6.3%	6.1%
1991	-0.1%	7.3%	3.1%
1992	3.5%	7.4%	2.9%

Table 12B   U.S. Government Deficit 1988–1992[99]

Year	Deficit (Billions)	Percent of GDP
1988	$ 155	2.9%
1989	$ 153	2.7%
1990	$ 221	3.7%
1991	$ 269	4.3%
1992	$ 290	4.2%

Congress demanded taxes be raised to combat the deficit. At first Bush refused, but ultimately, he agreed. A third tax bracket was added to the system, raising the highest marginal rate from 28% to 31%.[100] This increase in tax rates contradicted the tenet of Supply-Side Economics which asserted the way to increase tax revenues and cut government deficits was a reduction in tax rates. The increase in rates also cast doubt on Bush's claim that he had become a believer in Supply-Side Economics. Additionally, it broke his promise not to raise taxes.

When Bush ran for re-election against Bill Clinton in 1992 his broken promise not to raise taxes haunted him. Combined with the slow recovery from the recession, he lost the election.[i]

---

[i]   The third-party candidacy of Ross Perot also affected the election.

The Clinton Administration

Tax Policy and the Deficit

The Clinton Administration raised taxes to combat the deficit. The number of tax brackets was increased from three to five and the highest marginal rate was increased from 31% to 39.6%.[101] The economy recovered and the deficit fell dramatically, becoming a surplus by 1998 and reaching $236 billion by 2000. This further discredited the ideas of Supply-Side Economics and the Laffer Curve. Clinton had raised tax rates, increasing tax revenues not decreasing them, and reducing the deficit. The results are shown in Table 12C.

Table 12C   U.S. Government Deficit 1993–2000[102]

Year	Deficit (Billions)	Percent of GDP
1993	$255	3.7%
1994	$203	2.8%
1995	$164	2.1%
1996	$107	1.3%
1997	$22	0.3%
1998	-$69	-0.8%
1999	-$126	-1.3%
2000	-$236	2.5%

Economic Performance

Economic performance during the Clinton years was outstanding as shown in Table 12D. During this period, growth averaged 3.88%; unemployment 4.98%; and inflation 2.58%.

It is noteworthy to compare economic performance during the Clinton Administration with the Johnson and Reagan Administrations as shown in Table 12E. During the Reagan years, the economy consistently underperformed relative to both the Johnson years and the Clinton years in every major category. Supply-Side economists regularly reference the outstanding economic performance of the Reagan years as evidence that Supply-Side policies work. However,

147

the economy during the Reagan years consistently underperformed relative to the Johnson and Clinton periods in terms of growth, unemployment, and inflation. This can only further call into question the claims of Supply-Side economists.

Table 12D   Growth, Unemployment, & Inflation 1993–2000[103]

	GDP Growth Rate	Unemployment Rate	Rate of Inflation
1993	2.8%	6.5%	2.7%
1994	4.0%	5.5%	2.7%
1995	2.7%	5.6%	2.5%
1996	3.8%	5.4%	3.3%
1997	4.4%	4.7%	1.7%
1998	4.5%	4.4%	1.6%
1999	4.8%	4.0%	2.7%
2000	4.1%	3.9%	3.4%

Table 12E   Growth, Unemployment, & Inflation Johnson, Reagan, Clinton Administrations[104]

	GDP Growth Rate	Unemployment Rate	Rate of Inflation
Johnson 1964–1968	5.20%	4.00%	2.82%
Reagan 1980–1988	2.76%	6.73%	4.60%
Clinton 1992-2000	3.88%	4.98%	2.58%

Income and Wealth Concentration

Income inequality continued to worsen in the 1990s. The highest income fractiles saw the greatest increases. From 1992 to 2000 the income share of the top .01% increased 150%. For the top .1%, it was over 80%. The top 1% saw an increase of over 45%. The top 10% increase was nearly 17%. Meanwhile, the bottom 90% experienced a decrease of nearly 12%. Increases in income inequality are shown in Table 12F.

Table 12F   ***Share of Income by Income Fractile Selected Years 1992–2000***[105, 106]

	1992	1996	2000	% Change
Top .01%	2.00%	3.00%	5.00%	**150.00%**
Top .1%	6.00%	7.00%	11.00%	**83.33%**
Top 1%	15.00%	17.00%	22.00%	**46.67%**
Top 10%	38.40%	41.50%	44.90%	**16.92%**
Bottom 90%	61.60%	59.50%	55.10%	**-11.79%**

As with income, the top wealth fractile had the greatest increase. From 1992 to 2000, the top .1% fractile had an increase of over 23%. The top 1% was over 17% while the wealthiest 10% saw an increase of only about 7%. The bottom 90% of households experienced a decrease in their share of wealth of over 12%. Share of wealth is shown in Table 12G

Table 12G   ***Share of Wealth by Wealth Fractile Selected Years 1992–2000***[107, 108]

	1992	1996	2000	% Change
Top .1%	13%	13%	16%	**23.07%**
Top 1%	27.6%	28.6%	32.3%	**17.03%**
Top 10%	64.3%	66.4%	68.8%	**6.99%**
Bottom 90%	35.7%	33.6%	31.2%	**-12.60%**

Trade Policy

As discussed in Chapter 5, the Clinton Administration would attempt to deal with the problem of increasing inequality by expanding trade through trade deals. Both the North American Free Trade Agreement and the World Trade Agreement were negotiated during this time.

The Clinton Administration pursued trade deals in an attempt to deal with the problem of lower-income/middle-income/lower-wealth households falling further behind the faster rising living standards of higher-income/higher-wealth households. By increasing trade, production and consumption (living standards} would rise. It was mistakenly believed this would solve the problems of lagging growth in incomes and wealth for lower-income/middle-income/lower-wealth households

Unfortunately, the die had already been cast. The Reagan Oligarchic policies of lower tax rates for higher-income/higher-wealth households, the cuts in economic support programs, and the dismantling of economic opportunity programs meant that any gains from increased trade would disproportionately benefit higher-income/higher-wealth households. The foundation for a new era of Oligarchic Capitalism had been laid. Growth in income and wealth for lower-income/middle-income/lower-wealth households would fall further and further behind.

Financial Deregulation

One of the most consequential acts of the Clinton Administration was the repeal of the Glass-Steagall Act, which had been passed during the New Deal. As discussed in Chapter 9, the law disallowed Investment Banks from owning Commercial Banks. As a result of the repeal, Investment Banks formed holding companies and began taking over Commercial Banks. This led to a tremendous increase in the size of banks. When the Financial Crisis of 2008 occurred, the banks would be considered "too big to fail" since, as a result of their size, their bankruptcy would cause the economic system to collapse. The stage was increasingly being set for the second greatest economic crisis in the country's history.

The Second Bush Administration

Presidential Election 2000

In 2000 George W. Bush followed in his father's footsteps and was elected President. In one of the most disputed elections in history, Bush defeated Al Gore even though Gore won the popular vote. Contested voting results in Florida were taken to the Supreme Court, which ruled in Bush's favor. Bush became President, and new initiatives to strengthen and expand the Oligarchic Capitalist system were undertaken.

Social Security Reform

One of the first actions of the Bush Administration was to attempt to dismantle the foundational economic support program of the New

Deal, Social Security. Prior to the passage of Social Security, approximately 50% of the elderly lived in poverty. Today, that number is about 10%. It is estimated without Social Security about 43% of the elderly would live in poverty today.[109] The program ranks as one of the most successful economic support programs in history.

In 2001 Bush formed a bipartisan commission to study reform. One of his directives to the commission was to "…include individually controlled, voluntary personal retirement accounts…" as part of the system.[110] The intent was a partial privatization of the system by allowing younger workers to divert their payments to the system into private accounts they controlled. The commission issued a report in 2002.

> Social Security will be strengthened if modernized to include a system of voluntary personal accounts. Personal accounts improve retirement security by facilitating wealth creation and providing participants with assets that they own and that can be inherited, rather than providing only claims to benefits that remain subject to political negotiation.
>
> —GLASS, 2018, POLITICO, POLITICO.COM

Congress refused to act on the commission's recommendations. It was argued diverting resources from the program to fund private accounts was intended and, would ultimately, underfund the program and lead to its dissolution.

Bush refused to give up. After his re-election in 2004 Bush returned to Social Security reform as one of his priorities. In his State of the Union Address, he said,

> "As we fix Social Security, we also have the responsibility to make the system a better deal for younger workers. And the best way to reach that goal is through voluntary personal retirement accounts."
>
> —GLASS, 2018, POLITIC, POLITICO.COM

Polls continued to show the public disapproved of Bush's plans to privatize the system. Congress, again, refused to act on his proposal.

These attempts to privatize Social Security were a continuing attempt by opponents of Democratic Capitalism to undermine the role of the government in ensuring individuals had the economic support necessary to provide for themselves, especially in old age.

Protection of Public Resources

A second early action of the Bush Administration was to reduce government action to protect public resources. Bush announced he was withdrawing U.S. support of and participation in the implementation of the initiatives of the Kyoto Protocol on climate change. In 2001 one hundred and seventy-eight countries agreed to adopt the protocol; but the Bush Administration held the United States out. The intent of the treaty is to reduce greenhouse emissions to try to limit climate change. Christine Todd, administrator of the Environmental Protection Agency under Bush, responded to journalists: "No, we have no interest in implementing that treaty." (theguardian.com, 2001, *Bush kills global warming treaty*).

Going forward, the Bush Administration would cut enforcement and oversight of many areas of environmental protection including clean air, water quality, and endangered species. The Administration also opened up millions of acres of public land to greater mining, drilling, and logging operations by private interests.

Consumer Debt

Consumer debt reached a peak during the second Bush Administration. The extent of consumer debt is measured by its relationship to the size of the economy, i.e., to GDP. From 1960 to 1980 consumer debt as a percent of GDP had slowly increased from about 40% of GDP to about 50%. With the election of Ronald Reagan in 1980 and the adoption of Oligarchic Capitalist policies, consumer debt began to rapidly increase. By 1990 it was over 60%; by 2000, over 70%; and it reached a peak in 2007 at 98.63% of GDP. This reflected lower-income/middle-income/lower-wealth households struggling to maintain their living standards as increasing shares of income and wealth accrued to higher-income/higher-wealth households. Table 12H shows consumer debt as a percent of GDP.

Table 12H   Consumer Debt as Percent GDP Selected Years 1960–2008[111]

	Consumer Debt as % GDP
1960	40.72%
1970	43.89%
1980	49.70%
1985	53.69%
1990	60.77%
2000	70.58%
2007	98.63%
2008	96.10%

Financial institutions became concerned rising consumer debt could not be repaid. These institutions began lobbying the Bush Administration to reform bankruptcy laws. The Bankruptcy Abuse and Consumer Protection Act was passed in 2005. It reformed the personal bankruptcy process by adopting more stringent eligibility requirements for individuals to declare bankruptcy. Its intent was to force households to file bankruptcy under Chapter 13 of the bankruptcy laws rather than Chapter 7, which provided greater relief and protection for filers. Chapter 7 is more lenient in allowing unsecured debt to be forgiven and debts to be discharged in full with partial payment. Chapter 13 requires that all debt must be at least partially paid. The act requires filers to restructure their debt, creating a three-year to five-year repayment plan. Also, it made it easier for creditors to appropriate future income to pay off debt.

Tax Policy and Deficits

The Bush Administration cut taxes in both 2001 and 2003. The cuts were broad based, covering income, estate, gift and capital gains tax rates. The highest marginal income tax rates were cut from 39.1% to 38.6% in 2002, and again to 35% in 2003.[112] The capital gains tax rate was cut from 20% to 15% in 2003.[113]

Changes to the estate tax are shown in Table 12I. The top rate was cut from 55% to 45% and the amount exempted increased from $675,000 to $2,000,000. The initial rate remained unchanged. The cuts largely benefited high-income and high-wealth households.

Table 12I   *U.S. Federal Estate Tax 2000–2008*[114]

	Amount Exempted	Initial Rate	Top Rate
2000–01	$675,000	18%	55%
2002	$1,000,000	18%	50%
2003	$1,000,000	18%	49%
2004	$1,500,000	18%	48%
2005	$1,500,000	18%	47%
2006	$2,000,000	18%	46%
2007–08	$2,000,000	18%	45%

Gift tax rate cuts are shown in Table 12J. The top rate was cut from 55% to 45%. The annual exclusion was raised from $10,000 to $12,000; and the lifetime exemption from the tax increased from $675,000 to $1,000,000. The one caveat was the amount subject to the tax was decreased from $3,000,000 to $1,500,000. Like the estate tax cuts, these changes largely benefitted high-income and high-wealth households.

Table 12J   *U.S. Federal Gift Tax 2000–2008*[115]

	Annual Exclusion	Lifetime Exemption	Top Rate	Subject to Top Rate (Above)
2000–01	$10,000	$675,000	55%	$3,000,000
2002	$11,000	$1,000,000	50%	$2,500,000
2003	$11,000	$1,000,000	49%	$2,000,000
2004	$11,000	$1,000,000	48%	$2,000,000
2005	$11,000	$1,000,000	47%	$2,000,000
2006	$12,000	$1,000,000	46%	$2,000,000
2007–08	$12,000	$1,000,000	45%	$1,500,000

In March 2003, the United States invaded Iraq in retaliation for the attacks on the World Trade Center in New York on September 11, 2001. Using questionable intelligence reports, the Bush Administration falsely claimed Iraqi leader Saddam Hussein was behind the attacks. The combination of financing the war and the tax cuts caused the government surplus to be transformed into a deficit. A surplus of $236 billion was turned into a record deficit of $413 billion by 2004. The deficit would then be gradually reduced until 2008 when the Financial Crisis created a new record deficit of $459 billion. The record of the deficit during the Bush Administration is shown in Table 12K.

Table 12K   U.S. Government Deficit 2000–2008[116]

Year	Deficit (Billions)	Percent of GDP
2000	-$236	2.3%
2001	-$128	1.2%
2002	$158	1.4%
2003	$378	3.3%
2004	$413	3.4%
2005	$318	2.4%
2006	$248	1.8%
2007	$161	1.1%
2008	$459	3.1%

Income and Wealth Concentration

Changes in wealth inequality during the Bush Administration were significant as shown in Table 12L. The top .1% share increased nearly 19%; the top 1% share, nearly 12%; and the top 10%, almost 6%. At the same time, the bottom 90% share fell nearly 13%.

Table 12L   Share of Wealth by Wealth Fractile Selected Years 2000–2008[117, 118]

	2000	2004	2008	% Change
Top .1%	16%	16%	19%	18.75%
Top 1%	32.3%	33.2%	36.1%	11.76%
Top 10%	68.8%	68.6%	72.8%	5.81%
Bottom 90%	31.2%	31.4%	27.2%	-12.82%

Income inequality remained relatively unchanged for most groups as shown in Table 12M. The top .01% had no change in share of income. The top .1% dropped significantly, by 10%; and the top 10%, by over 2%. Both the top 10% and the bottom 90% saw little change.

Table 12M   Share of Income by Income Fractile Selected Years 2000–2008[119, 120]

	2000	2004	2008	% Change
Top .01%	5.00%	4.00%	5.00%	**0.00%**
Top .1%	11.00%	9.00%	10.00%	**-10.00%**
Top 1%	20.40%	18.30%	19.90%	**-2.45%**
Top 10%	44.90%	43.90%	45.30%	**0.89%**
Bottom 90%	55.10%	56.10%	54.70%	**-0.73%**

These rates reflected the greatest inequality in the country since just before the Stock Market Crash in 1929 and the years of the Great Depression. The stage was set. The final pieces were in place.

The Financial Crisis of 2008

The core problem of the Financial Crisis of 2008, which is typically ignored or downplayed, was the increasing inequality of income and wealth in the country which began in 1980 with the policies of the Reagan Administration. During the Bush Administration, this inequality reached its peak. Analysis of the crisis, instead, typically focuses on the housing and mortgage market, bank lending practices, securitization of mortgage debt through the creation of mortgage-backed securities, and the repeal of the Glass-Steagall Act allowing the creation of giant bank holding companies. While these are all important components of the crisis, they were not the foundational cause.

It must be emphasized that the Financial Crisis of 2008 and the resulting Great Recession, like the Stock Market Crash of 1929 and the resulting Great Depression, were primarily caused by the extent of income and wealth inequality resulting from Oligarchic Capitalist policies. Tax cuts (primarily for higher-wealth and higher-income individuals), cuts in economic support programs, and reductions in efforts to expand economic opportunity were the core policies leading to rising inequality. The increasing inequality forced lower-income/middle-income/lower-wealth households to increasingly rely on debt to try to maintain their living standards. And they were encouraged to do so, especially in the housing market.

The Bush Administration had embarked on a policy of encouraging home ownership. Bush stated:

"Now, we've got a problem here in America that we have to address. Too many American families, too many minorities do not own a home… And so here are some of the ways to address the issue…the single greatest barrier to first time homeownership is a high downpayment… And so that's why I propose and urge Congress to fully fund the American Dream Downpayment Fund. This will use money, taxpayers' money to help a qualified, low income buyer make a downpayment… A third major barrier is the complexity and difficulty of the home buying process. There's a lot of fine print on these forms. And it bothers people, it makes them nervous. And so therefore… has agreed to do is to streamline the process, make the rules simpler,…makes the closing much less complicated… And so one of the things that I'm going to talk about a little bit today is how to create a sustained commitment by the private sector that will have a powerful impact…we want to make sure that we help work to expand capital available to buyers… Fannie May and Freddie Mac, as well as the federal home loan banks, will increase their commitment to minority markets by more than $440 billion… Freddie Mac will launch 25 initiatives to eliminate homeownership barriers. Under one of these, consumers with poor credit will be able to get a mortgage with an interest rate that automatically goes down after a period of consistent payments."

—THE WHITE HOUSE, 2002, WHITEHOUSE.
ARCHIVES.GOV, *PRESIDENT CALLS FOR EXPANDING
OPPORTUNITIES TO HOME OWNERSHIP*).

Bush's home ownership initiative led to the creation of the subprime mortgage market. It lowered the requirements for individuals to qualify for a home loan. Practices like zero-down-payment mortgages, interest-only mortgage payments, and lower-income requirements to qualify for a mortgage became commonplace.

The Gramm-Rudman Act of 1985 allowed banks to begin developing and selling complex financial derivatives[ii] based on a basket of underlying financial securities. One result was the development of mortgage-backed securities; derivatives backed by home mortgages. In the beginning, these were considered relatively safe derivatives because of the rigors and demands required to buy a home and because one of the last payments a cash-strapped household quits paying is their home mortgage. The selling of financial derivatives was very lucrative for the banking industry. Other financial institutions were hungry to own them due to their perceived safety and rate of return. The Bush home ownership initiative began to undermine the safety of these derivatives.

Over time derivatives had become increasingly complex. Mortgages were sold and re-sold. Individual mortgages were divided and re-divided to create tranches, a security backed by small pieces of many different individual mortgages. It was presented and perceived that the tranches were safer investments than traditional mortgage-backed securities; while one individual mortgage might not be paid, the probability seemed extremely small that all or a significant number of the pieces of individual mortgages comprising a tranche wouldn't be paid. Ignored was the problem that as these mortgages were sold and re-sold; divided and re-divided; that it became increasingly difficult to identify exactly what an individual tranche was actually composed of. Also, homeowners would have an increasingly difficult time identifying who exactly owned their mortgages.

An insurance market developed to protect financial institutions against the perceived unlikely occurrence mortgages wouldn't be

---

[ii] Derivatives *derive* their value from an underlying asset. Mortgage backed securities derive their value from the underlying mortgages. The derivative itself is a contract between two parties for a cash payment based on the payments received from the underlying assets.

paid and the derivatives become worthless. The complex insurance product developed was the credit-default swap. The owner of the security "swaps" the risk the security won't be paid (credit-default) with an insurance company for a payment of money. Since the securities were tranches composed of many different mortgages from all over the country, it would take the perceived extremely unlikely event of a total collapse in the housing market for insurers to have to pay out any significant amount of money on the credit-default swaps.

The repeal of the Glass-Steagall act made it easier for Investment Banks to access mortgages through their Commercial Banks to create mortgage-backed securities. There was increasing pressure on Commercial Banks to make more mortgage loans to create more mortgage-backed securities for the Investment Banks to sell to other financial institutions. Combined with the Bush home ownership initiative, requirements to qualify for a mortgage were reduced.

Corrupt practices soon infected the housing market. Loan officers, pressured to make more mortgage loans, pressured assessors to over-value homes to ensure more mortgages got approved. Assessors had an incentive to do so because, the more generous they were in their assessments, the more loan officers were willing to hire them.

The Bush Administration home-ownership initiative easing mortgage-qualification requirements, the resulting development of the subprime mortgage industry, the almost insatiable demand for mortgage-backed securities by financial institutions, the development of derivatives in the form of mortgage-backed securities and eventually tranches, the development of credit-default swaps to insure the derivatives, the repeal of the Glass-Steagall Act and the forming of bank holding companies to combine Investment and Commercial Banks, the pressure of Investment Banks on Commercial Banks to make mortgage loans, and the eventual corruption permeating the housing market combined to create the Financial Crisis of 2008. *However, at the core of the crisis, was the increasing income and wealth inequality that forced lower-income/middle-income/lower-wealth households to use debt to try to maintain their living standards.*

The Great Recession

In effect, with the development of tranches, the mortgage-backed security market had morphed into a pyramid scheme. By 2007 more than $45 trillion in credit-default swaps existed. At the same time, there existed only $7.1 trillion of mortgages in the U.S. mortgage market.[121] The industry was incredibly leveraged. This resulted in much higher profits as housing prices rose but much greater losses if housing prices fell. But since housing prices had been rising for decades, it seemed extremely unlikely a collapse in housing prices would occur. Historically, housing had been a good investment as shown in Table 12N.

Table 12N   U.S. Housing Prices Selected Years 1940–2000[122]

	Median Price	Median Price Inflation Adjusted (2000 Dollars)
1940	$2,398	$30,600
1950	$7,354	$44,600
1960	$11,900	$58,600
1970	$17,000	$65,300
1980	$47,200	$93,400
1990	$79,100	$101,100
2000	$119,600	$119,600

Increases in housing prices led to a greater reliance on mortgage loans as lower-income/middle-income/lower-wealth households turned to the mortgage refinance market to try to maintain their living standards, further exacerbating the problem of consumer debt.

In 2007 housing prices began to ease as some subprime borrowers were unable to make their mortgage payments. Increasing numbers of borrowers defaulted on their mortgages and walked away from their homes. To protect themselves, lenders began tightening mortgage-qualifying requirements, which reduced the demand for homes and caused prices to fall further. The housing crisis had begun.

As increasing mortgage payments fell into arrears or were defaulted on, the value of mortgage-backed securities began to fall. The highly leveraged tranches created from the securities fell even more quickly. Financial institutions turned to the insurers that had sold them the credit-default swaps for payment due to the defaulted mortgage payments. Insurers, including one of the largest, American International Group (AIG), were unable to pay on the credit-default swaps they had sold, so, defaulted, and began to collapse.

As insurers collapsed financial institutions that had invested in the derivatives and tranches began to collapse, too. Bear-Stearns, Lehman Brothers, and Merrill-Lynch went bankrupt, merged with stronger banks, or were bailed out. The housing crisis turned into a financial crisis.

Financial markets around the world began to crash. The Dow Jones Industrial had peaked at 11,782 on August 11, 2008. By November 20 it had fallen 36% to 7,552. It would fall to 6,547 by March 3, 2009, a drop of 44.5% from its peak.[123]

Housing prices fell 12.4% in the United States during the fourth quarter of 2008.[124] They collapsed by 18% in October alone.[125] In the first quarter of 2009, they fell another 19%.[126] Decreases in some areas of California, Arizona, Florida, and Nevada were over 50%.[127]

The collapsing economy forced the Bush Administration and Congress to act. In October 2008 the Emergency Economic Stabilization Act was passed. It created the Troubled Asset Relief Program (TARP), a $700 billion government bailout of the banking industry. The Federal government would purchase "troubled assets," i.e., mortgage-backed securities and tranches, which were in default or in danger of defaulting. The Treasury Department used over $105 billion to purchase preferred stock in eight of the largest distressed banks; the government had now acquired an ownership interest to prevent the banks' collapse.[iii] Community and local banks received a $386 billion bailout. A $40 billion purchase of preferred stock was

---

[iii] Preferred stock provides the owner with a pre-determined, fixed dividend payment. The government would receive a 5% dividend until 2013, when it would rise to 9%. The eight banks involved were Bank of America/Merrill Lynch, Bank of New York Mellon, Citigroup, Goldman Sachs, J.P. Morgan, Morgan Stanley, State Street, and Wells Fargo.

combined with a $112 billion loan from the Federal Reserve to save insurance giant AIG. Also, General Motors and Chrysler received an $80.7 billion bailout. Lastly, $75 billion was provided to homeowners to refinance or restructure their mortgages.[128] It was the biggest government bailout in history.

As with the first era of Oligarchic Capitalism, the second faced financial calamity and economic collapse. As in the first instance, a newly elected Democratic President would implement Keynesian policies to resolve the crisis.

The Obama Administraton

American Recovery and Reinvestment Act

In the 2008 Presidential election Barak Obama defeated John McCain. The first order of business was to prevent a total collapse of the economic system and a second Great Depression. The TARP program was a short-term, stop-gap measure to save the banking industry. Economic recovery from the financial disaster would be another matter.

On February 17, 2009 Obama signed the American Recovery and Reinvestment Act. It was a classic Keynesian economic stimulus package to increase demand (spending) and move the economy into a recovery. It injected $787 dollars of spending into the economy. Eventually, the stimulus package would be raised to $831 billion. The program included:

- $260 billion in tax cuts and extended unemployment benefits
- $138 billion in health–care assistance
- $117 billion in education aid
- $83 billion in infrastructure projects
- $54 billion in aid to small businesses
- $22 billion in clean–energy projects
- $18 billion in science research129

The result was economic recovery, which began in July 2009. Deficits initially greatly increased as shown in Table 12O.

Table 120   Deficit, GDP Growth, & Unemployment Rate 2008–2016[130, 131]

Year	Deficit (Billions)	Percent of GDP	GDP Growth Rate	Unemployment Rate
2008	$459	3.1%	-0.1%	7.3%
2009	$1,413	9.8%	-2.5%	9.9%
2010	$1,294	8.6%	2.6%	9.3%
2011	$1,300	8.3%	1.6%	8.5%
2012	$1,087	6.7%	2.2%	7.9%
2013	$679	4.0%	1.8%	6.7%
2014	$485	2.7%	2.5%	5.6%
2015	$438	2.4%	2.9%	5.0%
2016	$585	3.1%	1.6%	4.7%

Just as predicted by Keynesian Economics, the increased deficit spending by the government resulted in recovery and falling unemployment. Also as predicted, as the economy recovered deficits were reduced. The deficit as a percentage of GDP initially skyrocketed to 9.8% of GDP; but as recovery unfolded the deficit fell to a low of 2.4% of GDP.

The problem was the recovery was very weak compared with previous recoveries with growth averaging only 2.17% per year. Growth during the 1980s recovery averaged 3.6%. In the 1990s recovery, it was 3.8%. Why was the recovery so slow? Economists in general agree the stimulus package was too small.

The Congressional Budget Office projections, which were very much in the mainstream of the economics profession, showed a combined drop in GDP for 2008 and 2009 of 1%, before the economy resumed growth again in 2010. This is with no stimulus. By contrast, the economy actually shrank by 3.1% in those years, even with the stimulus beginning to kick in by the spring of 2009. Given this background, it was easy to see that the stimulus was far too small. Compared with this loss of private sector demand, the stimulus was about $700 billion... Roughly $300 billion of this was for 2009 and

163

another $300 billion for 2010, with the rest of the spending spread over later years. In other words, we were trying offset a loss of $1.4 trillion in annual demand with a stimulus package of $300 billion a year. Surprise! This was not enough.

—BAKER, 2014, CNN, CNN.COM

The Obama administration envisioned a $1 trillion short-term deficit-spending…, had the administration known how big the problem would turn out to be, it would have sought a $2 trillion stimulus. And what did we get once Congress got through with it? A $600 billion stimulus—about one-third of what we needed.

—DELONG, 2010, WALL STREET JOURNAL,
ECONOMISTSVIEW.TYPEPAD.COM

It's a matter of basic math, says economist Dean Baker of the Center for Economic and Policy Research. The economy is currently losing—annually – $450 billion in housing wealth, $650 billion in consumer spending and $150 billion in commercial real estate value. You're talking about a gap on the order of twelve-hundred-fifty billion dollars, and we're trying to plug that with four-hundred-something, so we've got a long way to go," Baker says. (The stimulus package of roughly $800 billion doles out spending and tax cuts over two years.)

—GRIM, 2011, HUFF POST, HUFFPOST.COM

Why did the government not undertake sufficient deficit spending to ensure the economy would fully recover? Opposition of Congressional Republicans guaranteed any government stimulus package would be inadequate.

The GOP was so adamant about the deficit being bad for the country, for the economy and for their grandchildren that, even when deficit spending was justified by the Great Recession, they forced the 2009 stimulus bill to be much less than many

164

economists thought was needed. As a result, the recovery was slower and far less robust than it could…or should…have been.

—COLLENDER, 2016, FORBES, FORBES.COM

One key point being ignored by both sides is that the recovery might have been much more robust had the initial stimulus scheme been followed up by even more stimulus spending. That did not happen because Republican opposition limited the size of the recovery act and guaranteed that it would not have a sequel.

—HORSEY, 2014, LOS ANGELES TIMES, LATIMES.COM

But if the economists are right, the stimulus leg of that stool will need to be returned to. For Appelbaum, if this package shows results, it could help Obama argue for a second one. The president could cite the unanimous Republican opposition in the House and the strident objections of GOP senators that cut the stimulus down in size, she says. 'The most shocking thing to me has been to see the Republican Party playing chicken with the economy' says Appelbaum.

—GRIM, 2011, HUFF POST, HUFFPOST.COM

Just as with Great Depression, the government response to the Great Recession did not inject enough spending into the economy to ensure full recovery. This time, there would be no Second World War to provide the necessary additional spending. Instead, the economy was destined to recover very slowly. Unemployment remained unnecessarily high; and living standards, unnecessarily low.

Tax Policy

Tax policy was little changed during the Obama Administration. After recovery was underway, with the exception of the corporate income tax, rates were slightly raised. The top marginal income tax rate rose from 35% to 39.9%.[132] Top estate tax and gift tax rates were raised from 35% to 40%.[133, 134] The capital gains tax was increased from

15% to 20%.[135] These increases primarily impacted higher-income/higher-wealth households.

Income and Wealth Concentration

The slight increase in tax rates had no real effect on the problems of income and wealth inequality. Income inequality worsened during this period. While those at the very top had no change in their share of income, the top 10% had an increase of over 11% while the bottom 90% saw their share of income fall by over 7%. Table 12P shows income shares during the Obama years.

Table 12P   Share of Income by Income Fractile Selected Years 2008–2016[136, 137, 138]

	2008	2012	2016	% Change
Top .01%	5.00%	6.00%	5.00%	**0.00%**
Top .1%	10.00%	12.00%	10.00%	**0.00%**
Top 1%	19.90%	21.89%	21.00%	**5.50%**
Top 10%	45.30%	47.80%	50.31%	**11.05%**
Bottom 90%	54.70%	52.20%	50.69%	**-7.33%**

Wealth inequality also worsened considerably towards the end of Obama's term in office and at a much greater rate than income inequality. The top 1% saw an increase of nearly 10%. For the top 10%, it was over 8%. For the bottom 90%, this meant a drop of over a whopping 22%. This was the lowest share of wealth for the bottom 90% of households since 1939 when it was 19.7%. Table 12Q shows wealth inequality during the Obama Administration.

Table 12Q   Share of Wealth by Wealth Fractile Selected Years 2008–2016[139, 140]

	2008	2012	2016	% Change
Top .1%	19%	20%		
Top 1%	36.1%	38.9%	39.6%	**9.69%**
Top 10%	72.8%	74.5%	78.8%	**8.24%**
Bottom 90%	27.2%	22%	21.2%	**-22.05%**

The foundational problems of inequality remained; a foundation which had been laid during the Reagan years. Unless addressed, these foundational issues would keep preventing any real progress to lessen inequality.

The Trump Administration

In the Presidential election of 2008, Donald Trump shockingly defeated Hillary Clinton. In an election almost as contentious as the 2000 election, Trump became President despite not winning the popular vote. The result would be aggressive action to enhance and strengthen the Oligarchic Capitalist system.

Tax Policy and Deficits

In 2017 the Tax Cuts and Jobs Act was passed. It reduced the highest marginal tax rate from 39.6% to 37%.[141] More importantly, it cut the tax rate on corporate income from 35% to 21%.[142] Again, since 10% of households own 84% of stock the cut in corporate rates primarily benefitted higher-wealth households. The results of the tax cuts are shown in Table 12R.

Table 12R   Deficit & GDP Growth Rate 2016–2019[143, 144]

Year	Deficit (Billions)	Percent of GDP	GDP Growth Rate
2016	$585	3.1%	1.6%
2017	$665	3.4%	2.2%
2018	$779	3.8%	2.9%
2019 (est)	$780	4.6%	2.1%

The deficit increased dramatically as a result of the tax cuts, once again discrediting a fundamental tenet of Supply-Side Economics that lower tax rates lead to higher tax revenues. As Keynesian Economics predicted, the cuts did lead to an increase in the economic growth rate. The growth rate of 2.9% in 2018 equaled the best year of the Obama Administration in 2015. However, most economists agreed that the steep increase in the deficit was a heavy price to pay for such a modest increase in economic growth.

Income and Wealth Inequality

As shown in Table 12S, inequality during the first years of the Trump Administration worsened, reach some of the highest levels on record. Between 2015 and 2018, the top 20% of households saw a 1.7% increase in their share of income while the bottom 20% of households had a 2.5% decrease. The top two middle quintiles also experienced decreases of over 2%. The lowest of the middle quintiles saw an increase of less than 1%.

Table 12S   Share of Income by Income Quintile Selected Years 2013–2018[145]

	2015	2018	% Change
Top 20%	51.06%	51.96%	1.67%
Second 20%	23.22%	22.56%	-2.84%
Middle 20%	14.45%	14.12%	-2.28%
Fourth 20%	8.23%	8.28%	0.61%
Bottom 20%	3.14%	3.06%	-2.54%

Wealth inequality data for this period is not readily available at this time.

Trade Policy

As discussed in Chapter 5, the Trump Administration reversed the trade policies of earlier administrations. Unlike the Clinton Administration which saw increasing trade as a solution to the problems of inequality, the Trump Administration blamed increasing trade as the cause of rising inequality. However, as discussed previously, it was not increasing trade itself which caused rising inequality but, rather, the structure of the Oligarchic Capitalist system which caused the benefits of increased trade to disproportionately accrue to the highest-income, highest-wealth Americans.

Under the Obama Administration, the Trans-Pacific Partnership was negotiated. The intent was to increase trade between the U.S. and countries in the Americas and Pacific region. Immediately upon his election, Trump withdrew the U.S. from the agreement, arguing it, like previous trade deals, benefited other countries at the expense of the United States. The Trump Administration then turned its attention to re-negotiating or dismantling other trade agreements.

The United States was soon engaged in fractious disputes with its trading partners. Some of the country's biggest trading partners and closest allies such as Canada, Mexico, Japan, India, and the European Union were targets of the Trump Administration. They were continually accused of taking advantage of the United States and stealing jobs. As a result, other important agreements in such areas as security and defense became weakened due to the disagreements on trade.

The Trump Administration eventually turned its attention to the U.S.'s biggest trading partner and economic rival, China. A trade war soon began.

- April 2018: Trump ordered tariffs of 25% on all steel imports and 10% on all aluminum. China retaliated by placing 25% tariffs on 128 products from the United States. Trump responded with an additional 25% tariffs on a range of Chinese products.

- June 2018: China retaliated with additional tariffs on $50 billion of U.S. exports. In July the Trump Administration responded with 25% duties[iv] of $50 billion more on Chinese goods. China then imposed tariffs on another $34 billion of U.S. products.

- August 2018: the U.S. placed a 25% tariff on another $200 billion of Chinese imports. China responded with tariffs of 25% on $16 billion of U.S. goods.

- August 2019: the U.S. added a 10% tariff on another $300 Billion of Chinese imports. In response, China halted the purchase of some U.S. agricultural products.

[iv]   Tariffs are taxes imposed on other countries for imported goods. Duties are taxes imposed on individuals who buy the imported goods.

- China imposed 10% duty on U.S. crude oil imports. It also increased tariffs on soybeans from 25% to 30%. Tariffs on beef and pork increased another 10%.

—REUTERS, 2019, REUTERS.COM

It is estimated that the trade war will cost the average American household $1,000 per year[146] and result in a loss of 300,000 to 450,000 jobs.[147]

Protection of Public Resources

For the most part, the Trump Administration has weakened government protection of public resources. Actions included:

- February 2017: Stream Protection Rule revoked
- March 2017: Keystone XP Pipeline approved
- May 2017: EPA Budget cut 31%
- June 2017: U.S. withdraws from Paris Climate Accord
- January 2018: Toxic Air Pollution Rules eased
- April 2018: Auto Emissions Standards eased
- August 2018: Fuel Economy Rules eased
- August 2018: Coal Plant Emission Standards eased
- September 2018: Methane Emission Rules repealed
- October 2018: EPA Air Pollution Review Panel disbanded
- October 2018: Offshore Oil Drilling in Artic approved
- December 2018: Coal Plant Emission Standards reduced
- January 2019: Increased Logging on Public Lands approved
- April 2019: Pipeline Building Rules eased
- May 2019: Offshore Drilling Rules eased

—GRESHKO, ET AL., 2019, NATIONAL GEOGRAPHIC,
NATIONALGEOGRAPHIC.COM

Public resources were being opened up for greater appropriation and exploitation by private interests.

Attacking and Undermining Government

As President, Trump has undertaken the most virulent campaign to undermine, attack, and weaken the U.S. government compared with anyone who has ever held the office. This has included attacks and campaigns against the Justice Department, the State Department, the FBI, the CIA, and the U.S. Diplomatic Corps. These are the very agencies which oversee and provide protection for the basic security apparatus of the nation. Unfortunately, this was the inevitable place Oligarchic Capitalists almost certainly had to end up at.

In his first inaugural address to the nation, Ronald Reagan famously stated,

> "Government is not the solution to our problem; government is the problem."
>
> —ROSENBERG, 2019, THE THOUGHT
> COMPANY, THOUGHTCO.COM

In attacking and dismantling the Democratic Capitalist system, it was necessary for supporters of Oligarchic Capitalism to destroy the public's belief, confidence, and trust that government could be an effective force in improving their lives. Reagan's campaigns to be President began this process and it has continued throughout the last forty years. Trump's attack against government has taken the Oligarchic campaign against government to its logical and inevitable conclusion.

Summary

The post-Reagan era has seen a solidification and enhancement of Oligarchic Capitalism. Due to the foundation laid during the Reagan Administration, this was inevitable. Despite the elections of Bill Clinton and Barak Obama, who were largely inclined towards a Democratic Capitalist system, the polices of Oligarchic Capitalism were too firmly entrenched to allow any significant changes to the system. This was similar to the Progressive Era of 1900 to 1920 when progressive policies mitigated the worst excesses of Oligarchic Capitalism but did not eliminate them. It took the economic collapse of the Great Depression and the policies of the New Deal, combined with the expansion of government spending and deficits to fight World War II, to bring the first era of Oligarchic Capitalism to an end.

The second era of Oligarchic Capitalism also resulted in a financial collapse and an economic crisis. The lessons learned from the Great Depression led to a quicker application of Keynesian Economic policies to avert a second depression. So, instead of depression, the country experienced the Great Recession.

However, the forces of Oligarchic Capitalism had also learned a lesson from the Great Depression and New Deal. Unless concerted action was taken, long-term, significant changes could be undertaken to replace the Oligarchic system with a Democratic one. Supporters of Oligarchic Capitalism were better prepared and more willing to fight to prevent long-term, meaningful changes from being made to protect the Oligarchic Capitalist system and their privileged positions in it.

13

A New Era of Democracy

The Story of the Poker Game

Twelve individuals gathered to play poker. All the players started with the same amount of money. They each had enough money to play for a very long period of time. With the exception of one player, all the players were of equal ability. That one player was a one-percent-better poker player than all the others. How much of the money would the better player end up with? All of it.

Winner-Takes-All Economics

There is a tendency in Capitalism for a small group of individuals who are slightly better at "playing the game" (slightly more productive) to accumulate greater and greater shares of the income and wealth in the system. As this occurs, fewer and fewer individuals accumulate more and more wealth, resulting in great concentrations of income and wealth in fewer hands.

Various causes have been advanced for this inequality: unfair trade deals; political incompetence; foreigners; immigration; and a failing education system to name a few. *The real problem lies, however, in the natural trajectory of Capitalism itself, which, left to its own devices, trends towards income and wealth being increasingly concentrated in fewer and fewer hands and the development of an Oligarchic Capitalist system and Plutocracy.*

Capitalist Systems tend to evolve into Oligarchic Capitalism due to the development of winner-take-all compensation systems. In their book *The Winner-Take-All Society*, Robert Frank and Phillip Cook explain this tendency of Capitalism.[148] In a winner-take-all system,

> ...the value of what is produced...often depends on the efforts of only a small number of top performers, who are paid accordingly.
>
> —FRANK AND COOK, 1995, P. 2

Similar to the story of the poker game, a few people end up with almost all the money. As stated by Frank and Cook,

> Reward by relative performance is the single most important distinguishing characteristic of winner-take-all markets. In the markets that economists normally study, by contrast, reward depends only on absolute performance.
>
> —FRANK AND COOK, 1995, P. 24

> A second feature of winner-take-all markets is that rewards tend to be concentrated in the hands of a few top performers, with small differences in talent or effort giving rise to enormous differences in incomes.
>
> —FRANK AND COOK, 1995, P. 24

Sports leagues are a good example of this. The National Basketball Association (NBA) has 30 teams with 15 players on the roster of each team, a total of 450 players.[i] These are arguably the 450 best basketball

---

[i] NBA teams also have affiliate teams in the G League where some of their players participate as they develop their skills.

players in the world.[ii] With a global population of 7.7 billion, they are truly very elite, very productive individuals. NBA teams search the entire globe to find basketball talent.

The highest paid player in the NBA in 2019 was Stephan Curry with a salary of $37.46 million. The minimum salary allowed in the NBA in 2019 was $490,180. There is an enormous difference in salary between perhaps the best player in the world and the 450th best player in the world. The best player in the world makes 80 times the salary of the 450th best player in the world that has a global population of 7.7 billion.[iii] This is an example of a winner-take-all-market.

The forces leading to winner-take-all markets have permeated markets across the country. In addition to sports, entertainment, corporations, medicine, law, authorship, and education are all examples where a few individuals at the top may receive enormous compensation relative to others in the occupation who are relatively only slightly less productive. This process creates real dangers for our democratic system of government.

> A market winner-take-all attitude can, and has been, invading our polity, destroying norms and undermining the ability to reach compromise and consensus. If left unbridled, it will destroy national cohesion.
>
> —STIGLITZ, 2019 P. 30

The Role of Technology

Advances in communication and transportation technology have been the primary drivers of the spread and dominance of winner-take-all markets. In the late 1800s the best singer or actor or baseball player

---

[ii] Under the "One and Done" rule, some players who are younger than 19 years old who may be among the best in the world are forced to play one year in college or overseas before entering the NBA.

[iii] The disparity would be even greater except sports leagues like the NBA have adopted rules that limit the maximum amount the top players can be paid and the minimum amount the lowest paid player must be paid. These rules are discussed later in this chapter.

in a relatively small city like Grand Rapids, Michigan could make a living. People in Grand Rapids would pay to see these people perform.

With improvements in communication and transportation technology, people in Grand Rapids had a much wider choice of performers to select from. Improvements in transportation enabled performers from outside of Grand Rapids to come to Grand Rapids to perform. Radio enabled people in Grand Rapids to listen to singers, shows, and baseball games from far away. As people in Grand Rapids had access to see and hear better performers outside of the immediate Grand Rapids area, they became less willing to pay to see lesser performers from Grand Rapids. The incomes of these individuals fell. Meanwhile, higher-quality performers from around the country saw their incomes rise as people could now more easily access their performances.

Technological improvements, particularly in communication, in the late twentieth and early twenty-first centuries have exacerbated and intensified this process. People from across the globe can now access the performances of the best performers in the world. The incomes of these performers have soared to unprecedented levels. Meanwhile, the incomes of local and regional performers have greatly decreased. Marginal differences in ability result in enormous differences in income.

Communication technology has driven this trend across many occupations. Corporate executives can control and manage a greater breadth of processes across the globe. The top financiers, doctors, lawyers, educators, lecturers, marketers, and writers are available to individuals across the globe, greatly enhancing their incomes. Meanwhile, more local, marginally less-talented individuals see their incomes grow slowly, stagnate, or decline.

Capitalists vs Socialists

Advocates of Capitalism believe the inequality in a Capitalist system is due to productivity; individuals who are highly productive have high incomes and are wealthy. Their income and wealth are a reward for their high productivity. It is a just system.

Advocates of Socialism disagree. They believe the income and wealth of higher-income/higher-wealth individuals are not due to productivity but, rather, due to their power in the system; higher-income/higher-wealth individuals control the government and pass laws favorable to themselves, which protect and enhance their interests. Thus, the Capitalist system is exploitive, benefiting the capitalist class and harming lower-income/middle-income/lower-wealth individuals, i.e., the working class. The system is rigged. It is not a just system.

Ultimately, regardless of whether or not higher-income/higher-wealth individuals are rewarded for their productivity or whether they exploit others, the concentration of wealth and income in a Capitalist system culminates in a poorly functioning, failing system which undermines Democracy. The concentration of income, wealth, and, ultimately, power in fewer and fewer hands results in an unstable, non-sustainable system.

An additional problem in an Oligarchic Capitalist system is that Crony Capitalism becomes embedded in the system. Higher-income/higher-wealth individuals use their power to advantage their families, friends, colleagues, and acquaintances. Connections, not productivity (merit), increasingly determines who is hired, who gets promoted, who has access to a good education, and who gets access to capital through loans. The performance of an Oligarchic Capitalist system is further undermined by Crony Capitalism; individuals are not rewarded for their productivity; and resources are redirected to less-efficient uses, lowering overall productivity and living standards.

However, the most important failure of an Oligarchic Capitalist System is that it undermines and, ultimately, destroys a Democratic political system. As income and wealth become increasingly concentrated, it is used to take over the political system. As the political system becomes subjugated to higher-income/higher-wealth households, laws are passed protecting the income and wealth of those in power. Also, the wealthy and powerful gain control of the media to promote messages protecting their interests, further undermining a Democratic political system. *As a result, the political system naturally evolves into a*

Plutocracy. It is this destruction of Democracy that is the greatest threat of Oligarchic Capitalism.

Economic systems where income and wealth are concentrated in the hands of a small percentage of individuals inevitably become divisive, unstable, and undemocratic. The nature and preponderance of winner-take-all markets in modern economic systems, augmented and driven by communication and transportation technology, intensify the process by which income and wealth become ever-more concentrated. Capitalism must be either reformed or replaced to create a more equal distribution of income, wealth, and economic opportunity. Democratic Capitalism and Democratic Socialism are just those types of systems.

Democratic Capitalism, Democratic Socialism, and Oligarchic Capitalism

Table 13A compares Oligarchic Capitalism, Democratic Capitalism, and Democratic Socialism.

Table 13A   *Oligarchic Capitalism, Democratic Capitalism, Democratic Socialism*

	Oligarchic Capitalism	Democratic Capitalism	Democratic Socialism
Control of Production	More Concentrated Private Control	Less Concentrated Private Control	Greater Public Control
Economic Priorities	1. Protection of Wealth 2. Protection of High Incomes 3. Incentive to be Productive	1. Protection and Enhancement of Democracy 2. Incentive to be Productive 3. Equality of Opportunity 4. Economic Support	1. Protection and Enhancement of Democracy 2. Economic Support 3. Equality of Opportunity 4. Incentive to be Productive
Significantly Limits	1. Economic Support 2. Equality of Opportunity	1. Inherited Wealth 2. Cronyism	1. Inherited Wealth 2. Cronyism

	Oligarchic Capitalism	Democratic Capitalism	Democratic Socialism
Primary Determinant(s) of Individual Consumption	1. Inherited Wealth 2. Cronyism 3. Political Influence 4. Individual Productivity	1. Individual Productivity 2. Lesser Political Influence	1. Individual Productivity 2. Greater Political Influence
Income Tax System	Flat Rate	Progressive	Progressive
Key to Economic Power	Wealth and Political Control	Productivity with Lesser Political Control	Productivity with Greater Political Control
Form of Government	Plutocracy	Democracy	Democracy

Control of Production

In Oligarchic Capitalism, control of production lies in private hands and is highly concentrated. In Democratic Capitalism, control of production lies primarily in private hands but is less concentrated. The emphasis is on protecting and enhancing the Democratic system of government. Advocates of Democratic Socialism, on the other hand, support greater government control of production processes. They are more willing to have government take control of resources to solve problems in the economic system. Advocates of Democratic Capitalism prefer to leave resources in private hands and rely on the private sector to find solutions to problems.

Wealth, Income, & Democracy

Advocates of Oligarchic Capitalism put a great deal of emphasis on protecting wealth and high incomes. They support low marginal income, estate, and gift tax rates. They support low capital gains taxes and the elimination of the corporate income tax. Advocates of both Democratic Capitalism and Democratic Socialism, on the other hand, support a more progressive income tax, higher estate and gift taxes, equality between capital gains taxes and taxes on ordinary income, and the continuation of a corporate income tax for three reasons.

179

First and most importantly, the main priority of advocates of both Democratic Capitalism and Democratic Socialism is the protection and enhancement of Democracy. They recognize Democratic systems are undermined and corrupted when income and wealth become concentrated in the hands of a very small percentage of the population. Higher-wealth/higher-income households are able to gain control of the political system and the media, transforming a Democratic system into a Plutocratic system. Therefore, advocates of both Democratic Capitalism and Democratic Socialism believe it is crucially important to significantly limit inherited wealth and very high incomes. This is necessary to prevent the concentration of income, wealth, and the cronyism that results, from turning a Democracy into an Oligarchic, Plutocratic system.

> ...today's excessively low inheritance taxes mean that the United States is creating an inherited plutocracy.
>
> —STIGLITZ, 2019, P. XXVI

> Many among the top...achieved that success not by working hard but...by...large inheritances...we have been evolving into a twenty-first-century inherited plutocracy.
>
> —STIGLITZ, 2019, P. 43

Second, advocates of both Democratic Capitalism and Democratic Socialism support greatly limiting inherited wealth to reduce the importance of cronyism in the economic system. This better ensures the primary determinant of a person's living standard and the key to economic power is the individual's own productivity; not inherited wealth and cronyism. Individuals are much more likely to be hired and promoted based on their productivity (merit) rather than their connections. Advocates of both Democratic Capitalism and Democratic Socialism support both a progressive tax system and high estate and gift tax rates to prevent Democracy from being corrupted by the concentration of income, wealth, and the cronyism that results.

Third, advocates of both Democratic Capitalism and Democratic Socialism recognize inherited wealth creates a disincentive to be productive. Heirs are rewarded for the productivity of their ancestors, which greatly reduces the incentive for them to be productive. This negative impact on the incentive to be productive is another reason why advocates of both Democratic Capitalism and Democratic Socialism support higher estate and gift taxes.

> A growing portion of the non-working rich have never worked…They have inherited their wealth…the "self-made" man or woman…is disappearing… American is on the cusp of the largest intergenerational transfer of wealth in history… For the rich under the age of thirty-five…inherited wealth is more common…It is about to become the major source for a new American aristocracy.
>
> —REICH, 2015, P. 143-144

Rather than being productive in their own right, inheritors of great wealth are the beneficiaries of the productivity of their ancestors. This violates both the priority of preserving the individual incentive to be productive and the principle that the primary determinant of an individual's consumption (living standard) should be the individual's own productivity. Finally, there are also examples of the inheritors of great wealth living a profligate lifestyle of extravagance and excess, engaging in few acts of productivity of their own, to the detriment of both themselves and society.

Advocates of Oligarchic Capitalism derisively refer to inheritance (estate) taxes as a "Death Tax". They oppose inheritance taxes for two main reasons. First, they assert that restricting inherited wealth reduces the incentive to be productive for those who wish to provide for their heirs, particularly their children. If one cannot leave wealth to heirs, why would one put in the effort to build wealth? The result will be lower productivity and an economic loss to society. This violates a basic principle of Capitalism. Also, they assert that there are examples of inheritors of great wealth being productive and successful in their own right. In fact, the inheritance of great wealth may well enable them to be even more productive than they otherwise would have been.

Second, it is a matter of individual freedom. Advocates of Oligarchic Capitalism contend individuals should be free to leave their wealth, the fruit of their productivity, to whomever they desire. Why should the government limit the freedom of individuals to leave their wealth to the people of their choosing?[iv]

Economic Support & Incentives

The most important difference between advocates of Democratic Capitalism and advocates of Democratic Socialism is the different importance each place on the tradeoff between providing economic support and ensuring that the incentive to be productive be maintained. Advocates of both Democratic Capitalism and Democratic Socialism believe providing economic support to less productive (lower-income/lower-wealth) individuals is both necessary and appropriate. They recognize there can be a variety of reasons for a person having lower-income/lower-wealth. It could result from:

- Unavoidable low productivity due to unavoidable personal characteristics (youth, old age, physical disability, mental health, or psychological issues).

- Unavoidable low productivity due to institutional barriers (lack of educational or job training opportunities, sexism, racism, or prejudices due to ethnicity, religion, sexual orientation, or gender identity).

- Unavoidable low productivity due to exploitation in the system.

- Avoidable low productivity due to avoidable person characteristics (personal irresponsibility or laziness).

[iv] It is interesting to note while advocates of Oligarchic Capitalism support reductions in economic support due to the incentive effects of such support, they tend not to be concerned about the negative incentive effects of inherited wealth and gifts.

Advocates of Democratic Socialism tend to believe lower-income/lower-wealth is generally more likely due to unavoidable low productivity rather than avoidable low productivity. As a result, they tend to place greater importance on providing economic support to lower-income/lower-wealth households. Advocates of Democratic Socialism attribute low productivity to unavoidable personal characteristics, institutional barriers, or exploitation in the system. *Advocates of Democratic Socialism are, therefore, more willing to sacrifice the incentive to be productive to better ensure lower-income/lower-wealth households have needed assistance.* Advocates of Democratic Socialism tend to attribute the cause of low productivity and low income to failures in the system rather than failures of the individual.

Advocates of Democratic Capitalism, on the other hand, place greater importance on enhancing and ensuring individuals have the incentive to be productive. They tend to agree with advocates of Democratic Socialism that lower-income/lower-wealth are more likely to be the result of unavoidable low productivity, not avoidable low productivity, and to recognize the cause of low productivity is often the result of system failure, not individual failure. Despite this, advocates of Democratic Capitalism believe it is crucially important and necessary to maintain the incentive to be productive. *Therefore, advocates of Democratic Capitalism are more willing to sacrifice economic support provided for lower-income/lower-wealth households to ensure individuals have an incentive to be productive.*

Another important reason advocates of both Democratic Capitalism and Democratic Socialism support economic support programs is due to the long-run increases in productivity that result.

> One of the most important detractors from individual well-being is a sense of insecurity. Insecurity can also affect growth and productivity: individuals, worrying about whether they will be thrown out of their house or lose their job and only source of income, can't focus on the tasks at work in the way they should. Those who feel more secure can undertake riskier activities, often with the highest payoffs.
>
> —STIGLITZ, 2019, P. 188

In the long run, providing economic support for lower-income/ lower-wealth households such as food assistance, housing assistance, health-care assistance, access to quality public education, and access to public transportation increases the productivity, of lower-income/lower-wealth households resulting in higher living standards. Additionally, total productivity increases, causing overall living standards to rise. *Advocates of both Democratic Capitalism and Democratic Socialism believe whatever the short-run costs of implementing such programs, the long-run benefit in terms of higher levels of productivity more than outweigh the increase in short-run costs.*

Advocates of Oligarchic Capitalism believe that economic support for lower-wealth/lower-income individuals should be minimized. *Advocates of Oligarchic Capitalism attribute lower-wealth/lower-income to low productivity, which they believe is primarily caused by avoidable low productivity (personal irresponsibility or laziness), not unavoidable low productivity caused by either unavoidable personal characteristics (youth, old age, disability, etc..), institutional barriers (discrimination, lack of opportunity, etc..), or exploitation in the system.* Thus, low productivity is most likely due to an individual failing and, therefore, the responsibility for low productivity is caused by a personal failing of the individual. Advocates of Oligarchic Capitalism believe that providing economic support just incentivizes further low productivity and, therefore, must be minimized.

Economic Opportunity

For advocates of Oligarchic Capitalism, the individual freedom (right) to pass on wealth to others is more important than equality of opportunity. In addition, they believe economic opportunity is already plentiful for anyone who really wants it. Not taking advantage of existing economic opportunity is a personal failing.

Advocates of both Democratic Capitalism and Democratic Socialism believe there is a wide disparity in economic opportunity. In the story of the poker game at the beginning of this chapter, it was assumed everyone started the game with the same amount of money. However, it is more likely the case some individuals begin the game with much larger amounts of money than others. One player begins with $1,000; another with $10,000; a third with $100,000; a fourth with $1,000,000; a fifth with $10,000,000; a sixth with $100,000,000; and so on. Individuals beginning the game with significantly more money than others have a much greater opportunity to win the game than individuals who begin with less money.

The same is true in an economic system where some individuals inherit great wealth relative to others. These individuals start with a huge advantage that greatly reduces equality of opportunity. To more equalize economic opportunity, advocates of both Democratic Capitalism and Democratic Socialism believe inherited wealth should be greatly limited. The increasing equality of opportunity leads to better economic performance, i.e., higher levels of productivity. If people believe they have a legitimate opportunity to better themselves and move up the economic ladder, they will be more likely to put in the effort (be more productive) to do so.

Income Tax Rates

Advocates of both Democratic Capitalism and Democratic Socialism are in favor of a progressive income tax system, whereby higher-income individuals pay a higher tax rate (percentage) than lower-income individuals. This is in line with what Adam Smith, himself, advocated in *The Wealth of Nations*:

> It is reasonable, therefore, that they (the expense of defending the society) should be defrayed by the general contribution of the whole society, all the different members contributing, as nearly as possible, in proportion to their respective abilities.

> —SMITH, 1776/1937, P. 76

> The subjects of every state ought to contribute towards the support of government, as nearly as possible, in proportion to their respective abilities; that is, in proportion to the revenue which they respectively enjoy under the protection of the state.

> —SMITH, 1776/1937, P. 777)

185

Smith was a strong proponent of individual tax rates being based on the *ability* of a person to pay. *He understood it was the state that created the environment and protection for individuals to earn high incomes and attain great wealth.* Since higher-income/higher-wealth individuals more proportionately benefit from the economic environment created by the state relative to lower-income/middle-income/lower-wealth individuals, Smith argued higher-income/higher-wealth individuals should pay a higher rate of taxes than lower-income/middle-income/lower-wealth individuals. For Smith, it was an issue of fairness.

For advocates of both Democratic Capitalism and Democratic Socialism, an even more compelling reason for having a progressive tax system is, again, the protection and enhancement of the Democratic system itself. Like high levels of inherited wealth, high levels of income can have a destructive, corruptive impact on Democracy. Like high levels of wealth, high levels of income enable individuals to gain control of the political system, transforming a Democracy into Plutocracy. The protection of the Democratic system itself relies on a system of progressive taxes.

Advocates of both Democratic Capitalism and Democratic Socialism recognize that high, progressive tax rates can, to some degree, reduce the incentive to be productive. However, this is a necessary trade-off which must be made if a Democracy is to be preserved.

Advocates of Oligarchic Capitalism disagree with Adam Smith and oppose a progressive tax system, contending a fairer tax system would be a flat-tax system whereby all income levels pay the same percentage of tax on their income. They assert a progressive tax system inhibits the incentive to be productive by penalizing individuals with higher levels of income (productivity). As a result, people reduce their productivity (their willingness to put effort into work); and, so, consumption (living standards) fall. For the most part, advocates of Oligarchic Capitalism do not acknowledge or recognize the important role the state plays in creating and protecting the environment enabling the system to work.

Corporate Tax Rates

Advocates of both Democratic Capitalism and Democratic Socialism support significant taxes on corporate income. They believe there should be an emphasis on the closing of corporate tax loopholes. They contend it is a matter of fairness and equality to tax corporate income. Also, since 10% of households own 84% of stock, taxes on corporate income are effectively a tax on the wealthy, increasing wealth equality and protecting Democracy.

Advocates of Oligarchic Capitalists believe corporate income taxes should be very low or entirely eliminated. Their argument is two-fold. First, advocates of Oligarchic Capitalism contend corporate income taxes cause corporate investment and expansion to decrease, resulting in a slowing of economic growth (lower productivity), which lowers consumption (living standards). Second, they assert all income should be taxed on an individual basis; that a corporate income tax results in a "double taxation" of corporate profits. Corporate profits are first taxed on the corporate level and are eventually taxed a second time when those profits are passed on to the owners (stockholders). Advocates of Oligarchic Capitalism believe this leads to both an inefficiency in the economy and is unfair to corporate stock holders.

Advocates of both Democratic Capitalism and Democratic Socialism respond that any effects on corporate investment and expansion are outweighed by the resulting increases in economic equality and the protection of Democracy. Advocates of both Democratic Capitalism and Democratic Socialism also argue if business owners want to avoid "double taxation", they can simply not incorporate. Apparently, however, the benefits of incorporation are such it is worth the cost of double taxation.

The Lesson of Sports Leagues

In many ways professional sports leagues are a microcosm of the problems in Capitalist economic systems. Like Capitalism, sports leagues are confronted with the problem of winner-take-all economics. A few teams located in wealthy, densely populated metropolitan areas

187

such as New York, Boston, Los Angeles, and San Francisco would be able to pay significantly higher wages to the best athletes. People are interested in seeing the very best athletes play, so, these superstar athletes can command very high salaries relative to other players who are among the very best (most productive) and only marginally less productive than the superstars.

The problem for sports leagues would be that only these few teams in wealthy, densely populated areas would be competitive and have a real chance at winning a championship. Teams in less-wealthy, less-densely populated areas would have no chance. The result would be a sports league having far fewer fans and being much less profitable. An important aspect for a sports league's success is people across the country from many areas believing their local team has a shot at winning. Otherwise, there would be far fewer fans watching the sport.

Sports leagues adopt a number of rules to ensure their league is competitive and all teams have a shot at winning the championship. First, teams have a maximum budget they can use to hire players. Teams exceeding the budget pay a very high penalty, a "luxury tax," on the amount they exceed the budget.

Second, there is a salary cap, a maximum amount, that any player can be paid. Teams are not allowed to pay superstar players any amount they want.

Third, there is a minimum salary. The lowest-paid players must receive at least a certain minimum amount of money. There are some individuals who are so interested or desperate to play in a professional sports league they may be willing to play for virtually nothing. They are very good players; but given the winner-take-all aspect of the market, incomes would be concentrated to a very few superstar players.

These rules come at the expense of the teams in wealthy, densely populated areas and the superstar players who would otherwise receive the vast majority of the available income. *However, these teams and players are only harmed in the short run. In the long run these teams and the superstar players make more money.* Why is this the case?

In the long run, interest in the sports league will be more widespread if all the teams are competitive and are perceived to have a shot at winning a championship. If a sports league were dominated by only three or four teams in wealthy, densely populated areas and these teams were perceived as the only ones that have a chance of winning a championship, in the long run, there would be far fewer teams and far fewer fans; and the league would generate much less in profits. Both the teams and the superstar players would make less income in the long run. *So, these teams and players sacrifice their short-term interests (income and profits in the short run) to enhance their long-term interests (income and profits in the long run).*

Summary

Capitalist economic systems have a natural tendency to evolve into Oligarchic, Plutocratic systems. Policies must be adopted to ensure that income, wealth, and power do not become too concentrated and Democracy destroyed. Policies must be adopted to ensure economic opportunity and economic support exists for everyone. The provision of economic support must be appropriately balanced with the need to ensure individuals maintain the incentive to be productive.

Democratic Capitalism and Democratic Socialism both offer a path to a more democratic, equal society. The important differences lie in the extent of government involvement in overseeing production and the balance struck in providing economic support and preserving the incentive to be productive.

14

Where Do We Go from Here?

What Change?

The current state of affairs economically, both in the United States and globally, is a result of the failings of the Oligarchic Capitalist system. The increasing concentration of income and wealth, augmented by technology, is the natural trajectory of a Capitalist economic system unless moderating steps are taken. The increasing concentration of income and wealth leads to the destruction of a Democratic system of government and the development of a Plutocracy. As the vast majority of citizens find it increasingly difficult to meet their economic needs, the result is dissatisfaction, divisiveness, blame, and calls for change. But what change?

Rules of the Game

The foundation of all economic systems are the laws, the rules of the game, which determine how the system operates. Economic systems don't just appear out of nature. It is important to realize we have choices in what the rules are and how they are written.

> Few ideas have more profoundly poisoned the minds of more people than the notion of a "free market" existing somewhere in the universe into which the government intrudes.

> —REICH, 2015, P. 3

There can be no "free market" without government. The
"free market" does not exist in the wilds beyond the reach of
civilization…rules create markets, and governments generate
rules… A market—any market—requires that government
make and enforce the rules of the game… Government doesn't
"intrude" on the "free market." It creates the market.

—REICH, 2015, P 4

Economics is not a Natural Science. It is a Social Science; a science
dealing with human behavior. *Markets do not exist in nature; they result
from acts of human behavior.* Therefore, we have to decide how markets
are structured and how they operate.

Markets don't exist in a vacuum: they have to be structured,
and the way we structure them affects both the distribution of
market income and growth and efficiency.

—STIGLITZ, 2019, P. XXV

Presently our laws strengthen and enhance Oligarchic Capitalism.
They allow tremendous amounts of inherited wealth to be passed
from one generation to the next. The tax system has become increasingly less progressive. As a result, wealth and income have become
increasingly concentrated, enabling a small group of individuals to
gain enormous political power, transforming our Democracy into a
Plutocracy, and gaining ever greater economic and political control.

The result has been a system of laws which further strengthen the
hand of those at the top of the wealth and income ladder. As their
market power has increased, they have been able to push wages down,
greatly reduce economic support, and decrease challenges to them by
eliminating economic opportunity for others while using cronyism to
enhance the economic opportunity for those close to them.

Laws need to, first and foremost, enhance our Democratic system of
government and protect it from Plutocracy. These laws must ensure individuals are rewarded for their own productivity and effort, not through

192

cronyism and the past productivity of others. There needs to be a focus on equality of opportunity so that anyone sitting down at the poker table has a legitimate shot at winning the game. Adequate economic support needs to be provided for lower-productivity individuals to protect them in the short run and increase their productivity in the long run.

Power and Exploitation

The Socialist idea that power, not productivity, can be a key determinant of an individual's level of consumption (living standard) is finally receiving the recognition and acceptance it deserves among mainstream economists.

> The prevailing assumption that individuals are paid what they're "worth" is a tautology... Most fundamentally, it ignores power.
>
> —REICH, 2015, P. 94

> A close examination of why the pay of top executives...has soared...and why the compensation of managers and traders on Wall Street has skyrocketed...has less to do with any supposed surge in the value of their...skills than with their increasing power...
>
> —REICH, 2015, P. 156

> Put simply, large corporations, Wall Street, and wealthy individuals have gained substantial power over rules that generate outcomes favoring them—power that has been compounded as the additional wealth has accorded them even more influence over the rules.
>
> —REICH, 2015 P. 157

Even the taboo term "exploitation," long banned from the lexicon of most mainstream economists due to its association with Socialism and Karl Marx, is finally gaining acceptance among those brave enough to use it.

Look at the standard college economics textbook. The word *competition* is amply sprinkled through all of its chapters; the term *power* is reserved for but one or two. The term *exploitation* will likely be totally absent… Only recently have the epitaphs like *exploitation* and *power* been used to describe what is going on.

—STIGLITZ, 2019, P. 23

Market power allows firms to exploit consumers by charging higher prices than they otherwise would… Market power also allows firms to exploit workers directly, by paying lower wages than they would otherwise… The huge profits generated by market power allow corporations…to buy influence that further enhances their power and profits…

—STIGLITZ, 2019, P. 49

Individuals get wealthy by exploiting others… They can do it by the exercise of market power.

—STIGLITZ, 2019, P. 50

Unfortunately, the debt owed to socialists for the origin of this idea that power and exploitation help to explain our economic problems is, for the most part, ignored.

Adam Smith also warned of the danger of firms getting together to gain market power and secure control over prices and wages to the detriment of consumers and workers.

People of the same trade seldom meet together, even for merriment and diversion, but the conversation ends in a conspiracy against the public, or in some contrivance to raise profits.

—SMITH, 1776/1937, P. 128

Masters are always and everywhere in a sort of tacit, but constant and uniform, combination, not to raise the wages of labour above their actual rate... Masters, too, sometimes enter into particular combinations to sink the wages of labour even below this rate. These are always conducted with the utmost silence and secrecy...

—SMITH, 1776/1937 P. 66-67

Market power plays a particularly important role in an Oligarchic Capitalist system. With its focus on the protection of wealth and high incomes, it is little wonder that power, not productivity, is a major determinant of an individual's living standard. Socialist criticism around power and exploitation are valid. However, such criticisms do not necessarily apply equally to *all* Capitalist systems, particularly a Democratic Capitalist system.

Destruction of Democracy

The greatest threat of Oligarchic Capitalism is the destruction of our Democratic system fueled by the concentration of wealth, income, and power.

Market power...gets translated into political power: one cannot have a true democracy with the large concen-trations of market power and wealth that mark the US today.

—STIGLITZ, 2019, P. 77

It is...dangerous to our democracy, as dynastic wealth... accumulates even more political influence and power.

—STIGLITZ, 2019, P. 146

The most imperative task is the preservation and enhancement of our Democracy. This will require more stringent laws on the inher-itance of wealth and a more progressive income tax system. There is certainly a tradeoff to be made between the economic freedom to pass wealth on to heirs and to safeguard our democratic way of life. The same tradeoff exists between our income tax system and

Democracy. However, whatever the deleterious effects that might exist on the incentive to be productive and on the economic freedom of the wealthy few must be accepted if our Democracy is to survive and not be supplanted by Plutocracy.

Capitalist or Socialist?

In the search for answers to our economic problems, the solution has sometimes been presented as a choice between Capitalism and

Socialism. *This is a false choice.* The decision is really about the extent of government involvement in our economic system. It is helpful to think of it as a continuum as shown in Table 10A.

Democratic Capitalism has more government involvement than Oligarchic Capitalism and less government involvement than Democratic Socialism. Democratic Socialism has less government involvement than Socialism and more government involvement than Democratic Capitalism.

Table 14A   Government Involvement in Economic System

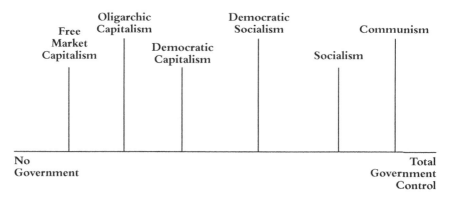

The Capitalist system has created the highest living standards the world has ever seen. People from across the globe have strived to emigrate to the United States, Canada, and Western Europe. This is due to the belief that economic opportunity exists and that a person's fate largely lies in their own hands; that there is a connection between an individual's productivity and how well they live. Unfortunately, this has become increasingly less true as our system has become more and more Oligarchist. Dealing with this problem will require changes to our economic system; changes that will require the government taking a more active role in ensuring economic opportunity exists for all and that our Democracy is protected.

It would seem the best way forward lies not in the replacement of Capitalism with Socialism, but rather in reforms to the Capitalist system itself: not the replacement of Oligarchic Capitalism with Democratic Socialism but, rather, a return to a system of Democratic Capitalism as existed in the past. Certainly, Democratic Socialism and Democratic Capitalism share much in common. The fundamental principle of protecting and enhancing Democracy is paramount in both.

Aside from the difference in economic priorities between Democratic Capitalism and Democratic Socialism, there is also the political challenge of changing people's perceptions of Socialism. The collapse of Socialism in the Soviet Union, China, and Eastern Europe happened. The failings of Socialism are real. There is a natural tendency on the part of the American public to distrust the idea of the United States becoming a "socialist" country. Socialism is a tough sell politically.

It can be argued people don't really know what Socialism is; that the Soviet Union and China weren't really socialist; that true Socialism has never been tried; and that Democratic Socialism is different from the type of Socialism practiced in the past. Even if these arguments are true, re-educating the American public to the "true" nature of Socialism is very problematic. It seems unlikely the American public will elect a socialist President, Democratic or otherwise, in the near future.

On the other hand, a return to a Democratic Capitalist system similar to the one that existed in the past is an idea that is more politically feasible. The American people are very receptive to the ideas of rewarding people for their work (connecting individual productivity to consumption), providing more equality of opportunity, providing appropriate economic support, protecting democracy, allowing private control of production (private ownership of resources), and preventing cronyism. Franklin Roosevelt is consistently ranked as one of the greatest Presidents ever. As a result, Democratic Capitalism is a much easier sell to the American public than Democratic Socialism. Americans already are inclined to believe the Capitalist system is superior to Socialism; past experience confirms it to them. This, along with the ideas of reward for work, equality of opportunity, private ownership, and success based on merit rather than connections, make it much more likely that an individual identifying themself as a Democratic Capitalist can be elected President.

Opposition to Change

Most beneficiaries of the current Oligarchic Capitalist system will fervently resist any meaningful changes to the system. They will employ whatever strategies are necessary to protect their interests.

In a speech in 1936 Franklin Roosevelt recognized the extent of the opposition of supporters of Oligarchic Capitalism to his efforts to create a system of Democratic Capitalism.

> "We had to struggle with the old enemies of peace—business and financial monopoly, speculation, reckless banking, class antagonism, sectionalism, war profiteering.
>
> They had begun to consider the Government of the United States as a mere appendage to their own affairs. We know now that Government by organized money is just as dangerous as Government by organized mob.
>
> Never before in all our history have these forces been so united against one candidate as they stand today. They are unanimous in their hate for me—and I welcome their hatred."

> —OURDOCUMENTS.GOV, *TRANSCRIPT OF PRESIDENT FRANKLIN ROOSEVELT'S RADIO ADDRESS UNVEILING THE SECOND HALF OF THE NEW DEAL 1936*

Few people have benefited more from the Oligarchic Capitalist system than our current President, Donald Trump. Inherited wealth and cronyism have been the primary means of his success. The tactics and techniques he has employed to date are indicative of what will be done to resist and prevent change.

The most important strategy opponents of change have used is the false choice of Capitalist or Socialist. Any changes in the system such as in health care, tax policy, economic support, or limiting the impact of money in elections is presented as overturning the Capitalist system and replacing it with Socialism. This false choice prevents us from dealing with the real problems of Oligarchic Capitalism and solving them.

Proponents of change need to emphasize the real choice is to decide how much additional government involvement is necessary to enhance and protect our Democratic system, equalize economic opportunity, ensure individuals are rewarded for their productivity, provide adequate economic support, and reduce the impact of cronyism. *Those who condemn Capitalism in general and call for its replacement with Socialism play into the hands of the opponents of change*

A second strategy used by opponents of change is to divert attention from the most important problem plaguing Oligarchic Capitalism, the inevitable concentration of income and wealth which corrupts Democracy and results in Plutocracy. The key is to place blame in other areas. Economic and social ills are the fault of immigrants, of minorities, of welfare recipients, of trading partners who take advantage of us, of elites, and of inept and corrupt politicians. It is important to create anger and division among people who actually share common economic interests by arousing racial and ethnic angst. Identity politics involving race, ethnicity, gender, sexual orientation, and gender identity are tools used to place blame on others and divert attention from the real economic problems that are at the core of our ills.

President Trump's vociferous attacks on trade agreements are one of the most revealing strategies used to defend the Oligarchic Capitalist system. Republicans have traditionally been very supportive of freer trade. They have long recognized and advocated the basic idea of

Adam Smith: increased trade increases production and increases living standards. Their willingness to stand aside while President Trump blames increased trade for our economic ills and our trading partners for taking advantage of us shows the extent to which opponents of change will go to prevent real change in the system. They are willing to deny basic principles they have always believed in to protect their interests.[i]

Alarmingly, President Trump has also shown a natural affinity for dictators and strongmen who share his propensity to control wealth and power and to rely on cronyism. Vladimir Putin is, perhaps, the wealthiest person in the world as a result of his power. Cronyism is the key to success in Russia. In North Korea, Kim Jong-un and those close to him live very well while many of their people starve. Xi Jinping and other leaders of the Communist Party in China live lives of luxury while the majority of people in China have lower living standards than they would otherwise have due to mercantilist policies. Crown Prince Mohammed bin Salman and the Royal Family in Saudi Arabia control vast wealth through inheritance and cronyism, denying others equality of opportunity. Meanwhile, allies who share our values are denigrated, blamed, and attacked as a major cause of our economic woes.

Whether or not high-income, wealthy liberals will support the necessary changes, particularly limiting inherited wealth, is an open question. Certainly, individuals like Warren Buffet recognize the deleterious effect that inherited wealth has on heirs.[ii] As a result, he is limiting the amount of wealth he will leave to his children and grandchildren and, instead, is leaving most of it for philanthropic purposes. (Though the amount being left to each of his children is still significant, in the neighborhood of $2 billion each).[149] However, many wealthy individuals who have liberal leanings may well be reluctant

---

[i] It must be noted whether or not President Trump's actions are a well thought out strategy to prevent change in the current system can be debated. It may be his actions are simply visceral and opportunistic.

[ii] It is not clear whether Buffet recognizes the deleterious effect inherited wealth has on the economic system as a whole and on Democracy.

to see their heirs denied the ability to inherit great wealth and will, therefore, resist any meaningful changes in the Oligarchic Capitalist system and its transformation into a Democratic Capitalist system.

Transforming our economic system from an Oligarchic one to a Democratic one will not be easy. In the next chapter, we will explore the policies that will be needed to effect the change.

15

Policy Prescriptions

Of Economic Expansions, Financial Crises, and Pandemics

A fundamental problem with the current Oligarchic Capitalist system is that when the economy is doing well, high income/high wealth households reap a disproportionate share of the gains. Meanwhile, when the economy is in crisis, responsibility and losses are disproportionately passed on to middle income/lower income/lower wealth households. In a sense, for high income/high wealth households it's a situation of heads we win, tails you lose.

When the economy is booming with corporate profits and stock prices significantly increasing, corporate executives see their compensation packages soar. The investment portfolios of the wealthy, who own the vast majority of stocks, rise dramatically. While middle income/lower income/lower wealth households also benefit during economic expansions, the extent they benefit is relatively much less than the benefit to higher income/higher wealth households. Table 15A shows the distribution of income gains during economic expansions during the post-World War 2 period.

The percentage of total income gains during economic expansions going to the highest income households has soared while the percentage of total income gains going to lower income households has plummeted during this time period. For the top 1%, it has risen from 1% of total income gains to 95% of the total increase in incomes. The top 10% share of income gains has risen from 20% to over 116%. This means that in the 2009 to 2012 expansion, the bottom 90% of households actually saw their share of total income fall. At the beginning of this period, the bottom 90% received 80% of the gains in total income. During the same time, the bottom 99% of households by income went from receiving 99% of income gains during economic expansions to only 5%. Economic expansions now lead to ever greater disparities in income distribution.

Table 15A   Share of Income Gains during Economic Expansions by Income Group[150]

Expansion	Top 1%	Top 10%	Bottom 90%	Bottom 99%
1949–53	1%	20%	80%	99%
1954–57	5%	23%	72%	95%
1959–60	8%	32%	68%	92%
1961–69	9%	33%	67%	91%
1970–73	11%	43%	57%	89%
1975–79	25%	45%	55%	75%
1982–90	45%	80%	20%	55%
1991–2000	47%	73%	27%	53%
2001–07	76%	98%	2%	24%
2009–12	95%	116%	-16%	5%

The disparity in the way gains in income were distributed during economic expansions became especially pronounced as a result of the tax reforms during the Reagan Administration. After the tax reforms of the 1980's, the top 1% had their share of income gains during economic expansions rise from 25% to 45%. The top 10% saw an increase from 45% to 80%. Meanwhile the bottom 90% share dropped from 55% to 20%, while the bottom 99% saw a drop from 75% to 55%. During the Clinton Administration this trend was slightly reversed, only to re-assert itself with the election of George W. Bush in 2000.

A similar situation exists for wealth. Since the Great Recession of 2008, household wealth has increased 80%. Federal Reserve research shows that one third of those gains has accrued to the wealthiest top 1% of households. Meanwhile, the bottom 50% of households in terms of wealth only saw a 2% increase in their wealth.[151] This is reflected in the median gains in wealth by quintile.

Table 15B   Median Increases in Wealth by Wealth Quintile 2009-2015[152]

Top 20%	$119,457
Second 20%	$17,091
Third 20%	$22,876
Fourth 20%	$5,942
Bottom 20%	$146
All Households	$11,930

So, when the economy is booming, higher income/higher wealth households reap a disproportionate share of the gains. The opposite is true during recessions; lower income/lower wealth suffer a disproportionate share of the losses. Several studies have confirmed this.

"The bottom of the earnings distribution falls off substantially relative to the median, causing earnings inequality to increase in recessions."

—HEATHCOTE, VIOLANTE, PERRI, 2010

"In this paper, we....measure the welfare losses of households across the wealth distribution, following a severe recession. We have argued that these losses are substantial, more than twice as high for wealth-poor relative to wealth-rich households...."

—KRUEGER, MITMAN, PERRI, 2016, P. 39

"In 2010, the bottom 20 percent of the U.S. earnings distribution was doing much worse, relative to the median, than in the entire postwar period. This is because their earnings (including wages, salaries, and business and farm income) fell by about 30 percent relative to the median over the course of the recession. This lowest quintile also did poorly in terms of wealth, which declined about 40 percent".

—PERRI, STEINBERG, 2012

Compounding these problems is that when financial calamity does strike with financial markets collapsing and corporations confronted with insolvency, the government must intervene to prevent total economic collapse. As discussed in Chapter 13, this was evident during the Financial Crisis of 2008 in the form of the Troubled Asset Relief Program (the government purchase of mortgage-backed securities and tranches which were collapsing in price), the Treasury Department purchase of stock in private banks, the government loan to and purchase of stock in the insurance giant AIG, and bailouts to General Motors and Chrysler. Rather than letting these markets and companies collapse and have the value of stocks and bonds go to zero (forcing high wealth households who own most of such securities to bear the cost), the markets and companies are bailed out by all Americans through government intervention. This is done to prevent the collapse of the economic system. So, on the upside of the economy, high income/ high wealth households pocket most of the gains, but on the downside they are protected from severe losses (the value of assets like stock going to zero) because we cannot allow the collapse of the economy and financial system.

We are seeing the same scenario now playout with the economic crisis precipitated by the coronavirus pandemic. The Federal government has passed a $2 trillion stimulus package, the biggest in history, to save the economy. The Federal Reserve has injected $1.5 trillion of liquidity into financial and money markets, dropping interest rates to zero. It has been announced that for the first time in its history the Federal Reserve is prepared to enter equity markets and purchase stocks to prevent markets from collapsing. These measures are necessary and prudent to prevent economic collapse and, unlike the bailouts in the 2008 Financial Crisis, have been structured to provide greater assistance to middle income/lower income/lower wealth households. However, it still results in higher income/higher wealth individuals being largely insulated from losses during the economic crisis, but to have reaped the majority of gains during the economic expansion.

What goes largely unrecognized during economic expansions is the societal infrastructure that is the necessary and critical foundation to any functioning economic system.[i] These include a functioning government that passes and enforces laws to sustain the system, the legal system, the criminal justice system, the military, the structural infrastructure (roads, water and sewer systems, the electrical grid, the internet, airports, seaports), the educational system, the health care system, and the many other ingredients which are necessary parts of a functioning economic system and which are built and financed by society as a whole. Instead, during economic expansions there is an over emphasis on the financial brilliance and business acumen of corporate leaders, financiers, bankers, entrepreneurs, and investors who are largely credited with the economic gains that occur during an expansion.

There can be no champion surfer without the wave. As talented and gifted as the surfer may be, if there is no wave, there is no performance to praise and admire. Without a functioning societal and economic infrastructure, there can be no business, entrepreneurial, and financial success. This infrastructure is built and financed by all of society, so there must be an equitable sharing with all of society of the gains reaped from this infrastructural foundation.

The problem is accentuated during times when the economic system is confronted with financial calamity and economic collapse. Such times are rarely attributed to the actions of corporate leaders, financiers, bankers, entrepreneurs, or investors. Rather, economic downturns are typically depicted as the natural course of events that inevitably happen in a capitalist economic system. And even if corporate leaders, financiers, bankers, entrepreneurs, or investors are seen as being at least partially responsible for an economic crisis, it is usually

---

[i] Increasing numbers of individuals, like Elizabeth Warren, have been calling attention to this.

argued that making high income/high wealth households bear the cost will lead to economic collapse so they must be bailed out by taxpayers. Heads they win, tails we lose.

If taxpayers are going to bear the preponderance of the costs of an economic crisis, they need to receive a far greater share of the economic gains during expansions. This can be done by increasing the progressivity of the tax system. Doing so means that during economic expansions, when the incomes and wealth of high income/high wealth households are soaring, they are required to pay an increasing share of those gains in taxes. If high income/high wealth households are going to be bailed out during an economic crisis to prevent the collapse of financial markets through government intervention financed by all Americans, then high income/high wealth households need to more broadly share the gains during economic expansions.

Tax Policy

There needs to be a general increase in taxes on the highest-income and highest-wealth Americans. These taxes are at historically low levels. Taxes should be modeled on the rates that existed during the period of Democratic Capitalism from 1945-1980. This would increase economic equality and economic opportunity and provide the resources necessary to fund needed government programs.

Personal Income Tax

There needs to be greater number of tax brackets created. From 1942 to 1978 there generally existed 24 tax brackets. Beginning in 1979, the number of brackets was reduced, eventually reaching a low of two brackets in 1988 at the end of the Reagan era. The number of tax brackets have gradually been increased since then and now stands at seven.

The reduction in brackets was done under the guise of "simplifying" the tax system. The idea has been presented that Americans should be able to file their taxes on a form the size of a postcard. However, the true purpose of "simplifying" the tax system has been to significantly lower taxes on very high incomes.

Middle-income and lower-income Americans already have an income tax system that is relatively easy to comply with, especially since their income is largely derived from wages. Also, modern tax-preparation software has also made complying with the requirements of filling out tax forms much easier and less expensive.

Reducing the number of brackets dramatically reduced the progressivity of the income tax system and has been the major contributor to increasing income and wealth inequality. The current seven brackets make it extremely difficult to tax very high incomes at a more significant and appropriate level than moderately high incomes.

At the same time, the highest marginal personal income tax, the rate of tax on an additional dollar of income, needs to be raised. The top rate currently is 37%. During Democratic Capitalism the rate was much higher. From 1954 to 1963, it was 91%. Throughout the 1960s and 1970s, it was 70% or higher. The rate in the highest bracket of the system, the 24th bracket, should be in the neighborhood of 70%.

Federal Estate (Inheritance) Tax

Under current law, the first $5,700,000 of inheritance is not taxed. The initial Federal Estate Tax is 18% with a top rate of 40%. From a historical perspective, this top rate is very low. From 1942 to 1976, the period of Democratic Capitalism, the top rate stood at 77%. The top rate needs to be raised to between the 70% and 80% range, which is more in line with what has existed in the past. The amount exempted should be decreased to $5 million. The history of the Federal Estate Tax is discussed in Appendix 4.

Federal Gift Tax

Currently there is an annual exemption on the Federal Gift Tax on the first $15,000 given to any individual. There is a lifetime exemption of $5,700,000 with a top rate of 40% on amounts above $5,7000,000. During the Democratic Capitalist period, the top rate was 57.75%. The top rate should be raised to 60% and the lifetime exemption from the being taxed decreased to $5 million. The history of the Federal Gift Tax is discussed in Appendix 5.

Corporate Income Tax

The corporate income tax rate is at 21%, its lowest rate since 1939. From the end of 1951 to 1986, it was around 50%. During the Reagan Administration, it was reduced to 34% and the was raised during the Clinton Administration to 35%, where it remained until it was cut by the Trump Administration in 2018.

The corporate income tax is primarily a tax on the wealthy since 84% of stock is owned by the top 10% wealthiest families. The corporate income tax rate needs be raised to its historical norm of around 50%. The history of the corporate income tax is discussed in Appendix 6.

Capital Gains Tax

A capital gains tax is a tax on the profit from the sale of a capital asset such as property or an investment. Capital gains taxes are primarily paid by high-wealth individuals. Historically capital gains have been taxed at a lower rate than ordinary income (personal income tax). There are numerous arguments as to why this should be the case. Most importantly, it is argued a low capital gains tax encourages savings and investment and, therefore, results in higher economic growth.

There are also several arguments against a lower tax rate for capital gains as opposed to ordinary income. First, capital gains are primarily earned by the wealthy. Therefore, a lower tax rate on capital gains creates greater wealth inequality. Additionally, a lower capital gains rate creates a more favorable environment for businesses to use and invest in capital rather than labor. Essentially, a lower tax rate on capital gains is a subsidy on income generated from capital. Combined with the fact that income generated from labor is also subject to payroll taxes which income from capital is not, an even greater advantage to capital is created relative to labor.

The top rate for the capital gains tax is currently 20%. During the period of Democratic Capitalism, it ranged between 25% and 27.5%.

210

Ideally capital gains should be eliminated and capital gains taxed at the same rate as ordinary income. The history of the capital gains tax is discussed in Appendix 7.

Wealth Tax

There has never been a Federal wealth tax in the United States although it has been used in other countries. A wealth tax, also known as a capital tax or an equity tax, is a tax on individual net assets; the value of their assets minus their liabilities (debts). Elizabeth Warren has proposed a 2% annual wealth tax on net assets valued at more than $50 million, which would risie to 3% on net assets worth more than $1 billion. It is estimated such a tax would raise $2.75 trillion over 10 years.[153] Critics' complaints include the difficulty of accurately determining the value of some assets and the problem of individuals hiding assets.

The relatively low tax rates of the last several decades have enabled the build-up of large fortunes and contributed to the big disparities in wealth that currently exist. Much of that build-up in wealth would now be insulated from other taxes. For example, Warren Buffet's wealth was estimated to be $82.5 billion in 2015; yet his tax return that year had an income tax of only $1.8 million paid on income of $11.6 million.[154] This is an extremely small amount relative to his wealth. A wealth tax would help correct this disparity between the taxes paid on income earned and accumulated wealth.

The political feasibility of adopting a wealth tax is very problem atic. The more important and accomplishable approach is to increase estate, gift, income, and capital gains taxes. If legislation were to be proposed to enact a wealth tax, it may be more likely to be passed if it included a sunset provision in it, whereby the tax would be enacted for a period of time, say ten years, at which time Congress would need to re-authorize it.

Trade Policy

One of the most difficult issues for economists to deal with is what to do when a country engages in inappropriate, unfair trade policies. If a country puts up barriers to the products from other countries such as tariffs and duties, or adopts other rules that make it difficult to trade with them, how should a country respond? There are no easy answers.

The typical response, the gut-level response, is that, if a country puts up trade barriers against another country, to respond in kind. If they won't let our goods in, we won't let their goods in. The problem with this response is that retaliation in kind hurts the country responding with barriers as much as it hurts the country who initiated barriers. Less trade results, sending production down, prices up, and living standards down. Then how does one respond?

The best response is almost certainly the response of every administration, both Republican and Democratic, prior to the Trump Administration; to engage countries like China in negotiations, to insist on greater access and to put pressure on them to reduce barriers. Engagement and diplomacy, over a long period of time, has consistently proven to be the most effective and least harmful path to greater cooperation and increased trade.

As a result, trade policy implemented by every administration since 1992, with the exception of the Trump Administration, should be continued and expanded. Trade deals like NAFTA and the World Trade Agreement have delivered exactly as Adam Smith said they would, increasing trade, production, and living standards across the globe, including in the United States.

The problem has been that the benefits have disproportionately benefited higher-income/higher-wealth individuals. The solution is not to walk away from trade agreements or to attack our trade partners for taking advantage of us but to adopt policies to ensure that the benefits of trade deals are more equally distributed. This can be done in several ways.

First, tax policy, as discussed above, needs to be reformed to raise taxes on higher-income/higher-wealth individuals who have reaped the majority of the benefits of increased trade. Second, the funds raised should then be used to provide economic support to those whose living standards are negatively impacted by the trade deals. This should include government assistance in terms of health care, education, job training, job creation, and other economic support programs. Such policies are discussed below.

Health Care Policy

The restructuring of our health care system is an important issue confronting our country today. There are basically five choices.

Private Insurance System

This system gives the entire responsibility for obtaining health care to the individual. It was the system in place prior to the passage of the Medicare program (government-provided health insurance for the elderly) and the Medicaid program (government-provided health insurance for the poor) during the Johnson Administration in 1965. Both the health care industry and the payment system are privately owned and operated.

Private Insurance with Government Subsidies

This is basically our current system. The health care industry is privately owned and operated. The payment system is primarily based on a system of private insurance which, for the most part, is provided through employers. Individuals without employer-provided insurance must purchase their own policies. Those who cannot afford private insurance are eligible for subsidies from the government so they can purchase policies. Elderly individuals are provided health care insurance by the government through Medicare. Qualifying low-income individuals are provided health insurance by the government through Medicaid.

An important issue is whether everyone should be required to have health care coverage. If not, healthier individuals, particularly young people, may opt not to buy coverage. Less healthy, older individuals will be more likely to buy coverage. Economists refer to this problem as "adverse selection"; those who are most likely to have health problems are more likely to buy health care insurance while those least likely to have them won't buy it. The result is individuals who buy insurance are more likely to become ill, so the cost of health care insurance increases.

As a result, advocates of Democratic Capitalism who support this solution contend that it must include a government mandate that everyone be required to purchase health care insurance. This will keep the costs of health care insurance lower. Also, even young, healthy individuals can have accidents or become ill. If they don't purchase health care insurance, the costs of their care will be borne by everyone else if they need health care, so it is appropriate and necessary to require that everyone purchase insurance. They also argue even young, healthy individuals will eventually require health care as they age. A system that requires that everyone purchase health care insurance ensures that everyone will have access to affordable health care insurance as they inevitably get older and will need it.

In general, advocates of Democratic Socialism are opposed to this system, with or without a mandate. They believe a profit-driven private insurance system inevitably results in higher costs and inefficiency. They believe a system with greater government involvement will provide better health care at a lower cost.

Many advocates of Oligarchic Capitalism oppose any governmental intervention in the health care insurance industry, including being opposed to programs such as Medicare and Medicaid. Advocates of Oligarchic who support the current system tend to be opposed to a government mandate that requires everyone to purchase health care insurance. Their opposition is based on free-market principles. They are opposed to government intervention that infringes on individual freedom to purchase or not purchase health care insurance. Critics contend that a system of private insurance with government subsidies without a government mandate is unsustainable.

Private Insurance with a Public Option

This would work as the above system with the addition of a government insurance program based on Medicare that would compete against private insurers. Individuals would have the option of purchasing insurance either from a private insurer or from the government. The idea is that the government could likely provide policies similar or better than private insurers at a lower cost. Most individuals would still receive health care insurance coverage through their employer. The system would include a government mandate that everyone is required to purchase health care coverage.

This is the system supported by most advocates of Democratic Capitalism. It gives individuals the choice to purchase either private insurance or a public plan. It incorporates the free-market capitalist principle of competition into the system. The public option would provide a low-cost alternative to private insurance.

Advocates of Oligarchic Capitalism oppose the inclusion of a public option since they are generally opposed to increased government involvement in the system. Also, they believe the government would have an unfair advantage in offering insurance over private companies that must make a profit. They fear the public option would eventually drive private insurers out of business and eliminate the system of employer-provided insurance that currently exists.

Advocates of Democratic Socialism generally believe the public option system will develop into a two-tiered system of health care with high-income/high-wealth households having access to a superior care system relative to everyone else. Therefore, they prefer a system of Medicare for all.

Medicare for All

Private health care insurance would be eliminated. All Americans would receive health care insurance through a government-provided insurance program based on Medicare. The health care industry itself would remain privately owned and operated. The cost of the administration of health care insurance would be reduced.

This is the system supported by most advocates of Democratic Socialism. They believe it will result in a more affordable, more efficient, higher-quality health care system. Removing private insurance company profits from the system will re-direct money to actually providing health care services. Also, administrative costs in the system would be reduced. The oversight and processing of health care claims would be greatly simplified. No longer would hospitals and physicians have to navigate the complex web of different private insurance plans.

While this system is acceptable to most advocates of Democratic Capitalism, they prefer the public option system. They prefer a system that includes competition among health insurance providers rather than one based on a government monopoly. They believe that, in the long run, the competitive system will be more efficient and provide better care. They also feel that individuals should be provided with choices in the system; Americans should not be forced into a government health insurance program. Individuals who want to continue to buy private health care coverage should have the opportunity to do so.

Advocates of Oligarchic Capitalism are opposed to this system. They believe eliminating competition from the health care insurance market will result in higher costs and poorer health care. They also believe government control of the payment system for health care will inevitably lead to government control of the health care industry itself.

Government Provision of Health Care

Government provision of health care means the health care industry itself would be operated by the government. Hospitals would be owned and operated by the government. Doctors, nurses, and other health care workers would be government employees hired and paid by the government. This would be like the health care offered by the Veterans Administration. There would be no need, strictly speaking, for health care insurance as all care would be directly provided by the government. Neither advocates of Democratic Capitalism nor advocates of Democratic Socialism support this solution; both believe that the industry itself should remain privately owned and operated. Advocates of Oligarchic Capitalists fundamentally believe there is little difference between government control of the payment system for health care and control of the industry itself. They generally equate a system of Medicare for all with a government-operated health care system.

216

Economic Benefit of Health-Care Reform

Advocates of both Democratic Capitalism and Democratic Socialism agree there are economic benefits to making health care more available and affordable. First, more healthy individuals are more productive, resulting in higher productivity and higher living standards. Second, removing the burden and concern of attaining affordable health care enables people to focus on things like work, education, and their career. This results in higher levels of productivity and living standards. Advocates of both Democratic Capitalism and Democratic Socialism contend such increases in productivity help offset any negative effects of providing health care to the entire population.

Conclusion

Our current payment system for health care is inefficient and costly. Health care providers devote an inordinate amount of resources navigating the complex network of private insurance plans. Private insurers can increase profits by turning down legitimate claims, and then make it complicated, difficult, and expensive to appeal rejections. Profits in the system could be redirected to actually providing health care.

The best choice is a private insurance system with a public option. It provides both competition and choice in the system. The public option would almost certainly result in a reduction in private insurance rates. All citizens need to be required to purchase health care insurance. It is also a more politically acceptable solution to the majority of the American public than a system of Medicare for all.

Social Security

The Success of Social Security

Social Security is the most important, foundational economic support program to come out of the New Deal. It is arguably the most successful economic support program, and one of the most successful programs in general, in the history of the United States. It has fully met all its payment obligations.

217

As already discussed, prior to the passage of the Social Security Act in 1935, nearly 50% of elderly Americans, those over the age of 65, lived in poverty. As of 2015 that number had been reduced to less than 10%. It has been calculated that without Social Security the number of elderly Americans living in poverty in 2015 would have been over 40%.

The Future of Social Security

The second Bush Administration presented inaccurate reports on the state of the Social Security Trust Fund. The administration attempted and failed to privatize a portion of Social Security. In contrast to what was presented by the Bush Administration, the fact is the Social Security Trust Fund is in relatively good condition and could be made secure with some straightforward adjustments.

Social Security is currently funded to ensure full payments through 2037. If no changes are made in the program before then, for the first time in history (over 100 years), Social Security will not be able to fully meet its obligations. At that point, continuing payments into Social Security will be able to pay about 76% of the payments due.[155] Two steps can be taken to secure the long-term viability of Social Security:

- **Raise the Cap on Incomes Subject to Social Security Taxes.** Currently earned income up to $127,200 is subject to the Social Security tax of 6.2%. Both the employee and the employer must pay this 6.2%. Any earnings over $127,200 are not subject to the Social Security tax. So, individuals earning $200,000, $300,000, $500,000, or millions of dollars pay the same amount in Social Security taxes as someone earning $127,200. The cap needs be significantly raised or eliminated.

- **Expand the Investments Social Security Can Invest In.** Currently Social Security funds can only be invested in U.S. Treasury securities such as Treasury Bonds, Treasury Notes, and Treasury Bills. Since these investments are very secure and are considered to be largely risk free, there is virtually no chance of losses. However, the returns on the fund are also very low. A portion of the Social Security Trust Fund should be invested in common stocks so a higher return is earned. The Trust Fund should create its own passive index fund based on a stock index such the S&P 500 Index or the Russell 2000 Index. The Trust Fund would be responsible for monitoring the fund just as it oversees the portfolio of Treasury securities it currently invests in. The portion of the funds invested in common stocks should initially be very limited to no more than, say, 10% or 20% of the funds. As time goes by, the amount could be increased.

Education Policy

Public Education

Both advocates of Democratic Capitalism and Democratic Socialism support a government-operated public-school system. They believe funding for public schools across the country needs to be more equalized. The current system of public schools being funded by local property taxes gives public schools in higher-income/higher-wealth areas very adequate funding while public schools in lower-income/lower-wealth areas (primarily inner cities and rural areas) are very inadequately funded. This exacerbates the disparity in economic opportunity afforded high-income wealthy households relative to everyone else.

Advocates of both Democratic Capitalism and Democratic Socialism support a broader-based funding system. This would entail state governments and/or the Federal government providing greater funding for lower-income/lower-wealth districts. They also support increasing salaries for public school teachers to attract more and better-qualified individuals to the field.

The primary difference between advocates of Democratic Capitalism and Democratic Socialism is their view towards school vouchers. Vouchers give parents the option to use public education funds to enroll their children in schools other than the public-school district where they live; either public schools outside the district they live in or private, charter schools. It is argued, by eliminating the local public-school monopoly and injecting competition into the system, the quality of education will be improved. Advocates of Democratic Socialism tend to oppose a voucher system while some advocates of Democratic Capitalism are more inclined to support it.

Advocates of Democratic Socialism believe a voucher system undermines public schools by siphoning money out of the system. They believe the problem is not a lack of competition in the system, but rather, that the system is underfunded and teachers are poorly paid. A voucher system merely exacerbates these problems.

Advocates of Democratic Capitalism are more divided on this issue. Most agree with advocates of Democratic Socialism. However, some advocates of Democratic Capitalism are more willing to accept the inclusion of vouchers. While they believe the primary problems lie in underfunded schools and poorly paid teachers, they also believe increasing the competition in the system could improve schools. They believe that parents should be given the opportunity to use their public-school tax dollars to send their children to the school of their choice.

Advocates of Oligarchic Capitalism oppose broader-based funding for the public-school system. They believe the system of local property tax funding is appropriate and gives parents more control over their local school district. Advocates of Oligarchic Capitalism support a voucher system enabling parents to use public school funding to enroll their children in any school of their choice, including religiously based ones. They believe, for the most part, the problems with public schools lie not in underfunding or underpaid teachers but, rather, with public school monopolies,[ii] the resulting lack of competition in the system, and a lack of parental involvement. The key to improving public education is increasing competition and giving parents more choice.

[ii]   Public Schools are not actually monopolies; parents can choose to send their children to private schools. Advocates of Oligarchic Capitalism complain parents may not be able to afford private school tuition and so should be subsidized with public school dollars. It is interesting to note that advocates of Oligarchic Capitalism don't have the same concern about individuals not being able to afford health-care insurance.

College Education

The cost of going to college has risen considerably over the last fifty years. Tuition at four-year public universities increased 140% between 1971 and 2016. Meanwhile, median income for women increased at about half that rate, 73.7%. Median income for men fell 5.4%. As a result, college cost as a percentage of median income increased 38.1% for women and 153.9% for men. This is shown in Table 15C.

Table 15C   Change in College Costs Four Year Public Universities 1971–2016[156]

	1971	2016	% Change
Cost of College	$8,734	$20,967	140.0%
Median Income			
Men	$42,757	$40,445	-5.4%
Women	$14,915	$25,901	73.7%
College Cost as % of Median Income			
Men	20.4%	51.8%	153.9%
Women	58.6%	80.9%	38.1%
Adjusted for Inflation 2017 Dollars			

At the same time, state government funding has not kept pace with the increased cost of higher education. State higher education expenditures have fallen approximately $1,000 per student from slightly over $7,000 per student in 1985 to slightly over $6,000 in 2010.[157]

Since 1965 Federal government assistance has largely taken the form of student loans rather than direct assistance to higher education institutions. This does not alleviate the problem of higher costs for students who incur debt which must eventually be paid off.

To deal with the problem, advocates of Democratic Socialism tend to be in favor of creating a system of tuition-free college. They believe a college education should be available to the children of lower-income/middle-income/lower-wealth individuals at no charge. They contend that it is economically beneficial to have a well-educated, well-trained population. Similar to health care, making higher education available

221

and affordable to everyone results in higher productivity and, therefore, higher living standards. Advocates of Democratic Socialism believe the increased costs of the system will be partially offset by the increases in productivity that result.

For advocates of Democratic Socialism, it is also an issue of economic opportunity and fairness. Children of higher-income/higher-wealth parents have a plethora of higher education opportunities. Children of lower-income/middle-income/lower-wealth parents have far fewer opportunities. A tuition-free system for such individuals levels the economic playing field, creating greater equality of opportunity.

Advocates of Democratic Capitalism tend not to be in favor of a tuition-free college system. They are concerned with costs of the system. They contend the costs of a tuition-free system far outweigh the benefits. Increases in productivity will be insignificant relative to the increase in costs.

Importantly, advocates of Democratic Capitalism are also concerned about the incentive effects of a tuition free college system. More students may be incentivized to go to college, but the incentives to be responsible and do well will be reduced. If college is tuition-free, students avoid the financial consequences of performing poorly and not taking their course work seriously. Advocates of Democratic Capitalism believe there has to be financial responsibility on students to ensure they are incentivized to take college seriously and perform well.

Advocates of Democratic Capitalism do believe the cost of a college education should be made more affordable. They believe both government funding of colleges and government direct aid to students should be increased.

Advocates of Oligarchic Capitalism largely believe there is little need to reform the current system. They believe obtaining a college education is a choice, not a right; so individuals themselves should largely bear the costs of a college education. They tend to oppose any increases in government funding of colleges or increased aid to students.

Student Debt Crisis

Advocates of Democratic Socialism generally support the forgiveness of college student loan debt. This is in line with their belief that students should not be charged tuition to attend college. The forgiveness program would tend to be very broad, although there would be some restrictions based on a student's, or their parents', income and wealth.

Advocates of Democratic Capitalism also believe there needs to be relief provided for student debt. However, they tend not to be supportive of the broad forgiveness of student debt supported by advocates of Democratic Socialism. Instead, advocates of Democratic Capitalism support reducing the burden of student debt by such steps as putting limits on the monthly payments that must be made, limiting the percentage paid based on income, or eliminating the student loan debt of certain targeted groups like public school teachers.

Advocates of Oligarchic Capitalism are generally opposed to mitigating the debt of college students. They argue the cost of such a program would be prohibitive. Also, they contend these individuals knowingly incurred the debt and should be held responsible for it.

Conclusion

Policies need to be adopted to increase funding to public schools. Funding to public schools needs to be more equalized so that economic opportunity is increased for lower-income/lower-wealth households. This will necessitate that the Federal and/or State government provide assistance to underfunded, poorer schools. Pay for public school teachers should be increased.

College education should be made more affordable for lower-income/ middle-income/lower-wealth households to improve equality of opportunity. Additionally, a more educated and, therefore, more productive population is in the country's interest. However, making a college education tuition free is a poor choice. Incentive effects are real; it must be ensured students are incentivized to take their college course work seriously and to do their best. Incentives are severely compromised in a tuition-free system; therefore, students must bear some of the cost of a college education.

Instead of a tuition-free system, student loans should be made at a much lower interest rate for lower-income/middle-income/lower-wealth individuals. There needs to be some interest charged to ensure there is an incentive to repay the loan but not so much as to deter students from going to college.

The current system of Stafford Loans[iii] includes both subsidized and unsubsidized loans directly to the student. Subsidized loans defer the charging of interest on the loan while the student is in school (followed by a brief grace period after graduation) while unsubsidized loans charge interest from the disbursement date. The amount of interest on undergraduate loans is set at the rate on the 10-year Treasury Note plus 2.05%.[158]

Three steps should be taken to lower the cost of college:

- All Stafford loans should be made subsidized; interest should not accrue while the individual is in school.

- The interest rate should be lowered. The rate should be dropped to equal the rate on the 10-year Treasury Note rather than 2.05% above it.

- Government funding for colleges, both at the Federal and state levels, needs to rise so that colleges are less reliant on tuition and fees to cover their costs.

The burden of current student debt also needs to be reduced. A program of total forgiveness of all student loan debt without consideration for individuals who have made payments on or paid off their loans would be divisive, inappropriate, and unfair. It is important individuals who have made payments or have paid off their student loans not be penalized relative to individuals who still owe money.

The following would be sensible and attainable steps:

- Going forward, the interest rate on current debt should be equal to the interest rate on the 10-year Treasury Note.

[iii] Named in honor of Senator Robert Stafford, a strong proponent of supporting education.

- Past interest payments above what the interest would have been if it had been equal to the interest on the 10-year Treasury Note should be applied to the principal.

- Tax credits should be given for interest payments made which exceed the amount of interest which would have been paid if interest had been equal to the rate on a 10-year Treasury Note.

Table 15D illustrates a possible system of tax credits. The system of credits should be on a sliding scale with more recent payments receiving a greater credit relative to more past payments.

Table 15D   Proposed Tax Credit on Student Debt Interest Payments

Time Since Interest Payment	Tax Credit
1 year or less	90%
1 to 2 years	80%
2 to 3 years	70%
3 to 4 years	60%
4 to 5 years	50%
5 to 6 years	40%
6 to 7 years	30%
7 to 8 years	20%
8 to 9 years	10%

Tax credits should be provided to both individuals who currently have debt and individuals who have previously paid off their college loans. Receipt of tax credits should be tied to income and ability to pay. Tax Credits should be applied up to the amount of taxes owed by an individual. Tax Credits above this amount should be applicable to future years' taxes. Such a program would be the equivalent of a tax cut for lower-income and middle-income individuals.

Economic Support Policies

Economic Support policies are intended to ensure lower-income/lower-wealth individuals have adequate financial resources to meet basic economic needs. Health care and education have been discussed above. The issue, then, concerns needs such as food, housing, transportation, and utilities.

There are two fundamental approaches to providing individuals with economic support: government provision or subsidies.

Government Provision versus Government Subsidies

Government provision means the government directly provides the good or service. The individuals in the industry are government employees hired and paid by the government. This can be done on the Federal, state, or local level.

An example of government provision is public education on the primary and secondary level. Public schools are built and run by the government. Teachers, administrators, and other public-school employees are government employees hired and paid by the government.

In some cases, the government requires individuals who use the good or service to pay use it. Their payment does not cover the full cost of the good or service but offsets the amount the government has to pay. This is viewed as fair or appropriate since the users of the good or service are the ones who must contribute. Examples of this are public transportation such as subways and higher education.

A subsidy approach means the government provides financial assistance but, the good or service is provided by the market. The recipient of the assistance must go into the private market and purchase the good or service. Examples of this are food assistance and housing assistance.

Individuals are provided food assistance through the use of Bridge Cards (formerly Food Stamps). Individuals receive the assistance from the government and then go to grocery stores to purchase food. The grocery stores are privately owned and operated; the employees are not hired and paid by the government.

Housing assistance is a mixture of government provision and subsidies. *Public Housing is housing owned by the Federal Government.* Public Housing is provided through the Department of Housing and Urban Development and controlled through a local housing authority. *The*

226

Housing Choice Voucher Program (Section 8) provides a subsidy (financial assistance) to individuals to access the private housing market and attain housing. It is assistance to rent privately owned and operated housing.

As discussed previously, voucher systems are also increasingly being used as an alternative to public schools. Rather than requiring parents send their children to the local public school owned and operated by the government, parents are provided vouchers enabling them to send their children to a school of their choice.

Advocates of government provision believe this system provides better access to the good or service at a lower cost and better ensures the good or service meets required standards. Advocates of subsidies believe the market is more efficient at providing the good or service. They believe injecting competition and choice into the system improves quality and will result in lower costs.

Targeted Subsidies versus Broad-Based Subsidies

There are two types of subsidies used to provide assistance to individuals: targeted subsidies or broad-based subsidies. *A targeted subsidy stipulates what the recipients must use the subsidy for. A broad-based subsidy allows the recipients to use the subsidy to purchase whatever they choose.*

Targeted subsidies are used for food and housing. The Bridge Card (formerly Food Stamps) *must* be used to purchase food. A Section 8 Housing voucher *must* be used to attain housing. The argument in favor of targeted subsidies is that it better ensures the recipients will use the assistance in an approved, appropriate manner. If the use of the assistance is not stipulated, the recipients could use the assistance in what is considered an inappropriate, unintended manner, e.g., illegal drugs, alcohol, gambling, or cigarettes.

Critics of targeted subsidies contend these subsidies can constrain recipients from obtaining more needed things. For example, recipients may need to buy shoes, clothing, or school supplies for their children. At the time, food assistance may be a less pressing need. Yet, assistance is being provided for something which is a less critical need for the recipients. The recipients may then be forced to choose

227

whether to illegally sell the subsidy (buy food that is not needed and sell it back to the grocery store owner at a lower cost than it was purchased for) and then use the subsidy for the more needed good or service or go without the more pressing need. A recipient could be turned into a criminal in conspiracy with the owner of the grocery store. As a result, critics contend, despite the risk a recipient may use the subsidy in what is considered an unapproved, inappropriate manner, it is more efficient and useful to provide recipients with a broad-based subsidy.

The main broad-based subsidy used is the Earned Income Tax Credit. To qualify for the Earned Income Tax Credit, individuals must have earned income, i.e., they must be working. Individuals who don't work are generally believed to be less deserving of assistance than those who do work. The Earned Income Tax Credit is intended for a group largely considered deserving of assistance; the working poor.

The working poor who are determined to have insufficient income to afford basic things like food and shelter are provided with a tax credit. The tax credit supplements their income and can be used in any manner desired by the low-income individual. Table 15E shows the current eligibility requirements and maximum credit that can be received.

Table 15E Earned Income Tax Credit Qualifying Income & Maximum Credit 2019[159]

| | Filing Status | Dependents | | | |
		0	1	2	3 or more
Qualifying Income	Single	$15,570	$41,094	$46,703	$50,162
	Married	$21,370	$46,884	$52,493	$55,592
	Maximum Credit $529		$3,526	$5,828	$6,557

Supporters contend eligibility for the program is too restrictive and penalizes individuals without dependents (children). Maximum income levels for individuals without children are set much lower than those with children, and the maximum benefit received is very low.

Supporters of the program believe both the eligibility for the program and the amount of credit should be expanded.

Critics of the program believe the costs of expanding the program are too high and recipients may use the subsidy in an inappropriate, unintended manner. They contend individuals without dependents should work more and should not be in need of the credit.

Earned Income Tax Credit versus the Minimum Wage

An alternative to a broad-based subsidy program like the Earned Income Tax Credit is the minimum wage. *A minimum wage stipulates the minimum amount a worker can be paid.*

A related idea is a living wage. *A living wage is a minimum wage which ensures a worker has sufficient income to cover the basic costs of living.* A living wage would be a relatively high minimum wage.

Supporters of a minimum wage rather than the Earned Income Tax Credit contend the Earned Income Tax Credit ultimately subsidizes the profits of private employers, particularly of large corporations. The largest employer in the United States is Walmart. It has been estimated that Walmart's profits are subsidized by $6.2 billion in public assistance for low-wage Walmart employees who qualify for programs like food and housing assistance.[160] Meanwhile, Walmart has been recording record profits over the last several years. Since the 10% of wealthiest Americans own 84% of all stock, this results in a huge subsidy to the wealthy.

Advocates contend corporations like Walmart should be required to pay wages which enable their employees to buy the necessities of life without having to rely on public assistance. They argue minimum wage laws force businesses to provide workers with a wage which enables them to support themselves rather than relying on taxpayers to support them through a subsidy program such as the Earned Income Tax Credit.

Critics of the minimum wage contend it ultimately increases unemployment. Employers will respond in the short run by hiring fewer workers and in the long run by replacing workers with capital (tools, machines, equipment). In the very long run, a minimum wage will encourage employers to develop new technology resulting in further substitution of capital for labor. As a result, the problem of low incomes and poverty will be aggravated for some people.

Universal Basic Income and the Negative Income Tax

A Universal Basic Income (UBI) is a subsidy payment by the government to all citizens to ensure they have the income required to purchase basic needs such as food, housing, and clothing. It is paid to all citizens regardless of work status, wealth, or income.

A program similar to the UBI is a Negative Income Tax (NIT). *A Negative Income Tax pays a subsidy to any citizen who has an income below a certain level.* Rather than owing the government taxes on their income, individuals eligible for the NIT would receive a payment from the government. Citizens are eligible for the payment regardless of work status. *A Negative Income Tax differs from a UBI because a NIT is only paid to low-income individuals while a UBI is paid to all citizens.*

A Universal Basic Income and a Negative Income Tax differ from the Earned Income Tax program because all citizens, regardless of work status, are eligible. With an Earned Income Tax program, only individuals who have earned income, i.e., working people, qualify.

Supporters of programs like the UBI and NIT contend these programs are the most efficient ways to provide assistance to low-income individuals. No distinction is made between deserving and underserving individuals based on whether or not they work. The cost of administration and oversight of these programs is less than in targeted subsidy programs.

Another benefit of the Earned Income Tax Credit, Negative Income Tax, or Universal Basic Income is that removing the insecurity, anxiety, and fear of not being able to meet basic need has important social and economic benefits. As a result of such programs, individuals are better able to focus on work, education, and their families, leading to individuals being more productive and improving family outcomes.

Finally, advances in technology and artificial intelligence put increasing numbers of jobs, particularly those held by lower-educated/lower-skilled individuals at risk of being eliminated. Workers in these jobs will have a very difficult time transitioning to the new jobs being created which will require higher skills and higher levels of education. Additionally, technology and artificial intelligence will reduce the total number of jobs available. A Universal Basic Income or a Negative Income Tax are the most effective ways to deal with this coming challenge.

Opponents of a UBI or NIT believe such programs would be too costly. They also contend programs such as these, as with all subsidy programs, reduce the incentive to work. Ultimately, it is the responsibility of all citizens to be productive members of society by working. An important principle of our economic system is the connection existing between an individual's productivity and their consumption (living standard). Altering such a basic criterion of our system, even for basic needs like food and shelter, undermines a fundamental foundation of our system. Assistance to low-income individuals needs to be limited to ensure all have an incentive to work and be productive.

Summary

Broad-based subsidy programs are more efficient than targeted programs. Ensuring recipients use the subsidy in an approved and what is deemed appropriate manner is difficult and expensive. While there is a risk the subsidy might be used in a manner deemed unacceptable and inappropriate, the benefit versus the cost of oversight is questionable. Additionally, it prohibits recipients from using assistance in the most beneficial manner to them such as buying shoes and clothing for children rather than food.

Distinguishing between deserving versus undeserving individuals such as whether or not they have earned income (i.e., they work) is also problematic. Individuals don't work for a myriad of reasons, both appropriate and inappropriate. It is probably more efficient and beneficial to simply determine whether or not individuals qualify for assistance based on their income, earned or not, even though this may somewhat increase the disincentive to work. A Negative Income Tax meets this criterion.

An NIT is a more feasible program than a Universal Basic Income program. Providing a subsidy payment to all citizens is unnecessary and expensive. Broad political support for such a program does not exist.

The issue of whether to use a minimum wage rather than subsidies is more difficult. It seems clear subsidies, targeted or broad-based, end up subsidizing the profits of corporations and their wealthy owners. On the other hand, it is also clear raising the minimum wage increases unemployment. When the price of something rises (workers), less of it will be bought. Increasing the minimum wage will result in companies hiring fewer workers. The issue is whether the benefits of increasing the minimum wage outweigh the costs.

Raising the minimum wage will result in those workers who remain employed earning higher incomes, reducing their dependence on public assistance. Those workers who lose their jobs will be more dependent on public assistance. *So, the issue is whether the reduction of public assistance to workers who remain employed outweigh the cost of increased assistance to those who lose their jobs.* It would seem it almost certainly does. The loss of jobs as a result of increasing the minimum wage, depending on how much it is raised, is projected to be relatively small. Therefore, the increase in assistance to those who lose their jobs will be relatively small. The increase in wages for the relatively large group of individuals who remain employed will be relatively more substantial and almost certainly outweigh the increased costs of the additional unemployed.

Policies

Broader-based subsidy programs should be expanded. Ideally, this includes the adoption of a Negative Income Tax. Alternatively, eligibility for the Earned Income Tax program needs to be made less restrictive; and the amount of the credit, increased. The bias against individuals without children needs to be reduced. Distinguishing between the undeserving and deserving poor is costly and inefficient. Targeted subsidy programs should be continued for the time being, but there should be a trend towards replacing them with more broad-based subsidy programs.

The minimum wage should be raised. The benefits of doing so outweigh the costs. Corporations need to pay their workers higher wages so they are less reliant on public assistance, which ultimately subsidizes corporate profits and the wealthy.

Job Creation, Urban Renewal, and Rural Support

Populations in urban and rural areas are often marginalized and are unable to fully participate in the economic benefits offered by our country. Decay of infrastructure, both public and private, plague many inner cities and rural communities. Residents often feel abandoned and forgotten. As a result, alcohol and drug addiction are major problems in many inner cities and rural areas. To help revitalize these areas and offer needed support, programs modeled after the Civilian Conservation Corps should be created to re-invigorate and support urban and rural areas that are suffering from decay.

An Urban Renewal Corps (URC) should be established that will offer employment, education, and job training to inner-city young adults who would be hired and trained to do revitalization of urban areas. Projects would include restoration and maintenance of public areas like parks, street cleaning, demolition of abandoned homes and buildings, replacement of damaged side-walks and other pedestrian pathways, and construction of bicycle routes. Aid could be provided in cleaning up and maintaining neighborhood schools. Training to inspect homes and buildings for lead and asbestos problems could be initiated. Environmental training to test air and water quality in neighborhoods could be undertaken. Such programs would provide jobs for residents and enhance public safety so that water tragedies as occurred in Washington, DC and Flint, Michigan, could be avoided. Program participants could be trained to call on elderly and disabled individuals within the community to provide companionship and assistance with needed activities. Program participants could be trained to provide guidance and support to those with alcohol and drug addiction diseases. As with the CCC, the program could include educational training enabling individuals to obtain their Graduate Equivalency Degree (GED) to complete high school, enroll in college preparatory classes, and even attend college.

A Rural Support Corps (RSC) should be established with similar opportunities for young adults in rural communities. Buildings in towns with dwindling populations could be maintained or demolished. Parks and public areas could be maintained. Public school grounds could be enhanced and maintained. More importantly, many rural communities have aging populations who are in need of support and help. A Rural Support Corps could call on these people to ensure they are okay, offer companionship, and provide transportation to get groceries, medical care, or whatever other services may be needed. Corps resources could be used to train program participants to provide guidance and support to help battle the drug and alcohol epidemic that plagues many rural communities. As part of the Corps, educational training could be offered through online classes offered by the Corps itself or through partnerships with public schools and colleges. Training would be provided in the process of taking online classes, including providing whatever equipment, primarily computers, that the participants may need.

Both the Urban Renewal Corps and the Rural Support Corps would first offer opportunities to people already living in the particular communities being served.

Bankruptcy Reform

As discussed in Chapter 12, the second Bush Administration reformed Bankruptcy laws strengthening the hand of Financial Institutions and Credit Card Companies at the expense of the general population. The law made it more difficult for individuals to file under Chapter 7 of the Bankruptcy Code, which offered greater relief and protection for filers and, instead, forced many to file under Chapter 13 of the Bankruptcy Code with its more stringent and demanding requirements which favor the financial industry. The financial industry was largely put in the driver's seat with the passage of the Bankruptcy Abuse and Consumer Protection Act of 2005.

Elizabeth Warren, one of the foremost authorities on bankruptcy law in the country, opposed the 2005 bill and has proposed important changes to it. She proposes a simplified process whereby the distinction between Chapter 7 and Chapter 13 would be replaced with a single system available to everyone. Individuals would have a menu of options to choose from. The costs for filing would be reduced. Under present law the ability to discharge student debt in a bankruptcy filing is extremely difficult. Under Senator Warren's proposal, student debt could be more easily discharged. Given the extent of the student debt crisis in the country, this seems a sensible approach. The plan better enables filers to keep their homes by allowing them to restructure their home mortgages.

Reform of the 2005 Bankruptcy law is overdue. The playing field needs to be better leveled so it is not so favorable to financial institutions and credit card companies. Individuals facing financial distress need reasonable accommodation when they file for bankruptcy to better enable them to get back on their feet.

Politics and Money

Ultimately, to protect our Democratic system requires that the influence of money on elections and the political process be limited. As long as the wealthy, corporations, and other groups are allowed to spend virtually unlimited amounts on election campaigns, our Democratic system will, over time, inevitably drift back to a Plutocracy.

Unrestricted spending on elections was triggered by the Supreme Court decision in Citizens United v. Federal Election Commission. There are two paths to reforming this decision. One is through a Constitutional Amendment; and the other, through the Supreme Court reversing its decision. Both paths need to be pursued. However, the passage of a Constitutional Amendment would be difficult and unlikely to be successful. The more likely path to success will be accomplished through the Supreme Court itself rendering a new decision reversing the Citizens United decision. Thus, the appointment of Justices who are likely to be supportive of reversing the decision is of paramount importance.

A New Era of Democracy

We do not need to create a new economic system or to replace our current system with one based on Socialism. We need a return to the types of policies which existed during the period of Democratic Capitalism, a system created by Franklin Roosevelt and expanded by Lyndon Johnson, a system which resulted in much greater income equality, wealth equality, and equality of economic opportunity.

Supporters of Oligarchic Capitalism used the economic problems of the 1970s, primarily caused by the oil crisis of that decade, to systematically dismantle the Democratic Capitalist system that had been created. The election of Ronald Reagan was a critical turning point in the re-establishment of the Oligarchic Capitalist system which had previously existed.

The era of Democratic Capitalism was not without its problems; many groups were prevented from reaping the full benefits of living in such a system. Due to discrimination based on race, ethnicity, gender, and sexual orientation, many individuals were unable to fully participate and enjoy the high living standards available in a Democratic Capitalist system. Fortunately, progressive social policies have been adopted ameliorating the systematic, institutionalized discriminatory barriers of the past. Although much still needs to be done, these will enable a much broader section of the American public to now have access to the benefits of living in a Democratic Capitalist economic system and help to alleviate the divisiveness and conflict now plaguing us.

In his acceptance speech at the 1936 Democratic Convention, Franklin Roosevelt, to a large extent, described the challenges we face today.

"For too many of us the political equality we once had won was meaningless in the face of economic inequality. A small group had concentrated into their own hands an almost complete control over other people's property, other people's money, other people's labor – other people's lives. For too many of us life was no longer free; liberty no longer real; men could no longer follow the pursuit of happiness.

Against economic tyranny such as this, the American citizen could appeal only to the organized power of Government. The collapse of 1929 showed up the despotism for what it was. The election of 1932 was the people's mandate to end it. Under that mandate it is being ended.

The royalists of the economic order have conceded that political freedom was the business of the Government, but they have maintained that economic slavery was nobody's business. They granted that the Government could protect the citizen in his right to vote, but they denied that the Government could do anything to protect the citizen in his right to work and his right to live.

Today we stand committed to the proposition that freedom is no half-and-half affair. If the average citizen is guaranteed equal opportunity in the polling place, he must have equal opportunity in the market place.

These economic royalists complain that we seek to overthrow the institutions of America. What they really complain of is that we seek to take away their power. Our allegiance to American institutions requires the overthrow of this kind of power. In vain they seek to hide behind the Flag and the Constitution. In their blindness they forget what the Flag and the Constitution stand for. Now, as always, they stand for democracy, not tyranny; for freedom, not subjection; and against a dictatorship by mob rule and the over-privileged alike."

—TEACHING AMERICAN HISTORY,
TEACHINGAMERICANHISTORY.ORG, *ACCEPTANCE SPEECH
AT THE DEMOCRATIC NATIONAL CONVENTION 1936*

We have little choice but to work for the necessary change, no matter how difficult it will be. If we fail, the future seems bleak. It is likely the United States will increasingly resemble many Third World countries where wealth and income are concentrated in ever fewer hands and cronyism is rampant, where a wealthy few live in gated communities with armed guards to protect them and their wealth, where the vast majority of the population live in poverty with little opportunity or power, struggling to get by.

The future is not determined. We have choices. We can create a fairer, more just system where productivity is rewarded, economic support is provided, economic opportunity for all exists, and Democracy is preserved. The choice is ours, as it was with an earlier generation. The issue is whether we are willing to fight for it.

APPENDIX 1

Marginal Revenue Product

Marginal Revenue Product (MRP) is the change in revenue that a firm receives that is the result of selling the additional output that is produced by hiring one more unit of an input. Generally, we assume that the additional unit of an input is a unit of labor. A more simplified way to think about it is that *Marginal Revenue Product is the change in the revenue that a firm receives that is the result of selling the additional output that is produced by hiring an additional worker.*

Mathematically MRP is a combination of two factors: Marginal Revenue (MR) and Marginal Product (MP) (often referred to as Marginal Physical Product). *Marginal Revenue is the change in the revenue of a firm from producing and selling an additional unit of output. Marginal Product is the change in output that results from hiring an additional unit of an input (i.e., hiring an additional worker).* Marginal Revenue Product is obtained by multiplying Marginal Revenue by Marginal Product:

$$\textbf{MRP = MR x MP}.$$

The value of a worker to a firm is the productivity of the worker (the amount the worker produces) times the amount that the production that the worker creates can be sold for (which in a competitive environment is the price of the product, i.e., in a competitive environment MR = price). Additionally, in a competitive environment, the wage the worker receives is equal to the MRP.

What an individual produces has to be wanted and valued (demanded) in the economic system. Being very productive in producing a product that few people want will result in very little income for the individual regardless of how productive the person is. Being productive is not enough; one must be productive in something that consumers want to buy.

APPENDIX 2

Marginal Income Tax Rate

The Marginal Tax Rate is the tax rate on an additional dollar of income. It is important to have an understanding of this important concept to understand how our income tax system works. As of 2019, there are seven tax brackets for the Federal Income Tax System. Table A2a shows these seven brackets for a married couple filing jointly.

Table A2a   Marginal Income Tax Rate 2019 Married Filing Jointly

Marginal Tax Rate	Married, Filing Jointly
10%	$0 to $19,400
12%	$19,401 to $78,950
22%	$78,951 to $168,400
24%	$168,401 to $321,450
32%	$321,451 to $408,200
35%	$408,201 to $612,350
37%	$612,351 or more

All married individuals filing jointly pay a 10% tax rate on the first $19,400 they earn, $1,940. This includes someone working at a fast-food restaurant or Warren Buffet. Married individuals filing jointly earning over $19,400 pay a 12% percent *marginal tax rate* on amounts earned between $19,401 and $78,950.

For example, a married couple filing jointly has income of $60,000.

They would pay a 10% tax on the first $19,400 they earned and a 12% tax on the next $40,600 ($60,000–$19,400). Their tax would be:

First $19,400 x 10% =	$1,940
Additional $40,600 x 12% =	$4,872

for a total tax of $6,812. The 12% rate is not applied to their *total income* but, rather, on their *marginal (additional) income,* that is, the amount above $19,400.

A married couple earning $130,000 would pay a 10% rate on the first $19,400, a 12% rate on the next $59,550 ($78,950–$19,400), and a 22% rate on the next $60,000 ($120,000–$59,500–$19,400). Their tax would be:

First $19,400 x 10% =	$ 1,940
Next $59,550 x 12% =	$ 7,146
Next $60,000 x 22% =	$13,200

for a total tax of $22,286. Again, the 22% rate is not applied to their *total income* but, rather, on their *marginal (additional) income,* that is, the amount above $78,951.

APPENDIX 3

Historical Federal Income Tax Rates

The first income tax was passed in 1862 to finance the Civil War. The tax was repealed in 1872, ten years after the war ended. The modern income tax was established with the passage of the Revenue Act of 1913.

Table A3a   Marginal Income Tax Rates United States 1913–1931[i]

	Number of Tax Brackets	Lowest Rate	Highest Rate
1913–15	7	1%	7%
1916	14	2%	15%
1917	21	2%	67%
1918	56	6%	77%
1919–21	56	4%	73%
1922–23	50	4%	58%
1924	43	2%	46%
1925–31	23	1.5%	25%

[i]   Tax Foundation. (2013, October 17). *U.S. Federal Individual Income Tax Rates History, 1862-2013 (Nominal and Inflation-Adjusted Brackets.* Retrieved from https://taxfoundation.org/us-federal-individual-income-tax-rates-history-1913-2013-nominal-and-inflation-adjusted-brackets/.

Initially rates were relatively low. With the advent of World War I, the highest marginal rates were significantly increased to finance the fighting of the War. The number of tax brackets were also significantly increased so that the highest incomes were most affected by the increase in rates. By increasing the number of brackets, marginal increases in rates could be structured so the impact of the higher rates more gradually affected higher income households, ensuring that only the highest income households paid the highest rates.

The Revenue Act of 1932 passed during the Hoover Administration significantly increased tax rates across the board. The lowest rate increased from 1.5% to 4%, an increase of 167%, while the highest rate increased from 25% to 63%, an increase of 152%. This was done to combat the increase in the Federal government deficit that resulted from the onset of the Great Depression. As discussed in Chapter 9, the increased tax rates drove the economy deeper into depression and did not reduce the deficit.

Table A3b **Marginal Income Tax Rates United States 1932–1933**[ii]

	Number of Tax Brackets	Lowest Rate	Highest Rate
1932–33	54	4%	63%

With the election of Franklin Roosevelt in 1932, higher marginal income tax rates were adopted for higher-income households, with the top rate increasing from 63% to 79%. Meanwhile, the lowest rate was held steady at 4%. Roosevelt believed that the high concentrations of wealth and income had contributed to the Stock Market Crash in 1929 and the Great Depression. Through the New Deal, he sought to create an economic system where income and wealth were more equally distributed. Under Roosevelt, the number of brackets was reduced from 54 to 30.

[ii] Ibid.

Table A3c   ***Marginal Income Tax Rates United States 1934–1945***[iii]

	Number of Tax Brackets	Lowest Rate	Highest Rate
1934–35	30	4%	63%
1936–40	33	4%	79%
1941	32	10%	81%
1942–43	24	19%	88%
1944–45	24	23%	94%

With the advent of World War II significantly higher rates were required to fight the War. By the end of the War, the lowest rate had risen 475% to 23%, while the highest rate rose 18.9% to 94%.

During the Post-World War II period, tax rates and the number of brackets would remain relatively unchanged.

Table A3d   ***Marginal Income Tax Rates United States 1946–1963***[iv]

	Number of Tax Brackets	Lowest Rate	Highest Rate
1946–50	24	20%	91%
1951	24	20.4%	91%
1952–53	24	22.2%	92%
1954–63	24	20%	91%

The U.S. economy had begun to stagnate during the late 1950s and early 1960s. When John F. Kennedy was elected in 1960, there was a movement to lower tax rates to stimulate the economy. Rates were reduced, with the lowest rate falling from 20% to 16% and eventually to 14%, a 30% reduction. The highest rate fell from 91% to 77% and eventually to 70%. In 1979 there were a reduction in the number of brackets from 25 to 15. Additionally, to aid the lowest income households, some income became exempted from the tax. It is important to note, that this income exemption applied to *all* households.

[iii]   Ibid.
[iv]   Ibid.

Table A3e   Marginal Income Tax Rates United States 1964–1978[v]

	Number of Tax Brackets	Lowest Rate	Highest Rate	Income Exemption**
1964	26	16%	77%	
1965–76★	25	14%	70%	
1977–78	25	14%	70%	$3,200

★Surtaxes increased the effective highest rate in some years:
1968: Surtax 7.5%, Effective rate 75.25%
1969: Surtax 10%, Effective rate 77%
1970: Surtax 2.5%, Effective rate 71.25%
**Married Filing Jointly

In the 1970s the number of brackets was reduced from 25 to 15. This resulted in the income tax system becoming less progressive by reducing the incremental (marginal) differences between brackets. The exemption amount was increased to $3,400.

Table A3f   Marginal Income Tax Rates United States 1979–1981[vi]

	Number of Tax Brackets	Lowest Rate	Highest Rate	Exemption Amount*
1979–81	15	14%	70%	$3,400

*Married Filing Jointly

With the election of Ronald Reagan and the re-institution of the policies of Oligarchic Capitalism, significant changes in the income tax system would be initiated. These changes would primarily benefit higher-income households and lead to significant increases in income and wealth inequality. Both the highest rates and the number of brackets would be significantly reduced. These changes would greatly protect the highest income households from substantial taxes on their incomes.

---

[v]   Ibid.
[vi]   Ibid.

Table A3g   Marginal Income Tax Rates United States 1982–1990[vii]

	Number of Tax Brackets	Lowest Rate	Highest Rate	Exemption Amount*
1982	12	12%	50%	$3,400
1983–84	**13**	**11%**	**50%**	**$3,400**
1985	13	11%	50%	$3,540
1986	13	11%	50%	$3,670
1987	6	11%	38.5%	$0
1988–90	2	15%	28%	$0

*Married Filing Jointly

The number of brackets were reduced from 12 to just two; very, very high-income individuals would now pay the same tax rate as many middle-income and upper-middle-income households. And the rate they paid would be reduced by from 50% to 28%. These were the lowest rates since 1931. Additionally, in 1987 the exempted income amount was eliminated, which had the largest impact on lower income households.

In 1991 there would be a third higher bracket added during the first Bush Administration as a result of the Gulf War, raising the highest rate to 31%. As discussed in Chapter 12, this would contribute to Bush losing the 1992 election to Clinton,

Table A3h   Marginal Income Tax Rates United States 1991–1992[viii]

	Number of Tax Brackets	Lowest Rate	Highest Rate
1991–92	3	15%	31%

With the election of Bill Clinton in 1992 the income tax system would be made very slightly more progressive. Two additional brackets would be added, raising the rate on the highest incomes to 39.6%, an increase of 27.7%. During the second Bush Administration, an additional bracket would be added and both the lowest and highest rates

---

[vii]   Ibid.
[viii]   Ibid.

would be reduced. The lowest rate would fall from 15% to 10%, a 50% reduction while the highest rate would fall from 39.6% to 35%, a reduction of 11.6%. Under the Obama Administration an additional bracket would be added, increasing the top rate to back to the 39.6% rate that existed during the Clinton years. The Trump Administration would reduce this highest rate to 37%.

Table A3i   Marginal Income Tax Rates United States 1993–2020[ix, x]

	Number of Tax Brackets	Lowest Rate	Highest Rate
1993–2001	5	15%	39.6%
2002	6	10%	38.6%
2003–12	6	10%	35%
2013–17	7	10%	39.6%
2018–2020	7	10%	37%

ix   Ibid.

x   Money Chimp. (n.d.). *Federal Tax Brackets.* Retrieved from http://www.moneychimp.com/features/tax_brackets.htm.

APPENDIX 4

Historical Federal Estate Tax Rates

The first use of a Federal Estate Tax was in 1862 to finance the Civil War. It was repealed in 1870, six years after the Civil War ended. The beginning of the modern estate tax was with the passage of the Revenue Act of 1916. This first period of enacting and refining the Estate Tax ran from 1916 to 1941.

Table A4a   Federal Estate Tax 1916 to 1933[i]

	Amount Exempted	Initial Rate	Top Rate
1916	$50,000	1%	10%
1917–23	$50,000	2%	25%
1924–25	$50,000	1%	40%
1926–31	$100,000	1%	20%
1932–33	$50,000	1%	45%

Initially, the first $50,000 of an estate's value was exempted from estate taxes. This was increased to $100,000 in 1926, reduced back to

[i]   U.S. Department of Treasury, Internal Revenue Service, U.S Department of Commerce, Bureau of Economic Analysis. (2004, January 16). *History of Estate Filing Requirements and Tax Rates, 1916-1948,* U.S. Dept of Treasury, Internal Revenue Service, U.S. Dept of Commerce, Bureau of Economic Analysis. Retrieved from www.heritage.org/taxes/report/estate-taxes-historical-perspective.

$50,000 in 1927, and then raised to $60,000 in 1942 where it remained until 1977. The starting rate was set at 1% with a top rate of 10%. The rates were increased in 1917 to 2% and 25% respectively. In 1924 the initial rate was reduced to 1% and the top rate was increased to 40%, thus reducing the tax on smaller estates while increasing it on larger ones. In 1926 the top rate was reduced to 20%.

As with the income tax, the Hoover Administration would increase the estate tax in an attempt to combat the increase in the Federal government deficit that resulted from the onset of the Great Depression. The top rate was increased to 45%.

With Franklin Roosevelt's election and the implementation of the New Deal, there would be further increases in the top rate: 1934 to 60%; 1935 to 70%; and 1941 to 77%; the highest it would ever reach. The initial rate would be increased in 1940 to 2% and in 1942to 3%.

Table A4b   Federal Estate Tax 1934 to 1945[ii]

	Amount Exempted	Initial Rate	Top Rate
1934	$50,000	1%	60%
1935–39	$50,000	1%	70%
1940	$50,000	2%	70%
1941	$611,076	2%	77%
1942–45	$566,608	3%	77%

The estate tax would then remain unchanged from 1945 to 1976.

Table A4c   Federal Estate Tax 1945 to 1976[iii]

	Amount Exempted	Initial Rate	Top Rate
1945–76	$60,000	3%	77%

The changes from 1977 to 1981 gradually increased the size of an estate exempted, eliminating many smaller estates from having to pay the tax. The exempted amount was doubled in 1977 from $60,000 to

---

[ii]   Ibid.
[iii]   Ibid.

$120,000. This was followed by series of continuing increases until it reached $175,000 in 1981. At the same time, the initial rate would be increased from 3% to 18%, greatly increasing the amount of tax that would have to be paid by estates that remained subject to the tax. However, the top rate was decreased from 77% to 70%, reducing the amount of tax paid by the wealthiest households. This combination of increasing the initial rate while reducing the highest rate was a net win for the highest-wealth estates.

Table A4d   Federal Estate Tax 1977 to 1981[iv]

	Amount Exempted	Initial Rate	Top Rate
1977	$120,000	18%	70%
1978	$134,000	18%	70%
1979	$147,000	18%	70%
1980	$161,000	18%	70%
1981	$175,000	18%	70%

With the election of Ronald Reagan in 1980 and the re-institution of Oligarchic Capitalist policies, significant reductions would be made in the estate tax benefiting the highest-wealth households. The top rate would be gradually reduced from 70% to 55%, and the size of an estate exempt from the estate tax would be increased from $175,000 to $600,000. These changes would have a significant impact on wealth inequality.

Table A4e   Federal Estate Tax 1982 to 1987[v]

	Amount Exempted	Initial Rate	Top Rate
1982	$225,000	18%	65%
1983	$275,000	18%	60%
1984	$325,000	18%	55%
1985	$400,000	18%	55%
1986	$500,000	18%	55%
1987	$600,000	18%	55%

[iv]   Ibid.
[v]   Ibid.

From 1988 to 1998, there would be no changes in the estate tax.

Table A4f   Federal Estate Tax 1987 to 1998[vi]

	Amount Exempted	Initial Rate	Top Rate
1987–98	$600,000	18%	55%

Beginning in 1999 there began a series of increases in the size of the estate exempted from the Federal Estate Tax, removing many estates from the rolls of those being taxed. In 1999 it was raised from $600,000 to $650,000. With the election of George W. Bush in 2000, changes in the estate tax would be accelerated, further benefiting the highest-wealth households. In 2002 the size of the estate exempted was increased from $675,000 to $1 million. In 2004 it was increased to $1.5 million; in 2006 to $2 million; and in 2009 to $3.5 million. Although the initial rate would remain at 18%, the top rate would be reduced from 55% to 50% in 2002, followed by a series of 1% cuts until it reached 45% in 2009. These actions greatly benefited highest-wealth households and further increased wealth inequality in the country.

Table A4c   Federal Estate Tax 1999 to 2009[vii]

	Amount Exempted	Initial Rate	Top Rate
1999	$650,000	18%	55%
2000–01	$675,000	18%	55%
2002	$1,000,000	18%	50%
2003	$1,000,000	18%	49%
2004	$1,500,000	18%	48%
2005	$1,500,000	18%	47%
2006	$2,000,000	18%	46%
2007–08	$2,000,000	18%	45%
2009	$3,500,000	18%	45%

[vi]   Ibid.
[vii]   Ibid.

The trend in increasing the amount of an estate exempted from the Federal Estate Tax would continue to climb between 2010 and 2019, though this was due to adjustments for inflation. The initial rate would remain at 18%. The top rate, on the other hand, would be reduced to 35% in 2010, the lowest it had been since 1926. It would be raised in 2013 to 40%, still well below its level for the previous 80 years.

Table A4d   Federal Estate Tax 2010 to 2019[viii]

	Amount Exempted	Initial Rate	Top Rate
2010	$5,000,000	18%	35%
2011	$5,000,000	18%	35%
2012	$5,120,000	18%	35%
2013	$5,250,000	18%	40%
2014	$5,340,000	18%	40%
2015	$5,430,000	18%	40%
2016	$5,450,000	18%	40%
2017	$5,490,000	18%	40%
2018	$5,600,000	18%	40%
2019	$5,700,000	18%	40%

Thus, over the years that the Federal Estate Tax has existed, the trend has been to exempt more estates from paying the tax by raising the exemption amount, increasing the rate on the estates on the low end of the scale that remain subject to the tax by raising the initial rate, and decreasing the rate on the largest estates by lowering the top rate.

[viii] Garber, Julie. (n.d.). *Federal Estate Tax Exemptions 1997 through 2019*. The Balance. Retrieved from *www.thebalance.com/ exemption-from-federal-estate-taxes-3505630.*

APPENDIX 5

Historical Federal Gift Tax Rates

The Federal Gift Tax was passed in 1924 in response to individuals transferring wealth while they were still alive to avoid the estate tax.

Table A5a   Federal Gift Tax 1924 to 1925[i]

	Annual Exclusion[ii]	Lifetime Exemption[iii]	Top Rate	Subject to Top Rate (Above)
1924–25	$500	$50,000	25%	$10,000,000

The gift tax was repealed in 1926 and then re-instituted in 1932 during the Hoover Administration. The annual exclusion was set at $5,000 and the top rate at 33.5%.

---

[i]   Tax Foundation. (2014, February 4). *Federal Estate and Gift Tax Rates, Exemptions, an Exclusions, 1916-2014.* Retrieved from https://taxfoundation. org/federal-estate-and-gift-tax-rates-exemptions-and-exclusions-1916-2014
[ii] The maximum amount that can be given by one person to another person in a calendar year.
[iii] The total amount that can be gifted by an individual over the course of their lifetime.

Table A5b   Federal Gift Tax 1932 to 1933[iv]

	Annual Exclusion	Lifetime Exemption	Top Rate	Subject to Top Rate (Above)
1932–33	$5,000	$50,000	33.5%	$10,000,000

The Roosevelt Administration would gradually increase the top rate to 57.75%. The annual exclusion would be gradually lowered to $3,000, subjecting more estates to the tax. The size of an estate subject to the highest rate would be $50 million from 1938 to 1941 reducing the effect of the tax on the largest estates, but would be lowered back to $10 million in 1942 raising the tax on the highest estates.

Table A5c   Federal Gift Tax 1934 to 1945[v]

	Annual Exclusion	Lifetime Exemption	Top Rate	Subject to Top Rate (Above)
1934	$5,000	$50,000	45.0%	$10,000,000
1935–37	$5,000	$40,000	52.5%	$10,000,000
1938–40	$4,000	$40,000	52.5%	$50,000,000
1941	$4,000	$40,000	57.75%	$50,000,000
1942–45	$3,000	$30,000	57.75%	$10,000,000

The gift tax would then remain unchanged from 1945 to 1976.

Table A5d   Federal Gift Tax 1945 to 1976[vi]

	Annual Exclusion	1.0755 in	Top Rate	Subject to Top Rate (Above)
1942–76	$3,000	$30,000	57.75%	$10,000,000

In 1977 the gift tax would be changed by increasing the top rate from 57.75% to 70%. In 1981 the estate size subject to the tax rate

iv Tax Foundation. (2014, February 4). *Federal Estate and Gift Tax Rates, Exemptions, an Exclusions, 1916-2014*. Retrieved from https://taxfoundation. org/federal-estate-and-gift-tax-rates-exemptions-and-exclusions-1916-2014
v Ibid.
vi Ibid.

would be lowered from $5 million to $4 million. The lifetime exemption would be raised from $120,000 to $175,000.

Table A5d   Federal Gift Tax 1977 to 1981[vii]

	Annual Exclusion	Lifetime Exemption	Top Rate	Subject to Top Rate (Above)
1977	$3,000	$120,000	70%	$5,000,000
1978	$3,000	$134,000	70%	$5,000,000
1979	$3,000	$147,000	70%	$5,000,000
1980	$3,000	$161,000	70%	$5,000,000
1981	$3,000	$175,000	70%	$4,000,000

With the election of Ronald Reagan more changes in the gift tax would be made to the benefit of high-wealth households. The annual exclusion was increased from $3,000 to $10,000, raising the amount that could be gifted tax-free. The top rate would gradually be reduced from 65% to 55%. The amount subject to the tax was reduced from $3.5 million to $3 million. The lifetime exemption was significantly increased from $225,000 to $500,000.

Table A5e   Federal Gift Tax 1982 to 1988[viii]

	Annual Exclusion	Lifetime Exemption	Top Rate	Subject to Top Rate (Above)
1982	$10,000	$225,000	65%	$3,500,000
1983	$10,000	$275,000	60%	$3,000,000
1984	$10,000	$325,000	55%	$3,000,000
1985	$10,000	$400,000	55%	$3,000,000
1986	$10,000	$500,000	55%	$3,000,000
1987-88	$10,000	$600,000	55%	$3,000,000

There would be no changes in the gift tax from 1988 to 1997.

[vii] Ibid.
[viii] Ibid.

Table A5e   Federal Gift Tax 1988 to 1997[ix]

	Annual Exclusion	Lifetime Exemption	Top Rate	Subject to Top Rate (Above)
1988–97	$10,000	$600,000	55%	$3,000,000

From 1998 to 2010 the main effect of legislation concerning the gift tax was to reduce its impact on high wealth households. Although the estate size subject to the top rate was reduced from $3 million to $1 million, the lifetime exemption was increased from $625,000 to $1 million and, most significantly, the top rate was reduced from 55% to 35%.

Table A5f   Federal Gift Tax 1998 to 2010[x]

	Annual Exclusion	Lifetime Exemption	Top Rate	Subject to Top Rate (Above)
1998	$10,000	$625,000	55%	$3,000,000
1999	$10,000	$650,000	55%	$3,000,000
2000–01	$10,000	$675,000	55%	$3,000,000
2002	$11,000	$1,000,000	50%	$2,500,000
2003	$11,000	$1,000,000	49%	$2,000,000
2004	$11,000	$1,000,000	48%	$2,000,000
2005	$11,000	$1,000,000	47%	$2,000,000
2006	$12,000	$1,000,000	46%	$2,000,000
2007–08	$12,000	$1,000,000	45%	$1,500,000
2009	$13,000	$1,000,000	45%	$1,500,000
2010	$13,000	$1,000,000	35%	$1,000,000

The trend of reducing the gift tax continued from 1998 to 2010. The annual exclusion and lifetime exemption were increased. The top rate was cut to its lowest level since 1932, 35%. The size of the estate subject to the top rate was reduced, countering the trend of a reduced gift tax.

Changes to the gift tax from 2011 to 2020 have been mixed. The top rate was increased from 35% to 40%, and both the estate size

ix   Ibid.
x   Ibid.

258

subject to the top rate and the lifetime exemption increased from $5 million to $5.7million.

Table A5g   Federal Gift Tax 2011 to 2019[xi]

	Annual Exclusion	Lifetime Exemption	Top Rate	Subject to Top Rate (Above)
2011	$13,000	$5,000,000	35%	$5,000,000
2012	$13,000	$5,120,000	35%	$5,120,000
2013	$14,000	$5,250,000	40%	$5,250,000
2014	$14,000	$5,340,000	40%	$5,340,000
2015	$14,000	$5,430,000	40%	$5,430,000
2016	$14,000	$5,470,000	40%	$5,470,000
2017	$14,000	$5,490,000	40%	$5,490,000
2018	$15,000	$5,600,000	40%	$5,600,000
2019	$15,000	$5,700,000	40%	$5,700,000

[xi]   Ibid.

APPENDIX 6

Historical Corporate Income Tax Rates

The first corporate income tax in the country was a 1% rate passed in 1901.

Table A6a   Highest Corporate Income Tax Rates 1909-2018[i]

	Rate
1909–17	Less than 10%
1918–39	10-20%
1940–49	24-40%
1950	38%
1951	51%
1952–63	52%
1964–69	48-52.8%
1970–86	46-49.2%
1987	40%
1988–1992	34%
1993–2017	35%
2018–19	21%

[i]   The Balance (n.d.). *U.S. Corporate Income Tax Rate, Its History, and the Effective Rate.* Retrieved from www.thebalance.com/corporate-income-tax-definition-history-effective-rate-3306024.

Initially the rate was set at 1%. By 1930, at the start of the Great Depression, it had risen to 12%. It was raised throughout the Depression when it reached 19% in 1939. With the start of World War II in 1940, it was raised until it reached 40% in 1949. It was raised in 1951 to 51% and would remain relatively steady between 46% and 52.8% from 1951 to 1986. With the Reagan tax reforms, it would be reduced to 40% in 1987 and to 34% in 1988. In 1983 there would be a very slight increase to 35% where it would remain until 2018. In that year it would be significantly reduced to 21%, the lowest rate since 1939.

APPENDIX 7

Historical Capital Gains Tax Rates

The capital gains tax was first adopted in 1922. Until then, capital gains were taxed as ordinary income, i.e., at the personal income tax rate.

Table A7a   ***Highest Capital Gains Tax Rates United States 1922–2019***[i]

Year	Rate
1922–1933	12.5%
1934–35	31.5%
1936–37	39.0%
1938–41	30.0%
1942–69	25%–27.5%
1970–78	32.3%–39.9%
1979–80	28.0%
1981	23.7%
1982–86	20.0%
1987–96	28%–29.2%
1997–2002	21.2%
2003–12	15%–16.1%
2013–19	25.0%

[i]   Wolters Kluwer (n.d.) *Historical Look at Capital Gains Rate.* Retrieved from www.taxna.wolterskluwer.com/whole-ball-of-tax-2019/historical-capital-gain

Prior to the years 1936–37, the rate was below 20%. In 1942 it was raised to 25%, which is approximately where it remained during the period of Democratic Capitalism. It was raised to over 30% during the 1970s. During the Reagan Administration, it was reduced to 20%. It was increased to 28% in 1987 where it remained for 10 years. In 1997 it was reduced to 20%; and during the G.W. Bush Administration, it was reduced to its lowest rate since 1941, 15%. In 2013 it was raised to 20%, where it stands today.

GLOSSARY

A

Absolute Advantage
  When a person can produce more of a product with a given amount of resources than another person can.

B

Broad-based Subsidy
  A subsidy which allows recipients to use the subsidy to purchase whatever they choose.

C

Capital
  A type of resource: machines, tools, equipment.

Capital Gain
  The profit from the sale of a capital asset such as property or an investment.

Colony
  An exclusive trading territory claimed by a country.

Commodity
  An output resulting from production used to satisfy the needs and desires of human beings. There are two types of commodities: goods and services.

Comparative Advantage
  When a person's opportunity cost of producing a product is less than someone else's.

Consumption

The act of using commodities to satisfy the needs and desires of human beings.

Credit-Default Swap

An insurance product whereby the owner of a security "swaps" the risk the security won't be paid (credit-default) with an insurance company for a payment of money.

D

Derivative

A security that *derives* its value from an underlying asset. It is a contract between two parties for a cash payment based on the payments received from the underlying asset.

Division of Labor

The way a job is broken down into parts.

Duty

A tax imposed on the individuals who buy imported goods.

E

Economic Process

The series of activities human beings must engage in to sustain themselves. Human beings use resources for production to make commodities for consumption.

Economic Problem

Scarcity of resources.

Entrepreneurship

Considered by some to be the fourth type of resource; a special type of human effort, economic leadership.

Earned Income Tax Credit

A broad-based subsidy which is paid to citizens who have earned income below a certain level. To qualify, individuals must have earned income, i.e., they must be working. It targets the working poor.

Exchange

The act of trading commodities.

Exploitation

Economic exploitation occurs when individuals are forced to produce more than they consume so that others can consume more than they produce.

F

Federal Funds Rate

The interest rate banks charge each other for an overnight loan.

G

Gains from Specialization

Increases in production that result when individuals concentrate their efforts on one area of production or on one component of a task (job).

Good

An output from production; physical and tangible.

K

Keynesian Economics

The belief that the key to the performance of the Macro economy is demand (spending).

L

Labor

A type of resource; human effort both physical and mental.

Laissez-faire

A French term for "Let it be". The belief that the macro economy is self-regulating and there is no need for government intervention on a macro level.

Land

A type of resource; the natural wealth of the physical environment. Now referred to as Natural Resources.

Living Wage
A minimum wage which ensures a worker has sufficient income to cover the basic costs of living.

M

Macro Economics
The study of the economic system as a whole; the study of system-wide issues.

Marginal Product
The change in output that results from using an additional unit of an input. For example, the additional output that results from hiring an additional worker.

Marginal Revenue
The change in revenue that results from producing and selling an additional unit of an output.

Marginal Revenue Product
The additional revenue a firm receives which is the result of selling the additional output that is produced by hiring one more unit of an input. Mathematically, MRP = Marginal Product x Marginal Product.

Micro Economics
The study of the operation of individual markets. The study of individual behavior in relation to the acts of production, consumption, and exchange.

Minimum Wage
The lowest amount a worker can be paid.

Mortgage-Backed Security
A type of derivative that is backed by and derives its value from home mortgages.

N

Negative Income Tax (NIT)
A broad-based subsidy which is paid to any citizen who has an income below a certain level regardless of employment status.

O

Oligarchy
> A system in which a small group of people have power and control, often based on great income and/or wealth.

Opportunity Cost
> The foregone benefit of the best available alternative. What is given up when one action is taken in lieu of another action.

P

Plutocracy
> A political system controlled by individuals of great income and/or wealth.

Production
> The act of making commodities or capital.

R

Reaganomics
> The popularized name for Supply-Side Economics.

Resource
> An input into production. Traditionally, economists have identified three resources: land, labor, and capital. Some economists contend there is a fourth resource: entrepreneurship.

S

Security
> A tradeable financial asset that represents a financial claim against the assets of a corporation or governmental entity.

Service
> An output from production; non-physical, intangible.

Stagflation
> The occurrence of high unemployment and high inflation at the same time.

Supply-Side Economics
> The belief that the key to the performance of the Macro economy is supply (production).

T

Targeted Subsidy
> A subsidy which stipulates what the recipient must use the subsidy for.

Tariff
> A tax imposed on other countries for the goods they sell (export) to the country imposing the tariff, i.e., for the goods imported by the country imposing the tariff.

Trade Monopoly
> An exclusive trading privilege granted to a company by a country.

Tranche
> A type of derivative that is composed of the small pieces of many different underlying securities.

U

Universal Basic Income (UBI)
> A subsidy payment by the government to all citizens, regardless of employment status or income level, to ensure they have the income required to purchase basic needs such as food, housing, and clothing.

V

Voucher
> A financial subsidy provided to the recipient to go into the private market place and purchase a particular product.

ENDNOTES

Introduction

[1]   Stone, Chad; Trisi, Danilo, Sherman, Arloc,; and Taylor, Roderick. (2018, December 18). *A Guide to Statistics on Historical Trends in Income Inequality.* Center on Budget and Policy Priorities. Retrieved from *www.cbpp.org/research/ poverty-and-inequality/a-guide-to-statistics-on-historical-trends-in-income-inequality.*

CHAPTER 4 Free Market Capitalism

[2]   Smith, Adam. (1776). *The Wealth of Nations,* New York, NY: Modern Library.

CHAPTER 5 The Expansion of Free Trade

[3]   knoema. (n.d.*) World GDP Ranking 2018 Country by Country Data and Chart.* Retrieved from *https://knoema.com/nwnfkne/ world-gdp-ranking-2018-gdp-by-country-data-and-charts.*

[4]   Smith, Rob. (2018, April 18). *The world's biggest economies in 2018.* World Economic Forum. Retrieved from *www.weforum.org/agenda/2018/04/ the-worlds-biggest-economies-in-2018/.*

[5]   Ibid.

[6]   Roser, Max. (n.d.). *Economic Growth*, Our World in Data. Retrieved from *https://ourworldindata.org/economic-growth.*

[7]   Statistic Times. (2019). *Gross World Product per capita.* Retrieved from. *www.statisticstimes.com/economy/gross-world-product-capita.php.*

[8]   knoema. (n.d.*) World GDP Ranking 2018 Country by Country Data and Chart.* Retrieved from *https://knoema.com/nwnfkne/ world-gdp-ranking-2018-gdp-by-country-data-and-charts.*

[9]   Amadeo, Kimberly. (n.d.). *U.S. GDP by Year Compared to Recessions and Events.* The Balance. Retrieved from *www.thebalance.com/ us-gdp-by-year-3305543.*

[10]   INEQUALITY.ORG. (n.d.). *Income Inequality.* Retrieved from *https:// inequality.org/facts/income-inequality/.*

[11]   INEQUALITY.ORG. (n.d.). *Wealth Inequality in the United States.* Retrieved from *https://inequality.org/facts/wealth-inequality/.*

[12]   TRADING ECONOMICS. (n.d.*). United States Corporate Profits* Retrieved from *https://tradingeconomics.com/united-states/corporate-profits.*

[13]   Wile, Rob. (2017, December 19). *The Richest 10% of Americans Now Own 84% of All Stocks.* Money. Retrieved from *http://money.com/money/5054009/stock-ownership-10-percent-richest/.*

CHAPTER 6 Socialism

[14]   Pusateri, C. Joseph. (1988). *A History of American Business.* Arlington Heights, IL. Harlan Davidson, Inc.

[15]   EH.net. (n.d.). *History of U.S. Telegraph Industry.* Economic History Association. Retrieved from *www.eh.net/encyclopedia/history-of-the-u-s-telegraph-industry/.*

[16]   Ibid.

[17]   Blackford, Mansel & Kerr, K. Austin. (1994). *Business Enterprise in American History.* Third Edition. Boston, MA. Houghton Mifflin Company.

[18]   Ibid.

[19]   O'Donnell, Edward T. (2019, January 31). *Are We Living in Gilded Age 2.0?* History. Retrieved from www.history.com/news/second-gilded-age-income-inequality.

[20]   Tax Foundation. (2013, October 17). *U.S. Federal Individual Income Tax Rates History, 1862-2013 (Nominal and Inflation-Adjusted Brackets.* Retrieved from https://taxfoundation.org/us-federal-individual-income-tax-rates-history-1913-2013-nominal-and-inflation-adjusted-brackets/.

[21]   Tax Foundation. (2014, February 4*). Federal Estate and Gift Tax Rates, Exemptions, an Exclusions, 1916-2014.* Retrieved from https://taxfoundation.org/federal-estate-and-gift-tax-rates-exemptions-and-exclusions-1916-2014.

[22]   Wolters Kluwer (n.d.) *Historical Look at Capital Gains Rate.* Retrieved from www.taxna.wolterskluwer.com/whole-ball-of-tax-2019/historical-capital-gain.

[23]   ProCon.Ogr. (2018, May 21). *Federal Corporate Income Tax Rates.* Retrieved from *https://corporatetax.procon.org/federal-corporate-income-tax-rates/,*

[24]   U.S. Department of Treasury, Internal Revenue Service, U.S Department of Commerce, Bureau of Economic Analysis. (2004, January 16). *History of Estate Filing Requirements and Tax Rates, 1916-1948,* U.S. Dept of Treasury, Internal Revenue Service, U.S. Dept of Commerce, Bureau of Economic Analysis. Retrieved from www.heritage.org/taxes/report/estate-taxes-historical-perspective.

[25]   Piketty, Thomas & Saez, Emmanuel, *Income Inequality in the United States. 1913-1998,* NBER Working Paper Series, Working Paper 8467, 2001.

[26]   Saez, Emmanuel & Zucman, Gabriel. (2014). *Wealth Inequality in the United States since 1913: Evidence From Capitalized Income Data,* NBER Working Paper Series, Working Paper 20625, 2014.

[27]   World Inequality Data Base. (n.d.). *Income & Wealth Inequality, USA, 1913-2014.* Retrieved from *https://wid.world/country/usa/.*

CHAPTER 9 The Birth of Democratic Capitalism

28 United States History. (n.d.). *Unemployment Statistic during the Great Depression.* Retrieved from *www.u-s-history.com/pages/h1528.html,*

29 Keynes, John Maynard. (1936). *The General Theory of Employment, Interest, and Money.* London, England: MacMillan & Co., LTD.

30 History.com. (2019, June 10). *Works Progress Administration (WPA).* Retrieved from *https://www.history.com/topics/great-depression/works-progress-administration.*

31 Ibid.

32 History.com (2019, June 10). *TVA.* Retrieved from https://www.history.com/topics/great-depression/history-of-the-tva.

33 History.com (2018, August 21). *Hoover Dam.* Retrieved from https://www.history.com/topics/great-depression/hoover-dam.

34 McClung, Christian. *The Great Depression in Washington State; Grand Coulee Dam.* Civil Rights and Labor History Consortium/University of Washington. Retrieved from https://depts.washington.edu/depress/grand_coulee.shtml.

35 The Living New Deal. (n.d.). *Rural Electrification Administration (REA) (1935).* Retrieved from https://livingnewdeal.org/glossary/rural-electrification-administration-rea-1935/.

36 Ibid.

37 The Living New Deal. (n.d.). *Rural Electrification Act (1936).* Retrieved from https://livingnewdeal.org/glossary/rural-electrification-act-1936/.

38 The Living New Deal. (n.d.). *Rural Electrification Administration (REA) (1935).* Retrieved from https://livingnewdeal.org/glossary/rural-electrification-administration-rea-1935/.

39 Ibid.

40 Tax Foundation. (2013, October 17). *U.S. Federal Individual Income Tax Rates History, 1862-2013 (Nominal and Inflation-Adjusted Brackets.* Retrieved from https://taxfoundation.org/us-federal-individual-income-tax-rates-history-1913-2013-nominal-and-inflation-adjusted-brackets/.

41 U.S. Department of Treasury, Internal Revenue Service, U.S Department of Commerce, Bureau of Economic Analysis. (2004, January 16). *History of Estate Filing Requirements and Tax Rates, 1916-1948,* U.S. Dept of Treasury, Internal Revenue Service, U.S. Dept of Commerce, Bureau of Economic Analysis. Retrieved from www.heritage.org/taxes/report/estate-taxes-historical-perspective.

42 Tax Foundation. (2014, February 4*). Federal Estate and Gift Tax Rates, Exemptions, an Exclusions, 1916-2014.* Retrieved from https://taxfoundation.org/federal-estate-and-gift-tax-rates-exemptions-and-exclusions-1916-2014.

43 Wolters Kluwer (n.d.) *Historical Look at Capital Gains Rate.* Retrieved from www.taxna.wolterskluwer.com/whole-ball-of-tax-2019/historical-capital-gain.

[44]   ProCon.Ogr. (2018, May 21). *Federal Corporate Income Tax Rates.* Retrieved from *https://corporatetax.procon.org/federal-corporate-income-tax-rates/.*

[45]   Amadeo, Kimberly. (2019, July 11). *U.S. Budget Deficit by Year Compared to GDP, Debt Increase, and Events.* The Balance. Retrieved from *www.thebalance.com/us-deficit-by-year-3306306.*

[46]   Amadeo, Kimberly. (2019, October 2). *Unemployment Rate by Year Since 1929 Compared to Inflation and GDP.* the balance. Retrieved from *www.thebalance.com/unemployment-rate-by-year-3305506.*

[47]   Ibid.

[48]   Amadeo, Kimberly. (2019, October 2). *Unemployment Rate by Year Since 1929 Compared to Inflation and GDP.* the balance. Retrieved from *www.thebalance.com/unemployment-rate-by-year-3305506.*

[49]   Piketty, Thomas & Saez, Emmanuel. (2001), *Income Inequality in the United States. 1913-1998,* NBER Working Paper Series, Working Paper 8467.

[50]   Saez, Emmanuel & Zucman, Gabriel. (2014). *Wealth Inequality in the United States since 1913: Evidence From Capitalized Income Data,* NBER Working Paper Series, Working Paper 20625, 2014.

[51]   World Inequality Data Base. (n.d.). *Income & Wealth Inequality, USA, 1913-2014.* Retrieved from *https://wid.world/country/usa/.*

[52]   Barchart. (2019, October 18). Retrieved from   *www.barchart.com/stocks/quotes/$DOWI/interactive-chart.*

[53]   Amadeo, Kimberly. (2019, July 11). *U.S. Budget Deficit by Year Compared to GDP, Debt Increase, and Events.* The Balance. Retrieved from *www.thebalance.com/us-deficit-by-year-3306306.*

CHAPTER 10 The Expansion of Democratic Capitalism

[54]   Piketty, Thomas & Saez, Emmanuel. (2001), *Income Inequality in the United States. 1913-1998,* NBER Working Paper Series, Working Paper 8467.

[55]   Saez, Emmanuel & Zucman, Gabriel. (2014). *Wealth Inequality in the United States since 1913: Evidence From Capitalized Income Data,* NBER Working Paper Series, Working Paper 20625, 2014.

[56]   World Inequality Data Base. (n.d.). *Income & Wealth Inequality, USA, 1913-2014.* Retrieved from *https://wid.world/country/usa/.*

[57]   Tax Foundation. (2013, October 17). *U.S. Federal Individual Income Tax Rates History, 1862-2013 (Nominal and Inflation-Adjusted Brackets.* Retrieved from https://taxfoundation.org/us-federal-individual-income-tax-rates-history-1913-2013-nominal-and-inflation-adjusted-brackets/.

[58]   Woods, Randall B, (2016). *Prisoners of Hope.* New York, New York. Basic Books.

[59]   History.com. (2018, August 28). *Great Society.* Retrieved from *https://www.history.com/topics/1960s/great-society.*

60 Amadeo, Kimberly. (2019, October 2). *Unemployment Rate by Year Since 1929 Compared to Inflation and GDP.* the balance. Retrieved from *www.thebalance. com/unemployment-rate-by-year-3305506.*

61 Wolters Kluwer (n.d.) *Historical Look at Capital Gains Rate.* Retrieved from www.taxna.wolterskluwer.com/whole-ball-of-tax-2019/ historical-capital-gain.

62 ProCon.Ogr. (2018, May 21). *Federal Corporate Income Tax Rates.* Retrieved from *https://corporatetax.procon.org/federal-corporate-income-tax-rates/.*

63 Tax Foundation. (2013, October 17). *U.S. Federal Individual Income Tax Rates History, 1862-2013 (Nominal and Inflation-Adjusted Brackets.* Retrieved from https://taxfoundation.org/us-federal-individual-income-tax-rates-histo- ry-1913-2013-nominal-and-inflation-adjusted-brackets/.

64 Piketty, Thomas & Saez, Emmanuel. (2001), *Income Inequality in the United States. 1913-1998,* NBER Working Paper Series, Working Paper 8467.

65 Saez, Emmanuel & Zucman, Gabriel. (2014). *Wealth Inequality in the United States since 1913: Evidence from Capitalized Income Data,* NBER Working Paper Series, Working Paper 20625, 2014.

66 World Inequality Data Base. (n.d.). *Income & Wealth Inequality, USA, 1913- 2014.* Retrieved from *https://wid.world/country/usa/.*

CHAPTER 11 The Rebirth of Oligarchic Capitalism

67 Macrotrends. (n.d.) *Crude Oil – 70 Year Historical Chart.* Retrieved from *www.macrotrends.net/1369/crude-oil-price-history-chart.*

68 Graefe, Laurel. (2013, November 22). *Oil Shock of 1978-79.* Federal Reserve History. Retrieved from *www.federalreservehistory.org/essays/ oil_shock_of_1978_79.*

69 Macrotrends. (n.d.) *Crude Oil – 70 Year Historical Chart.* Retrieved from *www.macrotrends.net/1369/crude-oil-price-history-chart.*

70 Amadeo, Kimberly. (2019, October 2). *Unemployment Rate by Year Since 1929 Compared to Inflation and GDP.* the balance. Retrieved from *www.thebalance. com/unemployment-rate-by-year-3305506.*

71 Tax Foundation. (2013, October 17). *U.S. Federal Individual Income Tax Rates History, 1862-2013 (Nominal and Inflation-Adjusted Brackets.* Retrieved from https://taxfoundation.org/us-federal-individual-income-tax-rates-histo- ry-1913-2013-nominal-and-inflation-adjusted-brackets/.

72 U.S. Department of Treasury, Internal Revenue Service, U.S Department of Commerce, Bureau of Economic Analysis. (2004, January 16). *History of Estate Filing Requirements and Tax Rates, 1916-1948,* U.S. Dept of Treasury, Internal Revenue Service, U.S. Dept of Commerce, Bureau of Economic Analysis. Retrieved from www.heritage.org/taxes/report/ estate-taxes-historical-perspective.

[73] Tax Foundation. (2014, February 4). *Federal Estate and Gift Tax Rates, Exemptions, an Exclusions, 1916-2014.* Retrieved from https://taxfoundation. org/federal-estate-and-gift-tax-rates-exemptions-and-exclusions-1916-2014.

[74] Saez, Emmanuel & Zucman, Gabriel. (2014). *Wealth Inequality in the United States since 1913: Evidence From Capitalized Income Data,* NBER Working Paper Series, Working Paper 20625, 2014.

[75] World Inequality Data Base. (n.d.). *Income & Wealth Inequality, USA, 1913-2014.* Retrieved from *https://wid.world/country/usa/.*

[76] Barchart. (2019, October 18). Retrieved from *www.barchart.com/stocks/ quotes/$DOWI/interactive-chart.*

[77] Piketty, Thomas & Saez, Emmanuel. (2001), *Income Inequality in the United States. 1913-1998,* NBER Working Paper Series, Working Paper 8467.

[78] Tax Foundation. (2013, October 17). *U.S. Federal Individual Income Tax Rates History, 1862-2013 (Nominal and Inflation-Adjusted Brackets.* Retrieved from *https://taxfoundation.org/us-federal-individual-income-tax-rates-history-1913-2013-nominal-and-inflation-adjusted-brackets/.*

[79] U.S. Department of Treasury, Internal Revenue Service, U.S Department of Commerce, Bureau of Economic Analysis. (2004, January 16). *History of Estate Filing Requirements and Tax Rates, 1916-1948,* U.S. Dept of Treasury, Internal Revenue Service, U.S. Dept of Commerce, Bureau of Economic Analysis. Retrieved from www.heritage.org/taxes/report/ estate-taxes-historical-perspective.

[80] Wolters Kluwer (n.d.) *Historical Look at Capital Gains Rate.* Retrieved from *www.taxna.wolterskluwer.com/whole-ball-of-tax-2019/historical-capital-gain.*

[81] ProCon.Ogr. (2018, May 21). *Federal Corporate Income Tax Rates.* Retrieved from *https://corporatetax.procon.org/federal-corporate-income-tax-rates/.*

[82] Tax Foundation. (2014, February 4). *Federal Estate and Gift Tax Rates, Exemptions, an Exclusions, 1916-2014.* Retrieved from https://taxfoundation. org/federal-estate-and-gift-tax-rates-exemptions-and-exclusions-1916-2014.

[83] Amadeo, Kimberly. (2019, July 11). *U.S. Budget Deficit by Year Compared to GDP, Debt Increase, and Events.* The Balance. Retrieved from *www.thebalance. com/us-deficit-by-year-3306306.*

[84] New York Times. (1976, Feb 15).'*Welfare Queen' Becomes Issue in Reagan Campaign.* Retrieved from *www.nytimes.com/1976/02/15/archives/welfare-queen-becomes-issue-in-reagan-campaign-hitting-a-nerve-now.html.*

[85] Ibid.

[86] Abramovitz, Mimi & Hopkins, Tom. (1983, November). *Reaganomics and the Welfare State.* The Journal of Sociology & Social Welfare.

[87] Campbell, Livie. (2017, September 13). *Here's what happened when Reagan went after healthcare programs. It's not good.* Timeline. Retrieved from *www.timeline. com/reagan-trump-healthcare-cuts-8cf64aa242eb.*

88 Rubin, Beth, Wright, James, & Devine, Joel. (1992, March). *Unhousing the Urban Poor: The Reagan Legacy*. The Journal of Sociology & Social Welfare.

89 Fredrickson, Lief, et. al, (2018, April) *History of US Presidential Assaults on Modern Environmental Health Protection*. American Journal of Public Health. Retrieved from *www.ncbi.nlm.nih.gov/pmc/articles/PMC5922215/*.

90 UPI Archives. (1984, August 2). *Anne Gorsuch Burford: Ex-EPA administrator*. Retrieved from *www.upi.com/Archives/1984/08/02/ Anne-Gorsuch-Burford-Ex-EPA-administrator/8223460267200/*.

91 Amadeo, Kimberly. (2019, October 2). *Unemployment Rate by Year Since 1929 Compared to Inflation and GDP*. the balance. Retrieved from *www.thebalance. com/unemployment-rate-by-year-3305506*.

92 Macrotrends. (n.d.). *Federal Funds Rate – 62 Year Historical Chart*. Retrieved from *www.macrotrends.net/2015/fed-funds-rate-historical-chart*.

93 Macrotrends. (n.d.) *Crude Oil – 70 Year Historical Chart*. Retrieved from *www.macrotrends.net/1369/crude-oil-price-history-chart*.

94 Amadeo, Kimberly. (2019, July 11). *U.S. Budget Deficit by Year Compared to GDP, Debt Increase, and Events*. The Balance. Retrieved from *www.thebalance. com/us-deficit-by-year-3306306*.

95 Saez, Emmanuel & Zucman, Gabriel. (2014). *Wealth Inequality in the United States since 1913: Evidence from Capitalized Income Data*, NBER Working Paper Series, Working Paper 20625, 2014.

96 World Inequality Data Base. (n.d.). *Income & Wealth Inequality, USA, 1913-2014*. Retrieved from *https://wid.world/country/usa/*.

97 Piketty, Thomas & Saez, Emmanuel. (2001), *Income Inequality in the United States. 1913-1998*, NBER Working Paper Series, Working Paper 8467.

CHAPTER 12 Oligarchic Capitalism in the Post-Reagan Era

98 Amadeo, Kimberly. (2019, October 2). *Unemployment Rate by Year Since 1929 Compared to Inflation and GDP*. the balance. Retrieved from *www.thebalance. com/unemployment-rate-by-year-3305506*.

99 Amadeo, Kimberly. (2019, July 11). *U.S. Budget Deficit by Year Compared to GDP, Debt Increase, and Events*. The Balance. Retrieved from *www.thebalance. com/us-deficit-by-year-3306306*.

100 Tax Foundation. (2013, October 17). *U.S. Federal Individual Income Tax Rates History, 1862-2013 (Nominal and Inflation-Adjusted Brackets*. Retrieved from https://taxfoundation.org/us-federal-individual-income-tax-rates-history-1913-2013-nominal-and-inflation-adjusted-brackets/.

101 Ibid.

102 Amadeo, Kimberly. (2019, July 11). *U.S. Budget Deficit by Year Compared to GDP, Debt Increase, and Events*. The Balance. Retrieved from *www.thebalance. com/us-deficit-by-year-3306306*.

[103]   Amadeo, Kimberly. (2019, October 2). *Unemployment Rate by Year Since 1929 Compared to Inflation and GDP.* the balance. Retrieved from *www.thebalance. com/unemployment-rate-by-year-3305506.*

[104]   Ibid.

[105]   INEQUALITY.ORG. (n.d.). *Income Inequality.* Retrieved from *https:// inequality.org/facts/income-inequality/.*

[106]   World Inequality Data Base. (n.d.). *Income Inequality USA.* Retrieved from *www.wid.world/country/usa/.*

[107]   Saez, Emmanuel & Zucman, Gabriel. (2014). *Wealth Inequality in the United States since 1913: Evidence From Capitalized Income Data,* NBER Working Paper Series, Working Paper 20625, 2014.

[108]   World Inequality Data Base. (n.d.). *Income & Wealth Inequality, USA, 1913- 2014.* Retrieved from *https://wid.world/country/usa/.*

[109]   Veghte, Benjamin. (2015, August 13). *Social Security's Past, Present, and Future.* National Academy of Social Insurance. Retrieved from *www.nasi.org/ discuss/2015/08/social-security%E2%80%99s-past-present-future.*

[110]   Glass, Andrew. (2018, May 2). *President George W. Bush pursues Social Security reform, May 2, 2001.* Politico. Retrieved from *www.politico.com/story/2018/05/02/ president-george-w-bush-pursues-social-security-reform-may-2-2001-559632.*

[111]   International Monetary Fund. (n.d). *Household debt, loans and debt securities.* Retrieved from *www.imf.org/external/datamapper/HH_LS@GDD/CAN/GBR/ USA/DEU/ITA/FRA/JPN.*

[112]   Tax Foundation. (2013, October 17). *U.S. Federal Individual Income Tax Rates History, 1862-2013 (Nominal and Inflation-Adjusted Brackets.* Retrieved from https://taxfoundation.org/us-federal-individual-income-tax-rates-histo- ry-1913-2013-nominal-and-inflation-adjusted-brackets/.

[113]   Wolters Kluwer (n.d.) *Historical Look at Capital Gains Rate.* Retrieved from www.taxna.wolterskluwer.com/whole-ball-of-tax-2019/ historical-capital-gain.

[114]   U.S. Department of Treasury, Internal Revenue Service, U.S Department of Commerce, Bureau of Economic Analysis. (2004, January 16). *History of Estate Filing Requirements and Tax Rates, 1916-1948,* U.S. Dept of Treasury, Internal Revenue Service, U.S. Dept of Commerce, Bureau of Economic Analysis. Retrieved from www.heritage.org/taxes/report/ estate-taxes-historical-perspective.

[115]   Tax Foundation. (2014, February 4*). Federal Estate and Gift Tax Rates, Exemptions, an Exclusions, 1916-2014.* Retrieved from https://taxfoundation. org/federal-estate-and-gift-tax-rates-exemptions-and-exclusions-1916-2014.

[116]   Amadeo, Kimberly. (2019, July 11). *U.S. Budget Deficit by Year Compared to GDP, Debt Increase, and Events.* The Balance. Retrieved from *www.thebalance. com/us-deficit-by-year-3306306.*

117　Saez, Emmanuel & Zucman, Gabriel. (2014). *Wealth Inequality in the United States since 1913: Evidence From Capitalized Income Data,* NBER Working Paper Series, Working Paper 20625, 2014.

118　World Inequality Data Base. (n.d.). *Income & Wealth Inequality, USA, 1913-2014.* Retrieved from *https://wid.world/country/usa/.*

119　INEQUALITY.ORG. (n.d.). *Income Inequality.* Retrieved from *https:// inequality.org/facts/income-inequality/*

120　World Inequality Data Base. (n.d.). *Income Inequality USA.* Retrieved from *www.wid.world/country/usa/.*

121　Amadeo, Kimberly. (2019, August 8). *Credit Default Swaps with their Pros, Cons, and Examples.* the balance. Retrieve from *www.thebalance.com/ credit-default-swaps-pros-cons-crises-examples-3305920.*

122　United States Census Bureau. (n.d.). *Census of Housing: Historical Census of Housing Tables Home Values.* Retrieved from *www.census.gov/hhes/www/housing/ census/historic/values.html.*

123　Barchart. (2019, October 18). Retrieved from *www.barchart.com/stocks/ quotes/$DOWI/interactive-chart.*

124　Christie, Les. (2009, February 12). *Home prices in record plunge.* CNN Money. Retrieved from *money.cnn.com/2009/02/12/real_estate/Latest_median_prices/.*

125　Christie, Les. (2008, December 30). *Home prices post record 18% drop.* CNN Money. Retrieved from *https://money.cnn.com/2008/12/30/real_estate/October_ Case_Shiller/index.htm.*

126　S & P Indices. (2010, January). *S&P/Case-Shiller Home Price Indices, 2009, A Year in Review.* Retrieved from *www.cmegroup.com/trading/real-estate/files/ SP-CSI-2009-Year-in-Review.pdf.*

127　Ibid.

128　Amadeo, Kimberly. (2019, June 25). *TARP Bailout Program.* the balance. Retrieved from *www.thebalance.com/tarp-bailout-program-3305895.*

129　Amadeo, Kimberly. (2019, July 30). *ARRA, Its Details, With Pros and Cons.* the balance. Retrieved from *www.thebalance.com/arra-details-3306299.*

130　Amadeo, Kimberly. (2019, July 11). *U.S. Budget Deficit by Year Compared to GDP, Debt Increase, and Events.* The Balance. Retrieved from *www.thebalance. com/us-deficit-by-year-3306306.*

131　Amadeo, Kimberly. (2019, October 2). *Unemployment Rate by Year Since 1929 Compared to Inflation and GDP.* the balance. Retrieved from *www.thebalance. com/unemployment-rate-by-year-3305506.*

132　Tax Foundation. (2013, October 17). *U.S. Federal Individual Income Tax Rates History, 1862-2013 (Nominal and Inflation-Adjusted Brackets.* Retrieved from https://taxfoundation.org/us-federal-individual-income-tax-rates-history-1913-2013-nominal-and-inflation-adjusted-brackets/.

[133] U.S. Department of Treasury, Internal Revenue Service, U.S Department of Commerce, Bureau of Economic Analysis. (2004, January 16). *History of Estate Filing Requirements and Tax Rates, 1916-1948,* U.S. Dept of Treasury, Internal Revenue Service, U.S. Dept of Commerce, Bureau of Economic Analysis. Retrieved from www.heritage.org/taxes/report/estate–taxes–historical–perspective.

[134] Tax Foundation. (2014, February 4*). Federal Estate and Gift Tax Rates, Exemptions, an Exclusions, 1916-2014.* Retrieved from https://taxfoundation.org/federal-estate-and-gift-tax-rates-exemptions-and-exclusions-1916-2014.

[135] Wolters Kluwer (n.d.) *Historical Look at Capital Gains Rate.* Retrieved from www.taxna.wolterskluwer.com/whole-ball-of-tax-2019/historical-capital-gain.

[136] INEQUALITY.ORG. (n.d.). *Income Inequality.* Retrieved from *https://inequality.org/facts/income-inequality/.*

[137] World Inequality Data Base. (n.d.). *Income Inequality USA.* Retrieved from *www.wid.world/country/usa/.*

[138] Baum, Rick. (2018). *Inequality Was Increasing Before Trump.* New Politics. Retrieved from *https://newpol.org/issue_post/inequality-was-increasing-trump/.*

[139] Saez, Emmanuel & Zucman, Gabriel. (2014). *Wealth Inequality in the United States since 1913: Evidence From Capitalized Income Data,* NBER Working Paper Series, Working Paper 20625, 2014.

[140] World Inequality Data Base. (n.d.). *Income & Wealth Inequality, USA, 1913-2014.* Retrieved from *https://wid.world/country/usa/.*

[141] Tax Foundation. (2013, October 17). *U.S. Federal Individual Income Tax Rates History, 1862-2013 (Nominal and Inflation-Adjusted Brackets.* Retrieved from https://taxfoundation.org/us-federal-individual-income-tax-rates-history-1913-2013-nominal-and-inflation-adjusted-brackets/.

[142] ProCon.Ogr. (2018, May 21). *Federal Corporate Income Tax Rates.* Retrieved from *https://corporatetax.procon.org/federal-corporate-income-tax-rates/.*

[143] Amadeo, Kimberly. (2019, July 11). *U.S. Budget Deficit by Year Compared to GDP, Debt Increase, and Events.* The Balance. Retrieved from *www.thebalance.com/us-deficit-by-year-3306306.*

[144] usgovernmentspending.com. (2019, October 26). *What is the Deficit as Percent of GDP?* Retrieved from *www.usgovernmentdebt.us/federal_deficit_percent_gdp.*

[145] Perry, Mark. (2019, September 11). *Explaining US income inequality by household demographics, 2018 update.* AEIdeas. Retrieved from *www.aei.org/carpe-diem/explaining-us-income-inequality-by-household-demographics-2018-update/.*

[146] Egan, Matt. (2019, August 20). *US tariffs on China could cost American households $1,000 per year, JPMorgan says.* CNN Business. Retrieved from *www.cnn.com/2019/08/20/business/tariffs-cost-trade-war-consumers/index.html.*

[147] Layne, Rachel. (2019, September 12). *Trump trade war with China has cost 300,000 U.S. jobs, Moody's estimates.* CBS New, Retrieved from *www.cbsnews.com/news/trumps-trade-war-squashed-an-estimated-300000-jobs-so-far-moodys-estimates/*.

[148] Frank, Robert and Cook, Phillip, *The Winner-Take-All Society,* (Martin Kessler Books, 1995).

CHAPTER 14 Where Do We Go From Here?

[149] Joyce, Kathleen. (2019, June 29). *These high-profile figures will not be leaving a lot of their fortunes to their children.* Fox Business. Retrieved from *www.foxbusiness.com/business-leaders/these-high-profile-figures-will-not-be-leaving-a-lot-of-their-fortunes-to-their-children.*

CHAPTER 15 Policy Prescriptions

[150] Irwin, Neil. (2014, September 26). *The Benefits of Economic Expansions Are Increasingly Going to the Richest Americans.* The New York Times. Retrieved from https://www.nytimes.com/2014/09/27/upshot/the-benefits-of-economic-expansions-are-increasingly-going-to-the-richest-americans.html

[151] Rugaber, Christopher. (2019, July 2). *Why the wealth gap has grown despite a record economic expansion.* Los Angeles Times. Retrieved from https://www.latimes.com/business/la-fi-wealth-gap-grows-20190702-story.html.

[152] Pressman, Steven. (2019, July 4). *The US economy likely just entered its longest ever expansion-here's who benefitting in 3 charts.* The Colorado Independent. Retrieved from https://www.coloradoindependent.com/2019/07/04/us-economy-expansion-income-wealth-inequality/.

[153] Frankel, Matthew. (2019, January 28). *Elizabeth Warren's Wealth Tax: Here's What You Need to Know.* The Motley Fool. Retrieved from *www.fool.c0m/taxes/22019/01/28/elizabeth-warren-wealth-tax-heres-what-you-need-t.aspx.*

[154] Ibid.

[155] Goss, Stephen C. (2010, Nov. 3). *The Future Financial Status of the Social Security Program.* Social Security Office. Retrieved from *www.ssa.gov/policy/docs/ssb/v70n3/v70n3p111.html.*

[156] PROCON.ORG. (2017, April 20). *Median Incomes v. Average College Tuition Rates, 1971-2016.* Retrieved from www.college-education.procon.org/median-incomes-v-average-college-tuition-rates-1971-2016/.

[157] Lederman, Doug. (2013, March 27). *State Budgeters' View of Higher Ed.* Inside Higher Ed. Retrieved from www.insidehighered.com/news/2013/03/27/state-state-funding-higher-education.

[158] CONGRESS.GOV (n.d.). *H.R 1911 – Bipartisan Student Loan Certainty Act of 2013.* Retrieved from www.congress.gov/bill/113th-congress/house-bill/1911.

[159] 20 Something Finance. (2019, March 17). *Earned Income Tax Credit Basics (2018 & 2019).* Retrieved from www.*20somethingfinance.com/ earned-income-tax-credit/.*

[160] Resnikoff, Ned. (2014, April 14). *Walmart benefits from billions in government subsidies: Study.* MSNBC. Retrieved from www. http://www.msnbc.com/ msnbc/walmart-government-subsidies-study#51652.

BIBLIOGRAPHY

20 Something Finance. (2019, March 17). *Earned Income Tax Credit Basics (2018 & 2019).* Retrieved from www.*20somethingfinance. com/earned-income-tax-credit/.*

Abramovitz, Mimi & Hopkins, Tom. (1983, November). *Reaganomics and the Welfare State.* The Journal of Sociology & Social Welfare.

Amadeo, Kimberly. (2019, June 25). *TARP Bailout Program.* the balance. Retrieved from *www.thebalance.com/ tarp-bailout-program-3305895.*

Amadeo, Kimberly. (2019, July 11). *U.S. Budget Deficit by Year Compared to GDP, Debt Increase, and Events.* the balance. Retrieved from *www.thebalance.com/us-deficit-by-year-3306306.*

Amadeo, Kimberly. (2019, July 30). *ARRA, Its Details, With Pros and Cons.* the balance. Retrieved from *www.thebalance.com/ arra-details-3306299.*

Amadeo, Kimberly. (2019, August 01). *U.S. GDP by Year Compared to Recessions and Events.* the balance. Retrieved from *www. thebalance.com/us-gdp-by-year-3305543.*

Amadeo, Kimberly. (2019, August 8). *Credit Default Swaps with their Pros, Cons, and Examples.* the balance. Retrieve from *www. thebalance.com/credit-default-swaps-pros-cons-crises-examples-3305920.*

Amadeo, Kimberly. (2019, October 2). *Unemployment Rate by Year Since 1929 Compared to Inflation and GDP.* the balance. Retrieved from *www.thebalance.com/unemployment-rate-by-year-3305506.*

AZ Quotes (n.d.). *Donald Trump Quotes About Trade.* (n.d.). Retrieved from *www.azquotes.com/author/14823-Donald_Trump/tag/trade.*

AZ Quotes. (n.d.). *Ronald Reagan.* Retrieved from *https://www.azquotes.com/quote/558788.*

Baker, Dean. (2014, February 20). *Why the stimulus couldn't do it.* CNN. Retrieved from *www.cnn.com/2014/02/20/opinion/baker-stimulus-anniversary/index.html.*

Barchart. (2019, October 18). Retrieved from *www.barchart.com/stocks/quotes/$DOWI/interactive-chart.*

Baum, Rick. (2018). *Inequality Was Increasing Before Trump.* New Politics. Retrieved from *https://newpol.org/issue_post/inequality-was-increasing-trump/.*

Blackford, Mansel & Kerr, K. Austin. (1994). *Business Enterprise in American History.* Third Edition. Boston, MA. Houghton Mifflin Company.

Brainy Quotes. (n.d.). *Ronald Reagan Quotes.* Retrieved from *https://www.brainyquote.com/quotes/ronald_reagan_382204.*

Bullinger, Jake. (2017, January 2). *Déjà vu at Interior and the EPA.* Outside. Retrieved from *www.outsideonline.com/2271306/zinke-and-pruitt-mirror-controversial-reagan-picks.*

Campbell, Livie. (2017, September 13). *Here's what happened when Reagan went after healthcare programs. It's not good.* Timeline. Retrieved from *www.timeline.com/reagan-trump-healthcare-cuts-8cf64aa242eb.*

Christie, Les. (2008, December 30). *Home prices post record 18% drop.* CNN Money. Retrieved from *https://money.cnn.com/2008/12/30/real_estate/October_Case_Shiller/index.htm.*

Christie, Les. (2009, February 12). *Home prices in record plunge.* CNN Money. Retrieved from *money.cnn.com/2009/02/12/real_estate/Latest_median_prices/.*

Collender, Stan. (2016, November 27). *Republicans Expose Themselves As Deficit Frauds.* Retrieved from *www.forbes.com/sites/stancollender/2016/11/27/republicans-expose-themselves-as-deficit-frauds/#5af913454dfe.*

Collins, Paul. (2013). *The Birth of the West.* New York, NY: Public Affairs, Perseus Books Group.

CONGRESS.GOV (n.d.). *H.R.1911 – Bipartisan Student Loan Certainty Act of 2013.* Retrieved from *www.congress.gov/ bill/113th-congress/house-bill/1911.*

DeLong, Brad. (2010, January 20). *Stimulus Too Small.* Wall Street Journal. Retrieved from *https://economistsview.typepad.com/ economistsview/2010/01/stimulus-too-small.html.*

Egan, Matt. (2019, August 20). *US tariffs on China could cost American households $1,000 per year, JPMorgan says.* CNN Business. Retrieved from *www.cnn.com/2019/08/20/business/tariffs-cost-trade- war-consumers/index.html.*

EH.net. (n.d.). *History of U.S. Telegraph Industry.* Economic History Association. Retrieved from *www.eh.net/encyclopedia/ history-of-the-u-s-telegraph-industry/.*

Elving, Ron. (2018, March 25). *Remembering 1968: LBJ Surprises Nation With Announcement He Won't Seek Re-Election.* NPR. Retrieved from *www.npr.org/2018/03/25/596805375/ president-johnson-made-a-bombshell-announcement-50-years-ago.*

Frank, Robert H. and Cook, Phillip J. (1995). *The Winner-Take-All Society.* New York, NY: The Free Press.

Frankel, Matthew. (2019, January 28). *Elizabeth Warren's Wealth Tax: Here's What You Need to Know.* The Motley Fool. Retrieved from *www.fool.c0m/taxes/22019/01/28/elizabeth-warren-wealth-tax- heres-what-you-need-t.aspx.*

Fredrickson, Lief, et. al, (2018, April) *History of US Presidential Assaults on Modern Environmental Heath Protection.* American Journal of Public Health. Retrieved from *www.ncbi.nlm.nih.gov/pmc/articles/ PMC5922215/.*

Garber, Julie. (n.d.). *Federal Estate Tax Exemptions 1997 through 2019.* The Balance. Retrieved from *www.thebalance.com/ exemption-from-federal-estate-taxes-3505630.*

Glass, Andrew. (2018, May 2). *President George W. Bush pursues Social Security reform, May 2, 2001.* Politico. Retrieved from *www.politico.com/story/2018/05/02/president-george-w-bush-pursues-social-security-reform-may-2-2001-559632.*

Goss, Stephen C. (2010, Nov. 3). *The Future Financial Status of the Social Security Program.* Social Security Office. Retrieved from *www.ssa.gov/policy/docs/ssb/v70n3/v70n3p111.html.*

Graefe, Laurel. (2013, November 22). *Oil Shock of 1978-79.* Federal Reserve History. Retrieved from *www.federalreservehistory.org/essays/oil_shock_of_1978_79.*

Greshko, Michael, et. al. (2019, May 3). *A running list of how President Trump is changing environmental policy.* National Geographic. Retrieved from *www.nationalgeographic.com/news/2017/03/how-trump-is-changing-science-environment/.*

Grim, Ryan. (2011, May 25). *Why The Stimulus Is Too Small.* HUFFPOST. Retrieved from *www.huffpost.com/entry/is-stimulus-too-small_n_165076.*

Heathcote, Jonathon; Violante, Gianluca; Perri, Fabrizio. (2010, February 2). *Inequality in times of Crisis: Lessons from the past and a first look at the current recession.* CEPR Policy Portal. Retrieved from https://voxeu.org/article/economic-inequality-during-recessions.

History.com. (2018, August 28). *Great Society.* Retrieved from *https://www.history.com/topics/1960s/great-society*.

History.com (2018, August 21). *Hoover Dam.* Retrieved from https://www.history.com/topics/great-depression/hoover-dam.

History.com (2019, June 10). *TVA.* Retrieved from https://www.history.com/topics/great-depression/history-of-the-tva.

History.com. (2019, June 10). *Works Progress Administration (WPA).* Retrieved from https://www.history.com/topics/great-depression/works-progress-administration.

Horsey, David. (2014, February 20). *Economic stimulus was too small from the start, thanks to GOP.* Los Angeles Times. Retrieved from *www.latimes.com/opinion/topoftheticket/la-na-tt-economic-stimulus-20140219-story.html.*

Hunt, E.K. (1986). *Property and Prophets, Fifth Edition.* New York, NY: Harper & Row Publishers.

INEQUALITY.ORG. (n.d.). *Income Inequality.* Retrieved from *https://inequality.org/facts/income-inequality/.*

INEQUALITY.ORG. (n.d.). *Wealth Inequality in the United States.* Retrieved from *https://inequality.org/facts/wealth-inequality/*

International Monetary Fund. (n.d.). *Household debt, loans and debt securities.* Retrieved from *www.imf.org/external/datamapper/HH_LS@GDD/CAN/GBR/USA/DEU/ITA/FRA/JPN.*

Irwin, Neil. (2014, September 26). *The Benefits of Economic Expansions Are Increasingly Going to the Richest Americans.* The New York Times. Retrieved from https://www.nytime.com/2014/09/27/upshot/the-benefits-of-economic-expansions-are-increasingly-going-to-the-richest-americans.html.

Joyce, Kathleen. (2019, June 29). *These high-profile figures will not be leaving a lot of their fortunes to their children.* Fox Business. Retrieved from *www.foxbusiness.com/business-leaders/these-high-profile-figures-will-not-be-leaving-a-lot-of-their-fortunes-to-their-children.*

Keynes, John Maynard. (2000). *A Tract on Monetary Reform.* Amherst, New York. Prometheus Books. (Original work published in 1923).

Keynes, John Maynard. (1964). *The General Theory of Employment, Interest, and Money.* London, England: MacMillan & Co., LTD. (Original work published in 1936).

knoema. (n.d.*) World GDP Ranking 2018 Country by Country Data and Chart.* Retrieved from *https://knoema.com/nwnfkne/world-gdp-ranking-2018-gdp-by-country-data-and-charts.*

Krueger, Dirk; Mitman, Kurt; Perri, Fabrizio. (2016, July). *On the Distribution of the Welfare Losses of Large Recessions.* NBER Working Paper Series. Retrieved from https://nber.org/papers/w22458.pdf.

Kuttner, Robert. (2018, October 7). *The Return of Keynes.* The American Prospect. Retrieved from *https://prospect.org/departments/return-keynes/.*

Layne, Rachel. (2019, September 12). *Trump trade war with China has cost 300,000 U.S. jobs, Moody's estimates.* CBS New, Retrieved from *www.cbsnews.com/news/trumps-trade-war-squashed-an-estimated-300000-jobs-so-far-moodys-estimates/.*

Lederman, Doug. (2013, March 27). *State Budgeters' View of Higher Ed.* Inside Higher Ed. Retrieved from www.insidehighered.com/news/2013/03/27/state-state-funding-higher-education.

Macrotrends. (n.d.) *Crude Oil – 70 Year Historical Chart.* Retrieved from *www.macrotrends.net/1369/crude-oil-price-history-chart.*

Macrotrends. (n.d.). *Federal Funds Rate – 62 Year Historical Chart.* Retrieved from *www.macrotrends.net/2015/fed-funds-rate-historical-chart.*

Marx, Karl. (1990). *Capital.* Middlesex England: Penguin Books. (Original work published in 1867).

McClung, Christian, *The Great Depression in Washington State; Grand Coulee Dam.* Civil Rights and Labor History Consortium/University of Washington. Retrieved from *https://depts.washington.edu/depress/grand_coulee.shtml*.

Money Chimp. (n.d.). *Federal Tax Brackets.* Retrieved from http://www.moneychimp.com/features/tax_brackets.htm.

Murse, Tom. (2019, July 3). *History of the US Federal Budget Deficit.* ThoughtCo. Retrieved from *www.thoughtco.com/history-of-us-federal-budget-deficit-3321439.*

National Park Service. (n.d.). *Lyndon B. Johnson and the Environment.*
Retrieved from https://www.nps.gov/lyjo/planyourvisit/upload/
EnvironmentCS2.pdf.

New York Times. (1976, Feb 15).*'Welfare Queen' Becomes Issue in
Reagan Campaign.* Retrieved from *www.nytimes.com/1976/02/15/
archives/welfare-queen-becomes-issue-in-reagan-campaign-hitting-a-
nerve-now.html.*

O'Donnell, Edward T. (2019, January 31). *Are We Living in Gilded
Age 2.0?* History. Retrieved from *www.history.com/news/
second-gilded-age-income-inequality.*

Perri, Fabrizio and Steinberg, Joseph B. (2012, June 15).
Inequality and Redistribution during the Great Recession.
Federal Reserve Bank of Minneapolis. Retrieved
from https://www.minneapolisfed.org/article/2012/
inequality-and-redistribution-during-the-great-recession.

Perry, Mark. (2019, September 11). *Explaining US income inequality by
household demographics, 2018 update.* AEIdeas. Retrieved from
*www.aei.org/carpe-diem/explaining-us-income-inequality-by-household-
demographics-2018-update/.*

Pew Research Center. (2012, August 22). *The Lost Decade of the Middle
Class.* Retrieved from *www.pewsocialtrends.org/2012/08/22/
the-lost-decade-of-the-middle-class/.*

Piketty, Thomas. (2014), *Capital in the Twenty-First Century.*
Cambridge, Massachusetts: The Belknap Press of Harvard
University Press.

Piketty, Thomas & Saez, Emmanuel. (2001). *Income Inequality in
the United States. 1913-1998,* NBER Working Paper Series,
Working Paper 8467.

Pippert, Wesley G. (1981, March 10). *Reagan cuts social programs.* UPI
Archives. Retrieved from *www.upi.com/Archives/1981/03/10/
Reagan-cuts-social-programs/6509353048400/.*

Pressman, Steven. (2019, July 4). *The US economy likely just entered its longest ever expansion-here's who's benefitting in 3 charts.* The Colorado Independent. Retrieved from https://www.coloradoindependent.com/2019/07/04/us-economy-expansion-income-wealth-inequality/.

ProCon.Org. (2018, May 21). *Federal Corporate Income Tax Rates.* Retrieved from https://corporatetax.procon.org/federal-corporate-income-tax-rates/.

Pusateri, C. Joseph. (1988). *A History of American Business.* Arlington Heights, IL. Harlan Davidson, Inc.

Reich. Robert B. (2015). *Saving Capitalism.* New York, NY: Vintage Books, Penguin Random House.

Resnikoff, Ned. (2014, April 14). *Walmart benefits from billions in government subsidies:* Study. MSNBC. Retrieved from *www.msnbc.com/msnbc/walmart-government-subsidies-study#51652.*

Reuters. (2019, September 5). *Timeline: Key dates in the U.S.-China trade war.* Retrieved from *www.reuters.com/article/us-usa-trade-china-timeline/timeline-key-dates-in-the-us-china-trade-war-idUSKCN1VQ24Y.*

Ricardo, David. (2004). *The Principles of Political Economy and Taxation.* New York, NY: Dover Publications. (Original work published in 1817).

Rosenberg, Jennifer. (2019, May 9). *32 Ronald Reagan Quotes You Should Know.* ThoughtCo. Retrieved from *www.thoughtco.com/ronald-reagan-quotes-you-should-know-1779926.*

Roser, Max. (n.d.). *Economic Growth.* Our World in Data. Retrieved from https://ourworldindata.org/economic-growth.

Rubin, Beth, Wright, James, & Devine, Joel. (1992, March). *Unhousing the Urban Poor: The Reagan Legacy.* The Journal of Sociology & Social Welfare.

Rugaber, Christopher. (2019, July 2). *Why the wealth gap has grown despite a record economic expansion.* Los Angeles Times. Retrieved from https://www.latimes.co/business/la-fi-wealth-gap-grows-20190702-story.html.

S & P Indices. (2010, January). *S&P/Case-Shiller Home Price Indices, 2009, A Year in Review.* Retrieved from *www.cmegroup.com/ trading/real-estate/files/SP-CSI-2009-Year-in-Review.pdf.*

Saez, Emmanuel & Zucman, Gabriel. (2014). *Wealth Inequality in the United States since 1913: Evidence from Capitalized Income Data.* NBER Working Paper Series, Working Paper 20625.

Smith, Adam. (1937). *The Wealth of Nations,* New York, NY: Modern Library. (Original work published in 1776).

Smith, Rob. (2018, April 18). *The World's Biggest Economies in 2018.* World Economic Forum. Retrieved from *www.weforum.org/ agenda/2018/04/the-worlds-biggest-economies-in-2018/.*

Statistic Times. (2019). *Gross World Product per Capita.* Retrieved from. *www.statisticstimes.com/economy/gross-world-product-capita.php.*

Stiglitz, Joseph E. (2019). *People, Power, and Profits.* New York, NY: W. W. Norton & Company.

Stone, Chad; Trisi, Danilo, Sherman, Arloc,; and Taylor, Roderick. (2018, December 18). *A Guide to Statistics on Historical Trends in Income Inequality.* Center on Budget and Policy Priorities. Retrieved from *www.cbpp.org/research/poverty-and-inequality/a-guide-to-statistics-on-historical-trends-in-income-inequality.*

Sumner, Scott. (n.d.). *How much did poverty rise under Reagan?* The Library of Economics and Liberty. Retrieved from *www.econlib. org/archives/2017/06/how_much_did_po.html.*

Tax Foundation. (2014, February 4*). Federal Estate and Gift Tax Rates, Exemptions, and Exclusions, 1916-2014.* Retrieved from *https://taxfoundation.org/ federal-estate-and-gift-tax-rates-exemptions-and-exclusions-1916-2014.*

Tax Foundation. (2013, October 17). *U.S. Federal Individual Income Tax Rates History, 1862-2013 (Nominal and Inflation-Adjusted Brackets.* Retrieved from https://taxfoundation.org/us-federal-individual-income-tax-rates-history-1913-2013-nominal-and-inflation-adjusted-brackets/.

Tax Policy Center, Urban Institute, & Brookings Institution. (2018). *Historical Highest Marginal Income Tax Rates.* Retrieved from *www.taxpolicycenter.org/statistics/historical-highest-marginal-income-tax-rates*.

Teaching American History. (n.d.). *Acceptance Speech at the Democratic Convention (1932).* Retrieved from https://teachingamericanhistory.org/library/document/acceptance-speech-at-the-democratic-convention-1932/.

Teaching American History. (n.d.). *Acceptance Speech at the Democratic National Convention (1936).* Retrieved from *https://teachingamericanhistory.org/library/document/acceptance-speech-at-the-democratic-national-convention-1936/*.

Teaching American History. (n.d.). *"Great Society Speech".* Retrieved from *teachingamericanhistory.org/library/document/great-society-speech/*.

The Balance (n.d.). *U.S. Corporate Income Tax Rate, Its History, and the Effective Rate.* Retrieved from *www.thebalace.com/corporate-income-tax-definition-history-effective-rate-3306024*.

The Guardian. (2001, March 29). *Bush kills global warming treaty.* Retrieved from *www.theguardian.com/environment/2001/mar/29/globalwarming.usnews*.

The Guardian. (2018, December 1). *'Read my lips. No new taxes' ; quotes from President George H. Bush.* Retrieved from *www.theguardian.com/us-news/2018/dec/01/read-my-lips-no-new-taxes-quotes-from-president-george-hw-bush*.

The Living New Deal. (n.d.). *Rural Electrification Act (1936).* Retrieved from https://livingnewdeal.org/glossary/rural-electrification-act-1936/.

The Living New Deal. (n.d.). *Rural Electrification Administration (REA) (1935).* Retrieved from https://livingnewdeal.org/glossary/rural-electrification-administration-rea-1935/.

The White House. (2002, June). *President Calls for Expanding Opportunities to Home Ownership.* Retrieved from *https://georgewbush-whitehouse.archives.gov/news/releases/2002/06/20020617-2.html.*

The White House. (2018, September 18). *Remarks by President Trump and President Duda of the Republic of Poland in Joint Press Conference.* The White House. Retrieved from *www.whitehouse.gov/briefings-statements/remarks-president-trump-president-duda-republic-poland-joint-press-conference/.*

TRADING ECONOMICS. (n.d.*). United States Corporate Profits.* Retrieved from *https://tradingeconomics.com/united-states/corporate-profits.*

United States Census Bureau. (n.d.). *Census of Housing: Historical Census of Housing Tables Home Values.* Retrieved from *www.census.gov/hhes/www/housing/census/historic/values.html.*

United States History. (n.d.). *Unemployment Statistic during the Great Depression.* Retrieved from *www.u-s-history.com/pages/h1528.html.*

UPI Archives. (1984, August 2). *Anne Gorsuch Burford: Ex-EPA administrator.* Retrieved from *www.upi.com/Archives/1984/08/02/Anne-Gorsuch-Burford-Ex-EPA-administrator/8223460267200/.*

U.S. Department of Treasury, Internal Revenue Service, U.S Department of Commerce, Bureau of Economic Analysis. (2004, January 16). *History of Estate Filing Requirements and Tax Rates, 1916-1948,* U.S. Dept of Treasury, Internal Revenue Service, U.S. Dept of Commerce, Bureau of Economic Analysis. Retrieved from *www.heritage.org/taxes/report/estate-taxes-historical-perspective.*

U.S. Equal Employment Opportunity Commission. (n.d.). *The Equal Pay Act of 1963.* Retrieved from *www.eeoc.gov/laws/statutes/epa.cfm.*

U.S. Equal Employment Opportunity Commission. (n.d.). *Title VII of the Civil Rights Act of 1964.* Retrieved from *www.eeoc.gov/laws/statutes/titlevii.cfm.*

usgovernmentspending.com. (2019, October 26). *What is the Deficit as Percent of GDP?* Retrieved from *www.usgovernmentdebt.us/federal_deficit_percent_gdp.*

US history.org. (n.d.). *Historic Documents: The Economic Bill of Rights.* Retrieved from *www.ushistory.org/documents/economic_bill_of_rights.htm.*

Veghte, Benjamin. (2015, August 13). *Social Security's Past, Present, and Future.* National Academy of Social Insurance. Retrieved from *www.nasi.org/discuss/2015/08/social-security%E2%80%99s-past-present-future.*

Volsky, Igor. (2009, July 29). *Flashback: Republicans Opposed Medicare in 1960s By Warning of Rationing, "Socialized Medicine".* THINKPROGRESS. Retrieved from *https://thinkprogress.org/flashback-republicans-opposed-medicare-in-1960s-by-warning-of-rationing-socialized-medicine-fad860d68e5c/.*

Weber, Max. (2002). *The Protestant Ethic and the Spirit of Capitalism.* New York, New York: Penguin Books, Inc. (Original work published in 1905).

Wile, Rob. (2017, December 19). *The Richest 10% of Americans Now Own 84% of All Stocks.* Money. Retrieved from *http://money.com/money/5054009/stock-ownership-10-percent-richest/.*

Wolters Kluwer (n.d.) *Historical Look at Capital Gains Rate.* Retrieved from *www.taxna.wolterskluwer.com/whole-ball-of-tax-2019/historical-capital-gain111.*

Woods, Randall B, (2016). *Prisoners of Hope.* New York, New York. Basic Books.

World Inequality Data Base. (n.d.). *Income Inequality USA.* Retrieved from *www.wid.world/country/usa/.*

www.ourdocuments.gov. (n.d.) Transcript of President Franklin Roosevelt's Radio Address unveiling the second half of the New Deal (1936). Retrieved from *https://www.ourdocuments.gov/doc.php?flash=false&doc=69&page=transcript.*